W9-AUZ-132

SPORTS AND GAMES OF THE ANCIENTS

SPORTS AND GAMES OF THE ANCIENTS

Steve Craig

Sports and Games Through History
Andrew Leibs, Series Adviser

Greenwood Press
Westport, Connecticut • London

Library of Congress Cataloging-in-Publication Data

Craig, Steve, 1961–
    Sports and games of the ancients / Steve Craig.
      p. cm.—(Sports and games through history)
    Includes bibliographical references and index.
    ISBN 0–313–31600–7 (alk. paper)
    1. Sports—History—To 1500. 2. Games—History—To 1500. 3. History,
Ancient. I. Title. II. Series.
    GV17.C73 2002
    796'.093—dc21   2001050101

British Library Cataloguing in Publication Data is available.

Library of Congress Catalog Card Number: 2001050101
ISBN: 0–313–31600–7

First published in 2002

Greenwood Press, 88 Post Road West, Westport, CT 06881
An imprint of Greenwood Publishing Group, Inc.
www.greenwood.com

Printed in the United States of America

The paper used in this book complies with the
Permanent Paper Standard issued by the National
Information Standards Organization (Z39.48–1984).

10 9 8 7 6 5 4 3 2

▦ CONTENTS

▦ SERIES FOREWORD

I am pleased to introduce Greenwood Publishing's Sports and Games Through History. I feel this new series offers readers the greatest geographical breadth and historical depth of any study on the games we play, how we play them, and what they tell us about the variations and the resounding similarities of the world's cultures.

The first four volumes in this series explore the sports, games, and physical activities during important periods in world history: from the first ancient Olympiad to the fall of Rome (776 B.C. to A.D. 476); from the start of the Middle Ages to the invention of printing (A.D. 476 to 1450); from the beginning to the end of the Renaissance (1450 to 1649); and from colonial America to the first modern Olympiad (1700 to 1896). The world's seven major regions (Africa, Asia, Europe, Latin America, the Middle East, North America, and Oceania) are all represented, though one of the series' great discoveries is how often sports and games cross geographic boundaries and historical time lines.

In the series' opening volume, Steve Craig notes that some sports, such as archery and wrestling, are indigenous to nearly all cultures in the ancient world. From the Great Pyramids of Egypt to the ruins of Rome, antiquity is strewn with references to, and artifacts from, what look like many sports and games we still play today. Although, the lack of detailed accounts and written rules often prevents absolute knowledge of sport history, the knowledge compiled by scholars such as Craig provide valuable insight into the nature of games played in the ancient world.

Each entry in the series provides a detailed description of sport, game, or activity, traces its development, explains how essential equipment can be made or adapted, and provides the rules of play. One goal of the series is to include enough information so students can recreate an activity as well as read about it.

Along with the simultaneous development of sports around the world, the shaping powers of military and cultural imperialism are the driving force behind the series' final volume on the eighteenth and nineteenth centuries. Bob Crego's book demonstrates the inexorable influence of Great Britain, both for the games they carried across their empire (the World Cup is awarded in soccer, not baseball), as well as the native games and traditions they banned while building colonies.

Above all, sports and games from all cultures offer insights that help us understand our own culture. One sees casinos on reservations differently after reading Sally Wilkins book on the Middle Ages, where we learn about the vital role that games of chance played in the spiritual and emotional lives of most Native American tribes.

Entries on major modern sports such as baseball and basketball are included, but the series ends with the first modern Olympiad in 1896. Thus, the series sets the stage for the twentieth century, during which sports were transformed by economic, cultural, and political realities into industries and their own myths, each needing its own encyclopedia.

One of the best things to take into the reading of this series is your own knowledge and love of the sports and games you play, watch, and follow. The ensuing pages offer many adventures in learning where these came from, and thus provide ideas on how to have the most fun as you explore the universe of play.

Andrew Leibs
Series Adviser

⊞ INTRODUCTION

In identifying and discussing notable sports and games that were popular around the globe at least 1,500 years ago, a few things should be noted:

- Encyclopedic sources naturally raise questions just as they attempt to answer them. Many books have been written about the Olympics alone. Multiple papers, chapters, and arguments have considered simply how victory in the pentathlon was decided, and there is still no clear answer. Conversely, in regions of the world where a written language was never developed, information can be spotty and prone to the mistakes of the original chroniclers, who were usually from a faraway land and imposed their own belief and moral system on their judgment of another race's pastimes. This is particularly true of the games played by the native peoples of the Americas and much of Oceania and Africa, all of whom were surely playing games and activities prior to outside interference.

- What constitutes sport in one culture would not be considered sport in another. That is one reason that this text includes the word "games" in its title. The intent is to give credence to physical activities (as well as those that were mental exercises that we might consider "tabletop" games) that are less structured and less rule-oriented than, say, the ancient Olympics but still generated significant participation from the populace where they originated.

- Virtually all people of the world seem to have participated in and practiced athletics, at least at some level. While this viewpoint is generally accepted by scholars in the various disciplines of social sciences, anthropology, and history, there is a tendency in sports history research (which is still in its relative infancy) to overemphasize the importance of the Greek Olympic Games. This book demonstrates that sports and games are not the creation of one race but rather a universal desire, a notion put forth eloquently by Wolfgang Decker: "A universalistic perspective comes inevitably to the conclusion that sport contests were in no sense a genuinely Greek invention. On the contrary they play a role in nearly every human culture and might well be termed an anthropological constant" (Decker 1992, 105).

- The emphasis of sports in different countries was reflective of their culture and environment. In the area now referred to as Oceania, which includes Australia, and the huge expanse of islands referred to as Polynesia, it is not surprising that the sea plays a role in the sporting culture. So, too, skiing was practiced in the northern reaches of Scandinavia. In the high steppes of the area once known as Persia and now including Mongolia, the horse was the primary mode of transportation. Therefore, horseback games, including polo, were the central activity.

- For all the dissimilarities, some sports seem almost universal, namely, archery and wrestling. Running was certainly as common worldwide, though it did not develop from a utilitarian purpose into a formal system of contests quite as frequently as both wrestling and archery. Leftovers from a time when survival counted for everything, wrestling, archery, and running became standards of training and preparation for military service.

Wrestling is a sport that appears throughout ancient history. In Egypt we have detailed depictions of wrestling 4,500 years old. In the Orient, the first *recorded* sumo match was in 23 B.C. Wrestling was a staple of the ancient Olympics in Greece, and the *palaestra*, or wrestling school, was a standard civic building. The Nubians were the most prominent of the African wrestlers and are depicted matched against Egyptians in temple carvings. Certainly, wrestling was a common training exercise for warriors of the Native American tribes when the white man first came to the shores of America. It is unlikely that one race or civilization was the sole creator of wrestling and then spread its practice from a central source. Rather, it was—like running and archery—an innate activity born from a human need to struggle, subdue, and at times escape foes, be they human or animal.

For that reason, the sports of wrestling, running, and archery are addressed in multiple sections of this book. To do less would be to slight their significance. Cross-references illustrate both their differences and similarities of practice and importance in different areas of the world.

Another general similarity across the globe should not come as a significant surprise, and that is the lack of information regarding the sports practices of women. As is still the case in many countries and among some cultural and religious groups, women in ancient times were, by and large, relegated to second-class status when it came to athletics. There are, however, some notable exceptions, and, when possible, the role of female athletes has been emphasized.

SOME PURPOSEFUL OMISSIONS

Some sporting practices have purposely been omitted, the most obvious being the gladiatorial contests of the Roman Empire. It is the intent of this series, as well as that of the author, to present a history that can also be put into practice, with some modification, by the modern student. That's one reason why the gladiators were not included. Conversely, some sports that had violent outcomes for the participant are discussed at length and given important credence. So why does the Mesoamerican ball game, which at times determined who would be offered as a human sacrifice, receive scholarly treatment and discussion, while the gladiators are left out? Inclusion was merited on a case-by-case basis. The Mesoamerican rubber ball games were unique games of skill and agility, deeply set into the Olmec, Mayan, and, later, Aztec religious and ritualistic ways of life. People aspired and were honored to play the games. In contrast, the purpose of the gladiator contests was to entertain the masses while purging the empire of criminals and Christians. Even though top gladiators were athletic, courageous, and at times the object of hero worship, this was not a career they chose. The closest comparison in our modern world is to the world of professional wrestling. Like the Colosseum games, it is hugely popular and sticks to a fairly strict script, and its practitioners are strong and athletic. But it is not a sport. It is entertainment. If the student wants to read about gladiators, and the social milieu that spawned them, there is plenty of information available elsewhere. With the same philosophy in mind, several animal-related sports that have ancient heritage have been excluded, notably, hunting and fishing, as well as using birds or dogs to aid in the hunt. The general fields of hunting and fishing have not been included primarily because for the majority of ancient people these were acts of food gathering, not diversions from day-to-day existence. Royalty, however, often hunted for the "sport" of it. Also hunting with falcons or hawks, which was a royal sport more than 3,000 years ago and had a wide range of influence, probably starting in China and then gaining popularity throughout the rest of Asia and into Europe, has not been included. In the case of falconry, coursing (a dog sport similar to a foxhunt on foot), and a wide variety of equestrian events, the decision not to include was based primarily on the difficulty that students would have emulating the sport.

SOME KEY DEFINITIONS

The entries are divided into seven distinct regions of the world: Africa, Asia, Europe, Latin America, Middle East, North America, and Oceania. While there may be a few more entries in one region compared to another, great effort was made to balance this book as much as possible between regions. Background information on each region's peculiarities and general traits is emphasized in separate regional introductions, and the text for each region attempts to offer a variety of activities that would fall into three subcategories labeled "Sports," "Play," and "Games."

For the purposes of this book, "sports" are activities that are rule-governed, have some degree of organization, and usually determine a victor or superior performers. Sports were often given significant social or religious meaning by the people who played them and often involved spectators. If the activity was prepared for, and/or used as preparation or training for some greater concern to the overall community it can be considered a sport. "Play," as this book defines it, is a loose collection of ludic activities where, generally, participation is stressed over victory. Usually, play activities were not associated with important cultural events but rather were played whenever the opportunity arose and did not require an audience. Children's games fit into this category. "Games" are essentially either board games or dice games, the latter being common in large portions of the world. These ranged from simple games of chance to take up idle time, to serious endeavors played for high stakes that could evoke strong emotions for both the players and spectators.

THE PURPOSE OF THIS BOOK

Sports and Games of the Ancients has set out to accomplish two primary goals: to provide students with a comprehensive, *worldwide* view of sports, play, and game activities that were indigenous, traditional, and/or ancient practices and to suggest, as often as possible, ways that these activities could be adapted for modern play. This book does not intend to create or support a general "world theory" on sports and games, other than to vividly portray that such activities were widespread in ancient times, whether they were the highly evolved contests of ancient Greece or a relatively unknown diversion for a small tribe in the Amazon.

This book shows the many different (and oftentimes similar) ways that men and women, both common and royal, from all regions of the world have devised strategies for play that have become central parts of their own respective cultures.

In an effort toward accuracy, Web sites were used infrequently as source material. To the best of the author's knowledge, any Web site cited as a source was viable at the time of publication.

Source

Decker, Wolfgang. 1992. *Sports and Games of Ancient Egypt*, translated by Allen Guttmann. New Haven, Conn.: Yale University Press.

▦ AFRICA

INTRODUCTION

Ancient and traditional sports and games in Africa are divided into two very unequal parts: Egypt and the rest of the vast continent. These parts are unequal in two primary ways: (1) though a large country, Egypt is still a very small part of a vast continent that has 52 nations as of this writing, most still in their infancy as independent states; and (2) disparity exists in the amount of information and concerted study of Egyptian sports compared to that done on the athletic practices of the many other various ethnic groups that create the heart of Africa.

Egypt was the proverbial gold mine for archaeologists, scholars, and adventure seekers from the time of ancient Greece until the middle of the twentieth century. Egyptians had a written language and left behind visual biographies. Generations upon generations of studious civilizations have looked to the Nile to see what they could learn from the makers of the great pyramids. Therefore, it was virtually impossible *not* to have gathered significant information about the Egyptians' enjoyment and participation in physical activities and mentally challenging games.

In comparison, the rest of Africa—particularly the sub-Saharan interior—is still a mystery. Travelers to the region who recorded the indigenous sporting practices weren't able to reach the central regions of the continent until the nineteenth century. Then, they seldom cared about how the native people comported themselves. Rather, "European colonizers saw in 'darkest Africa' merely a host of peoples to be subdued, exploited and enlightened by European standards" (Baker and Mangan 1987, vii).

This study of traditional African sports balances the information as best as possible but with an understanding that Egypt, situated as it is at the crossroads of Africa, Asia, and Europe, has always been an entity different from the rest of Africa. Egypt, through trade, warfare, and occupation of and by other nations, has been impacting other civilizations for more than 4,000 years. That simply is not the case with the vast majority of the continent.

Therefore, there is a still a relative lack of information about African traditional sports. There also is a tendency to define sports in a way that does not always fit with the framework of an African society. While big-game hunting was certainly considered a sport by the British colonists in East Africa, does that mean that the Masai's rite of passage of killing a lion should be considered a sport? Probably not, since for the Masai it is a ritualized, ceremonial, and required test of manhood that drew its importance from the need to hunt for survival. Very little about the act of the kill could be construed as fun or for simple enjoyment. In contrast, the practice with a spear or a bow and arrow probably should be considered a sport.

If the killing of a lion is not a sport, then what about the myriad numbers of African dances? They, too, were ritualized and ceremonial. They were certainly a required activity at special events. Sport, play, or neither? In this book, for the region of the world known as Africa, dance is considered a form of sportive play. This is based on a number of factors, including its often gymnastic characteristics, its intensity, its ability to raise the status of particularly good dancers within the community or group, and its prevalence across many nationalities.

As already suggested, what a Western audience probably views as a definition for sport—something along the lines of having two teams or two individuals competing with predefined rules in quest of victory—does not apply to some traditional African societies.

"Sport is a concept imported into Zaire" (Lema 1989, 232). This is a notion that parallels Blacking's more subtle suggestion in his overview of traditional African sportive and play practices that sport, in the Western sense, is not a concept that is innate.

However, what little information is available for the sub-Saharan part of the continent does indicate that physical competitions, particularly in the form of wrestling, were common social institutions that served important purposes across many different ethnic groups. Indeed, wrestling is the one activity that probably fits most easily into a modern view of what constitutes a sport. While practices differed greatly, there were some common themes, for example, practice within age groups and then an ascending order of matches from small, local affairs, to important, intertribal wrestling festivals where participation was an honor and where victory was worthy of celebration and often rewarded.

With all of the studies of sports in ancient and traditional societies contained in this book an effort has been made not to oversimplify or overgeneralize particular details. This needs to be especially the case when studying the sports, games, and play of the African peoples. Because of the paucity of information on the subject and the huge diversity of the continent, not enough is known about traditional African societies to represent individual instances as sweeping truths.

A quick look at Botswana points out the need for caution. This sparsely populated and landlocked country located in southern Africa is notable because of how often it deviates from the "norm" when it comes to African sports. For instance, there is virtually no wrestling. If wrestling is not the most widespread activity among traditional societies in Africa, then certainly gambling is. Again, Botswana has a relatively limited emphasis on gambling, and, in fact, the play activities of the San and Tswana groups are marked by the importance that they place on the mastery of skill, strategy, and physical prowess instead of stressing the aspect of luck or spirit influence.

One final word of caution again points to the differences between Egypt and the rest of the African continent. This has to do with the age of sports and games. Egypt affords us remarkably accurate dating, since much of what is known of ancient Egyptian sports and games comes directly from burial tombs of specific pharaohs or Egyptian elite.

With the rest of the continent, little archaeological or physical evidence can be dated to antiquity, with the omnipresent *mancala* boards being one notable exception. Instead, most of the information on sports and games of sub-Saharan populations comes from the reports of explorers and colonists from the nineteenth and early twentieth centuries. In many of these countries contact with the "white" or Western world was limited or nonexistent prior to this time. Therefore, a valid assumption can be made that what was considered a traditional physical activity, childhood game, or adult recreation had probably been played for many years. What is lost in many cases, however, is how these games developed and changed over the years.

Sources

Baker, William J., and James A. Mangan, eds. 1987. *Sport in Africa: Essays in Social History*. New York: Africana.

Blacking, John. 1987. "Games and Sports in Pre-Colonial African Societies." In *Sport in Africa: Essays in Social History*, edited by William J. Baker and James A. Mangan. New York: Africana.

Corlett, J. T., and M. M. Mokgwathi. 1989. "Sport in Botswana." In *Sport in Asia and Africa: A Comparative Handbook*, edited by Eric A. Wagner. Westport, Conn.: Greenwood Press.

Lema, Bangela. 1989. "Sport in Zaire." In *Sport in Asia and Africa: A Comparative Handbook*, edited by Eric A. Wagner. Westport, Conn.: Greenwood Press.

SPORTS

▦ Archery

In the long and varied dynastic eras of ancient Egypt one concept that remained relatively stable and unchanged was the unquestioned superiority of the pharaoh in everything. He was the smartest person, the most virtuous, and the strongest and most clever. In short, he was closer to being a god than a mortal man and was, thus, far superior to any mere mortal. By extension, that made him the best sportsman.

Archery gave the pharaohs a chance to prove it. At least that's what the legends supported by national propaganda and storytelling statues called *stelas* would have us believe.

While some scholars scoff at the overall effectiveness of the bows recovered in various tombs (Tutankhamen's among them), they do show a remarkable amount of craftsmanship and the use of compound materials, even if they are, for the most part, not of a recurved variety that produces a greater pull and velocity of the projectile. In the hands of the man-god pharaoh, however, bows were plenty powerful, particularly those of the Eighteenth Dynasty (1552–1306 B.C.). The Eighteenth Dynasty immediately followed the occupation of Egypt by the chariot-borne Hyksos who swept into the Nile valley about 1650 B.C. and controlled the region for more than a 100 years.

The omnipotence of the pharaohs had always been important. Now his powers as a warrior were stressed with more vigor. Thus, we have the stories of Amenophis II having a bow so strong that "there was none among them who could draw his bow" (Decker 1992, 90). Further, these supermonarchs were reportedly capable of shooting an arrow through sheets of copper ingots (which were commonly used as a form of exchange and have been uncovered in tombs) that were "three fingers thick." Truth? Almost certainly not, since the feat has not been able to be duplicated in modern times.

The pharaohs also engaged in target archery from chariots, particularly after being overrun by the Hyksos in just such a fashion. What they did not do, whether it was archery or any other form of athletic activity, was to compete against anyone. It simply was not permitted. Dogma and practicality did not allow for it. Since it was a foregone conclusion that any pharaoh was automatically superior, there would be no sense or reason for such a competition, and, if in reality the pharaoh was capable of losing such a contest, it would create mass hysteria since the outcome would contradict perceived standards.

Archery was also used as a means for hunting and, again, aggrandizing the pharaoh. Tuthmosis III, the father of Amenophis II, boasted that his arrows had killed seven lions in an instant.

In other parts of Africa, the bow and arrow usually was part of a style of hunting that relied mostly on stealth. Thus, the bows were generally not particularly strong or even well made but were adequate when the hunter was able to stalk his prey within close range. This trend is also found in North America, where the indigenous peoples—contrary to our Hollywood images—were not particularly good shots from great distances.

The bow still retained a level of mysticism and supernatural power and was often associated with the ruling class. C. G. Seligman (1873–1940), a British anthropologist, explained in an undated paper the striking similarity between the ancient enthronement ceremony of the pharaoh (as well as that of the Sed ceremony, which renewed the pharaoh's youth after 30 years) and coronation celebrations in other parts of Africa. Seligman describes how an arrow was shot to each of the four cardinal points in the Twenty-fifth Dynasty (712–633 B.C.) by Taharka and his queen, the latter actually loosing the arrows, signifying the taking possession of the kingdom. Seligman then notes that the king of Kitara (Unyoro) at his coronation took part in "shooting the nations." This was done with a royal bow, restrung with human sinews for each royal succession. After it was restrung, the bow and four arrows were handed to the king, and he shot them in four distinct directions. With each shot he named the nations that would be overcome by the arrows. The arrows were then searched for, returned, and placed in the quiver because it was an annual ceremony.

While documented well over 2,000 years apart, the influence of ancient Egypt into Africa would suggest that the Kitara people borrowed the practice, noting that the symbolism was still appropriate.

Sources

Burke, Edmund. 1957. *The History of Archery*. New York: William Morrow.
Decker, Wolfgang. 1992. *Sports and Games of Ancient Egypt*, translated by Allen Guttmann. New Haven, Conn.: Yale University Press.
Guttmann, Allen. 1992. "Old Sports." *Natural History*, July, Vol. 101, Issue 7.
Seligman, C. G. n.d. *Bow and Arrow Symbolism*. From Web site "Asian Traditional Archery Research Network."

⊞ Stick Fighting

Fighting with sticks was a form of military training and a self-defense art, but there are enough accounts of sword and stick competitions in ancient Egypt to suggest that it was also practiced as a form of safe competition.

A relief carving in the temple of Medinet Habu (near Luxor), which was built by Ramses III ca. 1900 B.C., shows what could pass for a modern fencing match. It records what could be considered a practice or perhaps a tournament but certainly not a duel since much care has been taken to avoid injuries. The swords have been well covered at the points, and the swordsmen wear protective masks as well as narrow shields strapped to their arms for defensive purposes. There are also judges and spectators on hand. This type of ritualized swordplay indicates that it was a tribute ceremony of some type, perhaps an international competition or part of an honorary funeral game.

While controlled sword fighting was probably a noble pursuit, most stick fighting was the domain of the common fishermen who patrolled the Nile River in papyrus reed boats and used long poles to propel themselves, much like the gondoliers of Venice. What resulted were relatively frequent battles between boats that could be called "fisherman jousting." These scenes are depicted in both Old (roughly 2920–2152 B.C.) and Middle Kingdom (1986–1759 B.C.) art. These would appear to be impromptu battles, as opposed to staged contests, that probably resulted out of either good-natured horseplay (sort of an aquatic, adult version of "king of the mountain") or to maintain territorial supremacy in a particularly fertile fishing area (similar to a lobsterman cutting traps that have invaded his area). The fisherman jousts could sometimes become bloody and violent, but the "victory" was won by knocking someone into the water. This was not always an easy defeat to accept, since not all fishermen knew how to swim.

Fighting with sticks was also an accepted and institutionalized activity in other parts of Africa, where training usually started early and continued through childhood. Consider this stanza concerning the Mpondo of South Africa: "Fighting with sticks is as constant an occupation of the Mpondo as is playing with a ball of the English. I have seen a mother playing with her son of 2 or 3, pretending to hit him so that he put up one arm for defense and tried to hit back; boys of 4 and 5 have their knobkerries, and begin to scrap. When out herding the elder boys arrange contests, pairing off couples and forcing them to fight." (Hunter 1936).

Stick fighting was also a standard pastime among the Nuba (see Africa: Wrestling). The Nuba are one of the traditional African groups that consider a wrestler's career to have ended upon his marriage. For the Nuba, the accepted postwrestling avenues for releasing the aggressive tendencies and challenging a man's strength and courage are stick dueling and spear fighting. It's worth noting that carved reliefs from the royal audience window of Ramses III in the Medinet Hubu area includes Egyptians doing battle against foreigners, including dark-skinned men who were usually referred to as Nubian. It seems plausible to suggest that the two stick-fighting societies may have had some international competitions nearly 4,000 years ago.

In Buganda, now a region of Uganda but once a separate entity controlled by the warring Ganda (or Baganda), a vicious game called "stick battle" was played by 100 of the king's pages and was a mock war. "The results were often almost as serious as though they had used spears instead of sticks. The side that lost most of its fighters by one casualty or another was driven from the scene and considered conquered" (Kagwa 1934, 136).

The Masai of modern-day Kenya and Tanzania would use meat as both the provocation for starting a stick fight and the reward for winning. This game was played by boys two or three years shy of circumcision (a vital initiation rite). The meat would be set out, and the opposing parties would fight for it. Apparently, this was a "favorite game of the boys" (Merker 1910, 72).

Meat and sticks also figure in a Masai ox-slaughtering feast to honor a "retiring" warrior who is about to be married. After everyone has their share of meat, the remainder is suspended from sticks over six feet in the air. Then the warriors and the girls and women fight for the meat, with the females having the advantage of being able to swing sticks. This is in contrast to the normal state of affairs, when the men carry fighting sticks and the women might be the target of a blow for disciplinary reasons.

Practicing the skillful use of the sword according to prescribed and mutually understood guidelines was an important activity in a number of the ancient civilizations, including the Egyptians, Greeks, Romans, and Persians as well as Near and Far East Asian cultures. Obviously, it was also practiced in sub-Saharan Africa. While there were situations where injury was frequent (the Baganda game pitting the king's pages seems especially designed to inflict injury), other stick-fighting games were designed to promote qualities needed in a warrior without the inherent intent of injuring the competitor.

Suggestions for Modern Play

Stick fighting can be considered the ancient predecessor to modern competitive fencing, an international sport that is part of the Olympic Games with classes for men and women. Fencing uses three different swords: the *foil*, which is an outgrowth of a practice weapon and is light and extremely flexible; the *épée*, which is closely associated to a dueling sword from years gone by; and the *saber* which is a heavier sword in the form most closely associated to military or cavalry swords. In the United States, fencing is best learned in the confines of a fencing club. Regional, national, and international competitions are held for young fencers in a junior (generally 20 years and under) division.

Another option is *kendo*, the traditional form of sword training for the samurai in Japan. Kendo (see Asia: Martial Arts) has experienced a renewed interest in Japan in the past few decades and is beginning to be a more popular pursuit in American martial arts schools.

Sources

Arlott, John, ed. 1975. *The Oxford Companion to World Sports and Games*. London: Oxford University Press.

Decker, Wolfgang. 1992. *Sports and Games of Ancient Egypt*. Translated by Allen Guttmann. New Haven, Conn.: Yale University Press.

Hunter, Monica. 1987 (1936). *Reaction to Conquest: Effects of Contact with Europeans on the Pondo of South Africa* Quoted in John Blacking, "Games and Sport in Pre-Colonial African Societies," in *Sport in Africa: Essays on Social History*, edited by William J. Baker and James A. Mangan. New York: Africana.

Kagwa, Apolo. 1934. *The Customs of the Baganda*. Translated by Ernest B. Kalibala. New York: Columbia University Press.

Merker, Meritz. 1910. *The Masai: Ethnographic Monograph of an East African Semite People*. Berlin: Deitrich Reimer.

⊞ Wrestling

As discussed in this book's introduction, wrestling is a universal sport, practiced by virtually every tribe and race in the world in some form. No ancient civilization dramatized and preserved its wrestling heritage any better than the Egyptians, thanks to the literally hundreds of detailed iconographs in the tombs of Beni Hasan, dating from 2,000 to 1,500 B.C.

While most sports—and especially the representation of sports—were the domain of the pharaohs and other exclusive members of the ruling elite, wrestling is one sport that seemed to at least flirt with crossing the socioeconomic boundaries in Egypt. Wrestling was practiced by private persons and soldiers for personal training purposes. Sometimes matches or exhibitions were held for the enjoyment of the pharaohs, and its presence was popularized by inclusion as relief art in the tombs at Beni Hasan as well as an audience viewing window of Ramses III.

The Beni Hasan wrestlers appear to be an educational display. Of the 30 or so graves of Middle Kingdom (ca. 1986–1759 B.C.) monarchs, four are decorated with wrestling scenes. One tomb is referred to as the "Six Phases of Practice Holds." Three are referred to as the Small Wrestling Area, the Middle-sized Wrestling Area, and the Large Wrestling Area, with 59, 122, and 219 pairs of wrestlers, respectively. This detailed artwork strongly suggests Egyptian wrestling was virtually no-holds-barred, and its emphasis was on throwing an opponent. Relatively speaking, there was no real basis for how to struggle once both wrestlers were on the floor or mat. While no point-scoring system has survived, it would appear that the contests were decided by a certain number of

This relief from the Royal Viewing Window of Ramses III located in Medinet Habu, Egypt, depicts the Egyptians competing in wrestling and stick fighting for the entertainment of the pharaoh and other foreign dignitaries. Inscriptions in the relief give evidence that these matches were international contests. (Courtesy of the Oriental Institute of the University of Chicago)

falls or, perhaps as Decker suggests, that wrestling is best seen as a training exercise for soldiers.

The Royal Window of Appearance of Ramses III shows that wrestling was one area where Egyptians competed against foreigners in athletics. Not surprisingly, Egyptians are shown defeating foreign wrestlers from conquered lands (Negroes, Libyans, Syrians), which could be a way to "buttress the royal dogma" (Decker 1992, 80) that the pharaoh is all-powerful (and, by extension that Egyptians are superior to conquered peoples) during a time in the New Kingdom when Egypt was actively stretching its borders.

The Ramses window included captions to go with the pictures, making the point hard to miss, as in one wrestler's taunt: "Woe to you, O Negro enemy! I will make you take a helpless fall in the presence of the Pharaoh." (Carroll 1988, 127).

The Ramses III Royal Window gives evidence that Nubian wrestlers competed against Egyptians, leading us to another stronghold of wrestling importance in Africa. While the Egyptians used the term "Nubian" to describe any brown- or black-skinned people, there is evidence that the wrestlers shown on the reliefs were the ancestral predecessors to a group of people who still place great importance on wrestling today—the Nuba of the southern Kordofanian hill country of Sudan. Here, clustered in a remote region, a "half million Nuba have practiced their tribal traditions, virtually uninterrupted for millennia" (Carroll 1988, 132). One of the most important traditions of the Nuba is wrestling, in a style that utilizes quick thrusts reminiscent of modern freestyle, with an emphasis on throwing the opponent.

According to oral tradition, the Nuba began to wrestle to mimic monkeys at play trying to throw one another. They still imitate animal and insect characteristics, rubbing hands on the ground like a baboon, stamping feet like a bull, flicking tongues like an insect: "the Nuba dances into the ring, not as a man, but representing the spirit of his cattle herd." (Carroll 1988, 133)

Matches are community affairs and include festive beginnings and a banquet of dance, food, and strong drink after the final match ends just before nightfall. Wrestlers are covered in white ash, symbolic of strength.

Young Nuba boys and men are trained daily while at cattle camp outside the village and are given the best food that the village has to offer. This is their schooling. There is one significant drawback. Since the Nuba believe that intercourse weakens the wrestler, it is very difficult from a social point of view for men in their late 20s to leave the cattle herd and start families.

The modern Nuba offer a glimpse into what ancient wrestling may have been like since there are known similarities between the ancient Nubians and the modern Nuba:

1. Both participated in wrestling and stick fighting.
2. Ball-like figures dangling from hems from the Nubian garments are similar to the gourds worn around the waists of the Nuba wrestlers.
3. They share the similar characteristic of wearing bounded, weighted tails and leggings.
4. The head of a cow in the only known representation of Nubian wrestlers in Egyptian iconography that takes place in a countryside setting could indicate that they were cattlemen, as are the modern Nuba.

The Ibo of Nigeria also put wrestling in a prominent position in village life, with many characteristics similar to those of the Nuba. The Brachama in northern Nigeria also actively participated in ceremonial wrestling matches to honor the various deities that controlled crop growth. The Brachama extended their festivals to invite neighboring peoples.

Wrestling is practiced in different ways in virtually every corner of Africa. In Ghana, the Ashanti, the Twi-speaking group that stood up to British rule for most of the nineteenth-century, practiced a stylized form of wrestling that one old observer compared to the Japanese martial art of judo because opponents meet arm-to-arm, leg-to-leg, and body-against-body with the object to throw or exhaust an opponent.

While this method could be rough, there were certainly more violent, dangerous varieties, according to Baker's (1999) review: "The Khoikhoi of southwest Africa engaged in bloody, no-holds-barred fights. Bambara wrestlers, in Mali, wore razor-sharp bracelets to intimidate and debilitate their opponents. Competitors in southeast Africa reportedly wrestled with only one arm and from a kneeling position at that. Boys in the same region grappled from a sitting position" (Baker 1999, 408).

For all of the differences in the various societies, some general similarities show up repeatedly in the field notes of observers of African wrestling. Wrestling was usually the reserve of young men, starting from the age of 10, when they first formed children's societies (more on this later), until they were married. Women did on occasion wrestle, though not in all cultures. Nuba and Ibo women wrestled once a year, when the harvest came in. In other areas, too, there is evidence of women's wrestling, and in each case the top wrestlers usually won attention, sometimes marriage, from the male wrestlers. (For more on one particular group of female wrestlers, see the section on the Kel Faduy tribe later.)

Older or former wrestlers often became "coaches" of the young wrestlers. Being a successful wrestler brought honor to one's kin. Often the rewards were tangible in the form of either gifts or a leadership position. When wrestling contests were held between villages, wrestlers usually were matched by age class with an emphasis on creating a fair match. The younger wrestlers would begin the festivities, with each successive match pitting older, larger, or more experienced wrestlers. It was not uncommon for a wrestler to refuse to wrestle if he felt his opponent was too strong. Wrestlers were often sequestered from the larger village group prior to important matches. Public and ceremonial wrestling usually took place in the dry season after the harvest on an even pitch of land where footing would be good. Practice matches and informal intravillage matches were held throughout the year. Most of the societies that placed significant importance on wrestling were agricultural communities, in part because these groups had the means to maintain specific wrestling grounds. They also tended to be larger groups, which meant they had the number of people to ensure that the wrestling tradition would be passed down and that young wrestlers could be evenly matched.

Another factor that has some consistency is that wrestling lessened in both its importance and its practice in areas of the continent where the Islamic religion had a strong grasp on the local populace. This effect is often viewed as the result of the Islamic leaders' viewing wrestling as a "pagan" ritual as well as frowning on the typical consumption of beer that went along with wrestling festivals.

An example of this effect is in Nigeria, where it has been contended that "Islamization devalued sporting events" (Paul 1987, 27). The Gungawa of the Yauri Division of the Nigerian Plateau still practiced traditional forms of wrestling as late as 1972, but when a Gungawa rose to a superior position among the Islamic Hasau who controlled the region, his new status would prevent him from participating in wrestling matches.

One of the more socially significant roles of wrestling was that it was often used as a means of deciding a group's leader, particularly among the children's societies in such tribes as the Lobi and Bobo in the Upper Volta (now Burkina Faso), the Mafa in northern Cameroon, and the Chaga of Kilimanjaro.

Children's societies could be compared to a college fraternity or sorority, a high school sports team, or even an inner-city gang. The children were placed together and with minimal direct adult conduct were expected to practice cooperation and to create their own governmental forms of control and order. Wrestling was often the means of choosing a leader and deciding rank within the group.

Lobi and Bobo lore tells of several legendary chiefs who became conquerors of the region as men who had gotten their start in a leadership position because they were the strongest of the group in their children's society. The Mafa boy who most excelled in wrestling was typically chosen as the play-group leader. The Chaga also used wrestling as a part of their leadership selection process, though it was incorporated into an overall evaluation of a boy's physical, mental, and social qualities. In this case, wrestling was one of the components that allowed a Chaga boy to rise above the rank of his parents and to make his own place in the greater society.

These champions from groups of similar age were the ones who were usually chosen to represent the greater community in any type of intervillage wrestling match. These matches were typically the more violent of the encounters but also offered the greatest acclaim for the victors. Among the Masakin Qisar, a sub-group of the Nuba located in modern central Sudan, the risks of the intervillage wrestling were offset by the extremely high regard given to one special village champion who was elected for a three-year period. This champion was awarded a rich outfit so special that it was stored in a separate hut throughout the wrestler's life. The special champion was entrusted with the process of training his successor, but his revered place in the society did not end with his retirement. Instead, he was highly honored, and when he died, a special and severe wrestling match would be held to honor his memory.

A society that bucks several of the noted standards of African wrestling is the Kel Faduy tribe of the pastoral Taureg people in the south-central area of the Sahara. Islamic in faith but still chiefly independent, the Kel Faduy favor women's wrestling, and it is performed, with great anticipation and glee, as part of the ritual celebration after the birth of a firstborn child to honor both the mother's coming-of-age and the naming of the newborn. The wrestling is a wild free-for-all, with several matches taking place at once, and can at times pit relatively young women against those who are as old as 70, with the wealthiest and most prestigious women of the tribe taking the central role. While the wrestling matches are fierce and usually preceded by a significant amount of boasting, they are accompanied by good cheer. They are viewed as a reaffirmation of the women's physical prowess and for their own benefit—not as a means of entertaining the men or apparently as a means to attract suitors. That the Kel Faduy approach things differently in general is attested by the fact that in this Islamic tribe the men wear veils, and the women do not.

Suggestions for Modern Play

Later in this book we suggest two ways high school wrestling teams could emulate traditional group wrestling matches (see Latin America: Wrestling; Middle East: Wrestling). Both of those have been suggested with the understanding that the vast majority, if not all, the wrestlers will be male. A girls' or women's athletic team could try to replicate the Kel Faduy and hold a group wrestling match. It would be vital to remember two key components to the event: it is done in celebration of an important event, and, most importantly, it is undertaken with a joyful spirit. Therefore, it should be an event that is offered as a "reward" for the team achieving something of value. Parents should be invited (and mothers could be encouraged to participate). The purpose of the event is not to declare a "champion" but rather as a means of gaining respect for other girls' strength and agility and to take pride in the overall fitness and competitive spirit of the group.

Sources

Baker, William J. 1999. "Traditional Sports, Africa." In *Encyclopedia of World Sport*, edited by David Levinson and Karen Christensen. Oxford: Oxford University Press.

Blanchard, Kendall, and Alyce Taylor Cheska. 1985. *The Anthropology of Sport*. South Hadley, Mass.: Bergin and Garvey.

Carroll, Scott T. 1988. "Wrestling in Ancient Nubia." *Journal of Sport History*, Vol. 15, No. 2.

Decker, Wolfgang. 1992. *Sports and Games of Ancient Egypt*. Translated by Allen Guttmann. New Haven, Conn.: Yale University Press.

Paul, Sigrid. 1987. "The Wrestling Tradition and Its Social Functions," In *Sport in Africa: Essays in Social History*, edited by William J. Baker and James A. Mangan. New York: Africana.

Worley, Barbara A. 1992. "Where All the Women Are Strong." *Natural History*, November, Vol. 101, Issue 11.

PLAY

▦ Ball Games Without Sticks

The amount of recorded information about formal games or sports involving the use of balls is relatively limited in traditional societies of

Africa. There does not appear to have been the early signs of a soccer-style game as in China (see Asia: T'su chu) or a regimented form of handball as in Europe during Greek dominance and then popularized during the Roman regime (see Europe: Episkyros and Europe: Harpastum). Certainly there is nothing close to the designated "stadium" for ball play as found throughout Central America where the games known as *tlachtli* and *pok-ta-pok* were played with great fervor (see Latin America: Mesoamerican Ball Games). There are examples of people playing with balls, however.

Not surprisingly, the ancient Egyptians left behind visual records of people using balls in different forms of play, and children's balls were buried with them. The types of balls uncovered in the burial ruins are typically made of leather strips sewn around a core of fiber, either hair or some type of grass. Others were shaped round from a solid natural element like clay or wood.

Catching and juggling games were apparently the domain of women. These quite possibly could have been part of court performances, as women have also been visually depicted in what appear to be acrobatic acts of dance. In depictions from two Middle Kingdom tombs there are displays of what would appear to be juggling, with a woman keeping three balls aloft with uncrossed and crossed arms. There are also images that show the women playing catch. Interestingly, one of these is a game where one woman sits on the back of another, facing two like women, with the ball passed between the women who are on top or "riding." There is also some evidence that playing with balls was a childhood activity. There is an often repeated theme of a ball-and-bat ritual that was done by the pharaoh to protect the kingdom because after the king has struck the ball, it has damaged the eye of Apophis, the enemy of the gods (Decker, 1992; 114–15).

There is even scantier evidence of playing with balls in the sub-Saharan region of Africa. Western Kenyan tribes called the Luo and Luhyas reportedly enjoyed seeing who could kick a ball the farthest. The Luo also participated in a rough approximation of hockey, using sticks to beat a ball around. (They also took part in another game where they did not bother with a ball and simply beat each other with sticks "with no rules at all" [Godia 1989, 268].)

In Somalia in the early twentieth century a game called *gonso* was recorded by Ralph E. Drake-Brockman. Played by the Esa and Gadabursi tribesmen it was compared to a handball version of rugby. The object of the game was to make two successful passes to a team member. Once the third distinct team member had the ball, he bounced it on the ground and then caught it on the back of his hand. This was worth 1 point, and the game was played to 10. The difficulty came in that each pass was contested, tackling was allowed, and the first two ball-handlers on a team could not bounce or drop the ball without forfeiting possession.

Once the man with the ball is collared fairly, the ball must be handed over to the other side. The tackling is usually very good indeed, and at times gets exceedingly rough. . . . Not the least amusing part of the proceedings is the amusement and interest of the spectators who crowd round, gradually drawing, in their excitement, a regular cordon round the players, who have no compunction in running headlong through them, upsetting men and boys in their endeavour to either get away and pass the ball or bounce it. (Drake-Brockman 1912, 136–37)

Because Somaliland was a British colony at the time of this detailed account, it is possible that this type of ball play was not completely indigenous but rather was a native interpretation of British games.

The San of South Africa had two formalized versions of ball playing that included some characteristics of group dancing and can be considered indigenous. The first was a game for women and involved two equal lines of women, usually between 5 and 10, facing each other 30 to 40 feet apart. The ball was about the size of an orange and was made out of a root. Essentially, it was a stylized game of catch that required dexterity. The game started when one of the women at the end of the line would toss the ball under her right leg to the woman standing across from her. The ball was caught and then returned to the original line but this time to the second woman, who would pass it back to the second woman in the opposite line and so forth. The original account does not say if any penalties were assessed for someone who dropped the ball. It appears that this was a fun, cooperative activity, as opposed to a means of declaring a winner.

The San also had a formalized game of ball played by the men, played with a specialized ball that was made from the thickest part of a hippopotamus hide cut from the back of the neck. The hide was then immediately pounded into a round shape. When finished, it had a measure of elasticity, allowing it to quickly rebound when thrown on a hard surface. This was vital to the game. Play began with a group of men circling a flat stone. The leader would start play by bouncing the hide-ball onto the stone, and then it would be caught by the next person in the circle. Play would continue until the ball had rotated around the circle and had come back to the leader, who at this point would throw the ball with extra might to produce a high enough bounce to allow all of the players to roll about on the ground imitating wild animals. The players would keep a wary eye out for the descending ball, however. Whoever caught the ball would then take the role of leader, and the game would continue.

The men's game was played in a more competitive, though still friendly, manner. At times just two men would be pitted against each other, and they would take turns bouncing and catching the ball until one person missed it. When that happened, one of the men watching the contest would quickly pick up or catch the ball, thus getting his turn to play.

Suggestions for Modern Play

Both of the ball games played by the San are easily adapted to the modern playground. Their very simple rules make the games fun for almost any age. Both could be played by either sex, or as coeducational games, but the suggested styles will stick with the San's same-sex approach.

The women's game can be viewed as either a cooperative exercise, as in the original, or as a means of slowly eliminating players who either drop the throw or misfire, until only one player remains from each row (or when one complete row is eliminated). Further difficulty could be added by making players throw the ball behind their backs or catch it behind their back once a high proficiency has been reached with the original style.

A common rubber ball the size of a baseball is a good choice for the men's game. Younger children might particularly enjoy the aspect of mimicking wild animals seen in the group game. This could help to promote good bounces that increase the likelihood of the player's neighbor actually being able to catch the ball since the wild animal noises can be made only if the ball goes full circle back to the leader.

Sources

Blacking, John. 1989. "Games and Sport in Pre-Colonial African Societies." In *Sport in Africa: Essays in Social History*, edited by William J. Baker and James A. Mangan. New York: Africana.

Decker, Wolfgang. 1992. *Sport and Games of Ancient Egypt*. Translated by Allen Guttmann. New Haven, Conn.: Yale University Press.

Drake-Brockman, Ralph E. 1912. *British Somaliland*. London, Hurst and Blackett.

Godia, George. 1989. "Sport in Kenya." In *Sport in Asia and Africa: A Comparative Handbook*, edited by Eric A. Wagner. Westport, Conn.: Greenwood Press.

Sfeir, Leila. 1989. "Sport in Egypt: Cultural Reflection and Contradiction of a Society." In *Sport in Asia and Africa: A Comparative Handbook*, edited by Eric A. Wagner. Westport, Conn.: Greenwood Press.

▦ Dance

Early ethnographic researchers as well as other firsthand witnesses found African dance to be as mesmerizing as it is strenuous. Consider George Basden's account from his 1938 book, *Niger Ibos*: "Great muscular development is necessary, because the movements are not only complicated, they are also extraordinarily difficult to execute. Muscles that are not usually highly developed are brought into use. The dance involves a prolonged series of body contortions carried through at high speed" (Basden 1938, 345–46).

Using ritualized dance as an integral ingredient of important social events was by no means a practice uniquely African. Certainly, traditional North Americans practiced dance as both an important social outlet as well as part of the preparation for sporting events themselves. The ancient Greeks at times included dance competitions in their Panhellenic Games.

Still, the dance, as both recreation and athletic game, stands out in many African tribes as being *the most important* form of physical and social expression. Many modern scholars feel that the adoption of modern sports like soccer in African countries could be a "substitute for ceremonial and recreational dancing," (Blacking in Baker and Mangan 1987, 7). Blacking himself does not agree with the "sport-replacing-dance" hypothesis but does agree that in at least some cases traditional African dances can be regarded as a sport.

For many racial groups in what is sometimes called black Africa, or the Africa that is south of the Sahara Desert, dance was truly a form of play—sometimes very important play. One important ingredient that separates the African dance form from either the event-specific dances of the Native Americans or the dance "competitions" of ancient Greece was the amount of creative freedom allowed and actually encouraged in some forms of the dance. While there were dances where the steps and the eventual outcome were predetermined and known by both the participants and the audience, others were a creation of improvisation.

This open window of interpretive behavior left the outcome in doubt. The dancers had a series of choices to make throughout a dance, and those choices would determine where, when, and how the dance would end. In this way, the dance was like an athletic contest, which can hinge on a myriad number of decisions and actions from a rather subtle direction in the opening moments, to one dramatic swing of events in the closing stages.

As with any sport or form of play practiced in a vast area by a large number of ethnic or societal groups (as in Africa), it is important to withstand the lure of making sweeping generalizations.

Dances had different purposes, styles, and—at least in some societies— special terminology that described the differences between one dance and another. Dance was practiced by men and women, in large groups and by soloists. Among the Ibo that Basden described, some men were considered to be professional dancers, while the women played the lead role in the dances connected to religious festivals.

Some types of dances also appear to have been spread across societal groups and at times were transformed into types of play, with the dance element becoming less important. Blacking notes that a distinctive dance style that was part of the Venda (South Africa) girls' puberty rites, accompanied by a song about the pains of childbirth, consisted of the same movements recorded over 50 years previously as a boys' game played by the Ila of Zambia that mimicked a battle fought on marshy ground. Both dances featured a distinctive motion of having two lines of facing dancers who began with one knee on the ground and their foot placed in front. Then the line dancers would energetically move toward the middle by alternating their leg positions back and forth.

At times dance could become a competition. This could happen between members of the same society and also at specially organized events that pitted dancers representing different "ethnic groups, chiefdoms, neighborhoods, or voluntary associations" (Blacking 1989, 13). In the latter cases practices were held to prepare the dance team. Along these same lines were the relay song-and-dances, which put a premium on the back-and-forth, call-response cadence. This produced consecutive solo dances, each in reaction to the previous one performed.

Dance was also a vital part of the initiation process in many African societies, which required boys and girls to learn and perform specific dances. Many of these could be considered ritual dances and thus could easily be classified as an endeavor outside the realm of sports, though certainly vital to the cultural group. Others, however, were of a more game-like quality. Among the Venda, they were called *nyimbo dza mitambo*, or "game songs."

Groups of youth dancers took on many of the characteristics of team sport units that would be recognizable to Western athletes: they at times traveled outside their own "home" region to dance; they did this to bring honor to their tribe and themselves; they prepared for these "road-trip" dances; and the process of the preparation and the trip itself usually enhanced the camaraderie among the group of dancers.

In Rwanda in the 1960s, dance was still considered an "appropriate sport for conduct in warfare," because the dances continually brought in new characters that created new choices. This helped to demonstrate to the soldier-dancers how one good (or bad) decision could affect the outcome of a battle.

While this section has dealt mostly with the prevalent and important forms of dance in sub-Saharan Africa, dance was a significant form of recreation in ancient Egypt, where it often bordered on acrobatics. These physical displays of athletic ability and joy shared an aspect with the more ritualized forms of dance in black Africa. They were performed most often with a specific intention of pleasing some deity. Egyptian dancers have been depicted as early as the Sixth Dynasty (2325–2155 B.C.); In one tomb a group of five female dancers have simultaneously kicked their left legs into the air while leaning so far back that their backs are nearly horizontal to the floor. The depiction, complete with one female standing and possibly clapping in time, has a striking similarity to the synchronized leg kicks that are the trademark finale of the Radio City Music Hall Rockettes in New York City. Other tomb engravings show a variety of gymnastic positions, which can be interpreted in a number of different ways, though the progression of the motifs suggests that the Egyptians were adept at forward flips, somersaults, pirouettes, cartwheels, and even no-hands headstands.

Sources

Basden, G. T. 1938. *Niger Ibos*, 1966 edition. New York: Barnes and Noble.
Blacking, John. 1989. "Games and Sport in Pre-Colonial African Societies." In *Sport in Africa: Essays in Social History*, edited by William J. Baker and James A. Mangan. New York: Africana.
Decker, Wolfgang. 1992. *Sports and Games of Ancient Egypt*. Translated by Allen Guttmann. New Haven, Conn.: Yale University Press.
Sfeir, Leila. 1989. "Sport in Egypt: Cultural Reflection and Contradiction of a Society." In *Sport in Asia and Africa: A Comparative Handbook*, edited by Eric C. Wagner. Westport, Conn.: Greenwood Press, Inc.

▦ Running

In no modern sporting endeavor is the success of African nationals more pronounced than in the area of long-distance running.

Since Abebe Bikila, a member of the Ethiopian Imperial Guard, shocked the sporting world by winning the 1960 Olympic marathon while running barefoot (and then repeating the feat four years later with ease while wearing socks and shoes), the greatness of African runners has been acknowledged. When Kipchoge "Kip" Keino of Kenya blitzed American favorite and world-record holder Jim Ryun to win the 1968 Olympic gold medal in the 1,500 meters, it marked the beginning of a constant presence of African runners among the world's elite distance athletes. In fact, the runners from the mountainous areas of East Africa— particularly the Kenyans who have followed Keino—have become dominant. From 1991 to 2000 a Kenyan man won the Boston Marathon, and even in 2001, when their winning streak was snapped by South Korean Bong-Ju Lee, six Kenyans were among the top 12 finishers, and the women's race was won for the second year in a row by Kenyan Catherine Ndereba.

The marathon success has been relatively recent (Kenyan coaches used to discourage their athletes from running the marathon), but long-distance running is such a revered part of the culture that a runner appears on the country's 20-shilling note.

Is this only a twentieth-century phenomenon, a result of the Kenyans' willingness to work extremely hard with the hopes of escaping impoverished conditions combined with the natural edge of living and training at altitudes of 6,000–10,000 feet? Or does some ancient historical information suggest that the Africans had been preparing for greatness for centuries and just needed the political and economic resources to allow them to compete on the world stage?

Certainly, the modern Kenyan runner does benefit from constant altitude training, much as the mountainous home of the Tarahumara of northern Mexico contributes to their remarkable feats of endurance running (see North America: The Tarahumara Kickball Races). But many other groups of people from all over the globe have lived at altitude for centuries yet have not produced any great distance runners. That Kenya is a relatively poor state and that running offers a path to otherwise unachievable riches are also true now, though when Keino and the other early East African stars were making the initial inroads to superior international performances, there were no professional meets, appearance fees, endorsement contracts from shoe and apparel manufacturers, or even college scholarships in the equation.

As William J. Baker points out, "Distance running seems 'natural' for Africans, who have known a minimum of mechanized, motorized transportation" (Baker 1987, 280). Because the success of modern Kenyan runners is highly concentrated among the Nandi people of the Kalenjin tribe, there has also been widespread temptation to suggest that physiological traits predispose this particular tribe to success. This has not been proven or even particularly validated beyond the traits of a slender frame (found advantageous to distance runners across many nationalities) and the excellent cardiovascular fitness that is also found in virtually any group of people who live at altitude.

So, the question is begged, Are there ancient or at least traditional cultural precedents for Africans' modern success in distance running? It's a question seldom tackled in the literature reviewed. When running is mentioned—other than the previously quoted remark—it is in relation primarily to modern military sports training or the training options open to modern African athletes. Ethnographic studies of the Masai in Kenya and the Amhara of Ethiopia, the latter of which does offer some useful information on games, are similarly barren when it comes to footracing.

In Kenya, which became a British protectorate in 1895 and gained independence in 1963, many of the native groups are herdsmen. Physical exercises were simply part of the daily routine. Since young children were often the shepherds or herdsmen of the cattle flocks, running long distances in the mountainous regions was both ordinary and expected when they were looking after the cattle or hunting. When schools were built, it was often necessary for the widely dispersed school-age population to run long distances to and from the schoolhouse. This was considered "natural training," not so much a sport as it was a precondition of daily life that eventually would be well adapted to a more formalized sports setting. As a pastoral people, they also had a relatively high proportion of protein (particularly through milk) in their diet compared to other African groups.

Some more specific traditional attributes of the Nandi people certainly emphasized discipline, tolerance for discomfort, and indeed long-distance running itself. Discipline was learned and stressed by participation in age group-based societies, from which the warrior class would come. (For another example of age-class societies and their impact on sport, see Africa: Wrestling.) Circumcision was a ritual initiation rite for manhood and had to be undertaken without even a hint of pain or fear creeping over the initiate's face, or else he would be ostracized and ridiculed for the rest of his life. Once a boy became a full warrior, he then could take part in cattle raids, some of which covered over 100 miles. Success in raiding cattle led to prestige and subsequent benefits—like the wealth needed to keep multiple wives.

Ritual circumcision, age-group societies, and cattle raids were common throughout Africa. Still, they would have helped lay the foundation for disciplined endurance athletes. The British colonial government may have given the tribes of Kenya the final extra prod to actual athletic success by instituting organized track meets as an alternative to cattle raiding.

For truly ancient references to running in Africa one has to look to Egypt. In Egypt running served multiple purposes from the important and regimented training of troops, to the highly ceremonial Jubilee Run by the pharaohs' that was a specific means of demonstrating to the masses the pharaohs continued strong health and superiority. There are also references in ancient texts to runners serving as bodyguards of prominent men, with the runners gliding along beside the wealthy man who was in a chariot, as well as soldiers who were ascribed the honorary title of "swift runner," possibly achieving this title by means of a contest.

In the Jubilee Run, which was part of the Jubilee Festival (also known as the Festival of Sed, the Renewal Festival and the Ritual of Renewal), the pharaoh would make a ceremonial and solo run. There were no competitors because the Egyptian man-god worship of the pharaoh both precluded and made unnecessary the existence of rivals.

The reasons for the Jubilee Run were probably threefold. It was held after a span of 30 years of being in power and it is possible that an aging king did the run to prove his adequacy, though the overall feeling of a pharaoh's being a god would seem to make this unnecessary. More likely, the run had symbolic and magical overtones. It was a reenactment of the run that the pharaoh had made when he first seized power. In this way it was a physical reminder of the pharaoh's greatness on a special anniversary. It has also been suggested that the completion of the run magically renewed the king's power. This seems like a reasonable hypothesis since, even though they were viewed as something of a god, the pharaohs were still mortal men, and there had to have been an understanding that the body that housed their spirit and will would eventually wither and die. It should be noted that the aging pharaoh was probably not overly taxed by this mostly symbolic act. A running track unearthed at the funerary tomb of Djoser (Third Dynasty, ca. 2624–2605 B.C.) was slightly less than 140 meters long, even though the courtyard in which it was housed could have accommodated a significantly larger structure.

More significant from a purely athletic perspective is the running *stela* of Taharqa (ca. 685–684 B.C.), which offers strong evidence of a 100-kilometer run completed by an Egyptian military troop after it had undergone daily training. This was done as a feat of fitness after the pharaoh had come to inspect his troops and found them to be in a high state of readiness, as opposed to an athletic competition, since no spectators were on hand. The stela, meaning an inscribed statue, states that the best runners completed the distance in approximately nine hours, running the 50-kilometer distance from Memphis to the oasis of Fayum, taking a two-hour break, and then running back to Memphis. While at first glance the completion of such a long race in nine hours may seem unlikely, it is a distance-time comparison that is achievable, at least by modern standards, especially when the factors of the runners starting in the coolness of night and being afforded a lengthy rest period upon reaching the turnaround point are considered. Of equal amazement is that the pharaoh Taharqa actually got out of his chariot and ran with the troops for an hour.

Interestingly, this event took place in the Twenty-fifth Dynasty (ca. 690–664 B.C.), which was a time period when Egypt was ruled not by Egyptians but by conquerors. This happened from time to time in the over 2,000-year history of the pharaohs. In this case, the ruling family had hailed from Nubia, with Taharqa being a second-generation pharaoh. Nubia had long been part of the Egyptian rule. It is an area that extended into modern Sudan. Further, Egyptians routinely referred to any person of dark skin as Nubian. Decker (1992) makes a point of saying that the Twenty-fifth Dynasty was not the reign of the Ethiopians, as some early Greek scholars contended. Still, there is a fascinating possible connection between the native home of the pharaohs in this time period, this unique piece of evidence, and the greatness of modern East African distance runners.

For some specific suggestions on how to turn ancient running practices into modern play, see North America: Running, and North America: Tarahumara Kickball Races.

Sources

Baker, William J. 1987. "The Meaning of International Sport for Independent Africa." In *Sport in Africa: Essays in Social History*, edited by William J. Baker and James A. Mangan. New York: Africana.

Decker, Wolfgang. 1992. *Sports and Games of Ancient Egypt*. Translated by Allen Guttmann. New Haven, Conn.: Yale University Press.

Godia, George. 1989. "Sport in Kenya." In *Sport in Asia and Africa: A Comparative Handbook*, edited by Eric A. Wagner. Westport, Conn.: Greenwood Press.

Layden, Tim. 2001. "Long-distance Land." *Sports Illustrated*, April 23, Vol. 94, Issue 17, p A4, 6s, 6c.

Manners, John. 1975. "In Search of an Explanation." In *The African Running Revolution*, edited by Dave Prokop. Mountain View, Calif.: World Publications.

Merker, Meritz. 1910. *The Masai: Ethnographic Monograph of an East African Semite People*. Berlin: Deitrich Reimer.

Messing, Simon D. 1985. *Highland Plateau Amhara of Ethiopia*. Edited by M. Lionel Bender. New Haven, Conn.: Human Relations Area Files.

Wallechinsky, David. 1996. *Sports Illustrated Presents the Complete Book of the Summer Olympics, 1996 edition*, Boston: Little, Brown.

⊞ Games with Stick and Ball

As mentioned in the "Ball Games Without Sticks" section, ball games were not at the core of the African's world of sport and play compared to other regions of the world.

Still, the notion of knocking a ball around with a club or stick is plainly evident at the immensely enlightening tombs of Beni Hasan, ca. 2000 B.C. Most noted for their extensive depictions of wrestling, other sports are also represented in the ancient drawings in this Nile Valley region, one of which certainly has the appearance of being an ancient ancestor of a "hockey" type of game.

Two men, standing square to each other, are holding curved sticks that are similar to early twentieth-century field hockey sticks. Between the men is something that can be interpreted as either a ball or a small hoop. Their stances are similar to a stance that would be taken in modern field hockey when the ball is put in play between two players, what is known as the "bully," which initiates play at the beginning of a game and after a goal is scored.

Especially in Eastern Africa there are other examples of stick-and-ball games. Some are associated with specific festivals, some with early cult beliefs, and others are little more than rudimentary examples of a fairly natural inclination to hit a stone or round object with a stick. These games are possibly due to dissemination from Egyptian sources. Others suggest that they aren't even traditional games but rather were games passed on by early colonial or trade influences. Even if the latter is the case, there are still some cases where the game has been incorporated enough into the cultural framework to merit mention.

Among the peasant population of the Amhara in modern Ethiopia the common word for Christmas is *ganna*, which is the name of an outdoor game played with sticks and a wooden puck. That a special day would be linked with a rough-and-tumble game is owed, in part, to the relaxation of the social rules on this particular day and the fact that boys, young men, and even elders on occasion will play together on Christmas Day. The game is virtually without rules, and any usual norms for showing respect to older members of the community are forgotten while the game is in progress. The ganna game continues until darkness. Players suffering serious injuries (broken arms or legs) are not uncommon. When the game ends, the winners serenade the losers with "abusive limericks" (Levine 1965, 62). These games can sometimes go on for more than one day.

The Amhara also have a boys' game that uses both a stick and a ball while combining some of the characteristics of baseball and soccer and one distinctive physical movement normally associated with the spiritually important rubber ball game of Mesoamerica.

This game is called *kwas* and is played throughout the dry season. In this case the teams are evenly distributed, a like number of small and big boys on each team. The ball is knocked with a stick, and there is running from base to base (like baseball), but there is also a goalkeeper (like soccer). The interesting thing is that the goalkeeper can stop the ball only with his hip. The use of the hip for stopping, controlling, and propelling the ball is a vital aspect of the Mesoamerican game but otherwise not a common requirement for other ball games around the world. The game of kwas is accompanied by an abundant amount of boasting and taunting in imitation of adult Amhara men.

The Somali, who live not only in Somalia but also in large numbers in Ethiopia, Kenya, and Tanzania, have a simple variation of a hockey game with a goalie protecting a goal that is usually a bush, and they also play a two-stick game where the object is to use a larger stick to bounce a smaller stick a specified number of times. The image would be similar to a tennis player bouncing the ball repeatedly on his own racket.

Suggestions for Modern Play

Two of the African stick games offer at least a starting place for modern play. The free-for-all aspect of the ganna would be a fun, single-day activity that could involve male and female parents, teachers, and older children. Play on a football field, use hockey sticks, wear soccer-style shin guards, and substitute a softball for a wooden puck. To increase safety, add one field hockey rule: the sticks cannot be swung above the waist. The goals can be the football goalposts. Because ganna encourages boasting and taunting these aspects should be included with the provision that profanity is not allowed. Encourage clever and insightful verbal sparring with a small post-match award for the "wittiest" comment.

As a simple physical education activity, test students' coordination with the two-stick game of bouncing one stick with the other. Line students up in a well-spaced row and see who can bounce his or her small stick the longest.

Sources

Arlott, John, ed. 1975. *The Oxford Companion to World Sports and Games.* London: Oxford University Press.

Decker, Wolfgang. 1992. *Sports and Games of Ancient Egypt.* Translated by Allen Guttmann. New Haven, Conn.: Yale University Press.

Levine, Donald N. 1965. *Wax and Gold: Tradition and Innovation in Ethiopian Culture.* Chicago: University of Chicago Press.

Marin, G. 1931. "Somali Games." *Journal of the Royal Anthropological Institute of Great Britain and Ireland,* 499–511.

Messing, Simon D. 1985. *Highland Plateau Amhara of Ethiopia.* Edited by M. Lionel Bender. New Haven, Conn.: Human Relations Area Files.

⊞ Swimming

The Nile River provided a natural defining point for settlement in ancient Egypt and made a significant impact on the sporting culture of the Egyptians. Swimming was known to be a respected and valued ability among the Egyptian elite. While it never reached the same high level as in Greece, where Plato specifically mentions the ability to swim as a vital part of an education in his *Laws*, the ability to survive once in the water was seen as a measure of a person's cultural refinement.

As was their way, the Egyptians tended to judge other peoples by whether and how well those peoples had mastered certain skills that the Egyptians themselves deemed to be significant. Such was the case with swimming. If a person of different descent—say a Hittite prince—was unable to swim, then that person was inferior to the pharaohs and by extension the Egyptians themselves.

While swimming was seen as a skill for the educated, it is likely that most Egyptians knew how to swim. As Decker writes, "It is probable that nearly all Egyptians, living as they did on the Nile or on one of the canals branching from the river, knew how to swim for utilitarian purposes" (Decker 1992, 90).

The type of stroke practiced by the Egyptians is a question easily debated. Hieroglyphics from as far back as the First Dynasty give the impression of the modern crawl stroke, but the drawings are rudimentary.

The oldest written reference lends credence to the importance of swimming among both the elite and even the pharaohs. In the tomb of Kheti, a prince from Siut ca. third millennium B.C., his personal biography proudly proclaims that in his youth he was allowed to take swimming lessons with the king's own children. This indicates that the king took an interest in his children's being able to swim as well as the children of other high-ranking officials.

This does not mean that swimming contests were the norm. Just as in ancient Greece, the ability to swim was seen as important, but actual races are considered very rare indeed. Swimming could certainly be considered a form of athletic "play" and was also apparently undertaken by both men and women, if archaeological findings are viewed as evidence.

The motif of a naked, swimming girl is found repeatedly in Egyptian art, especially in the form of wooden spoons, with the girl and her outstretched legs forming the handle and her arms supporting the spoon. Often the spoon is shaped in the form of a fish or a duck, adding legitimacy to the notion that the girl is "swimming." Swimming girls cavorting among fish and fowl are also seen as decorative art in bowls, shards, and on an ointment bowl as well as appearing in love poetry where the "maid pulls a fish from the water and hands it to her beloved" (Decker 1992, 92). In the Old Kingdom there was even a goddess of swimming, called *Wajdet*.

As previously stated, swimming was also a necessity. Fishing was both a favored pastime as well as an occupation. Being able to swim could mean the difference between life and death, especially if one was the loser in another popular form of Egyptian physical entertainment known as "fisherman jousting," which was akin to fencing with sticks or the medieval martial art of doing battle with a quarter-staff.

Swimming was not the sole property of the Egyptians. Even older than the First-Dynasty hieroglyphs mentioned earlier are cave paintings depicting swimming in what is now modern Libya.

In other parts of the continent swimming was certainly a traditional form of both play and survival. In Zaire most people begin swimming at an early age, but competitive swimming is not stressed today, nor apparently was it ever, despite the large number of lakes, streams, and rivers, including the Zaire River, which, like the country itself, was once known as the Congo and cuts a wide swath through the country.

In Nigeria, a West African country that was formerly a British colony, "traditional swimming" has been identified as a form of recreational sport. One of the few writers from the colonial era to even comment on sports or physical pastimes of sub-Saharan Africans was British missionary George Basden. He wrote *Among the Ibos of Nigeria* in 1921 and *Niger Ibos* in 1938 and detailed that particular ethnic group's participation in sports. He wrote that swimming was commonly a recreation for adult men. If the village was near a river, children of both sexes became expert swimmers.

Interestingly, it is reported that makeshift competition is very common among the swimmers. While the type of strokes varies, and there are no rules, swimming to a specified target is common, as are underwater swimming contests. Looked at from a Westerner's perspective, this seems a wholly natural outcome of having a group of people—particularly if they are of similar age and/or gender—swim together in a river or a lake. Sooner or later one person is going to challenge another or the group as the whole to see "who will be first" to swim to the other side or "who can stay underwater the longest."

It is quite likely that such an event was of such ordinary occurrence that it would not merit being recorded in Egyptian writings. Therefore, to categorically say that swimming could not be a competitive recreation or activity would be presumptuous. It is fair to say that traditional swimming on the African continent was not a sport that merited organized and recorded results of competition.

In Africa today there are scattered formal swimming programs, some of which are set up in countries that had strong ties with the old Soviet Union, which opened its sports training doors to many African nationals.

Sources

Baker, William J., and James A. Mangan ed. 1987. *Sport in Africa: Essays in Social History*. New York: Africana.

Basden, G. T. 1938. *Niger Ibos*, 1966 edition. New York: Barnes and Noble.

Decker, Wolfgang. 1992. *Sports and Games of Ancient Egypt*. Translated by Allen Guttmann. New Haven, Conn.: Yale University Press.

Wagner, Eric A., ed. 1989. *Sport in Asia and Africa: A Comparative Handbook*. Westport, Conn.: Greenwood Press.

GAMES

⊞ Abbia: An Example of the Gambling Culture

Games that used two-sided chips made from some natural material like wood, seeds, stones, bark, or shells are relatively common around the world, particularly in cultures that practiced and especially accepted gambling as a legitimate form of entertainment. The Native American tribes had a variety of games built around two-sided "dice," which were usually seeds or specially marked wooden sticks (see North America:

Moccasin Game; Gambling). The use of knucklebones, called *astragali*, was prevalent in many cultures, including the ancient Greeks.

The manner of play was usually similar. The chips, dice, or sticks would be marked in a distinctive manner on one side and left either completely or relatively unmarked on the other side. They were then thrown into the air, and some wager would be made on the pattern or count that they formed when they landed. It was relatively common for the "best" or most advantageous throws to be those where all of the chips fell with the marked side facing up or with all of them facing down.

In northern Africa, ancient Egypt, and the Middle East, the games of choice were *astraglis, senat* in Egypt (see Africa: Senat), or one of the other 20-plus board games that have been identified with traditional peoples in the Middle East.

Popular in the rain forest belt of the sub-Saharan African continent was the game of abbia, a very fast-paced pitch-and-toss gambling game that required intense concentration, good eyesight, and steely nerves from the players. *Abbia* is both very old and very popular among the people of West and Central Africa, who use the wooden chips from the hard nut of a common rain forest tree. Players bet constantly and repeatedly on the way the wood chips (usually four at a time) would land. As quickly as they landed, they were scooped up, bets were won or lost with money exchanged, new bets were made, and the process started again. This was a game that was given importance by the players but not because of any inherent skill involved (though, as we'll see, there were ways to improve or lose one's luck). Rather, it was the thrill of the gamble, the prospect of a quick haul balanced against the danger of a big loss that produced the excitement.

George Basden, who spent significant time documenting the play patterns of the Ibo of Nigeria in the first quarter of the twentieth century, wrote about the pitch-and-toss games that he witnessed, noting that it was "one of the fastest ways of winning and losing money ever devised by man," and "the play becomes exceedingly fast and soon a cloud of dust encircles each group of gamblers" (1938, 352–53).

That the game was taken seriously is evidenced by how intricately the pieces were carved. The abbia chips often had images of the natural, mechanical, and the physical world. The game played by farmers and trappers of southwestern Cameroon is probably the best-known variant of this type of wood-chip game.

The playing pieces are shaped like the outer boundary of a human eye—oblong with pointed ends. The nuts are split in two, and the delicate carvings are made in the outer shells. Because they are drawings of animals, machinery, and important plants, these wood chips have served as important sources of information regarding original African art and today are made into jewelry, especially for the tourist trade.

Once a symbol of the elite due to the masterful carving that set them apart from the more common "chips" made out of cowrie shells, they are now a symbol of Cameroon and its relatively successful transition into an African nation that has been able to create its own identity and international markets. The abbia chip has become a popular secular item, even though the game itself is now rarely played.

One reason for its decline may be that it has begun to succumb to an antigambling sentiment. This is an opinion that is strongly espoused in the Koran, the holy text of the Islamic religion, which says that gambling is a sin. Before Islam's spread into Africa, there was probably already a group of people who sought to put an end to gambling—women. Quite frequently the stakes for the game were women, for the purpose of being a wife or a slave worker.

Since gamblers often wagered such high stakes, they took whatever means were available to them to win. These included cheating and deception. They also included invoking the spirit powers of gods and deceased ancestors. Abbia players were particularly wary and respectful of the powers of spirits and often spent the night before a gambling session dining on a diet of specially prepared foods. Burrs were tossed in with whatever was being staked or wagered in order to "snare a win." While women did not gamble, some wives were recognized by not only their husbands but also other gamblers as being good-luck wives, and therefore they would be present at the matches.

The abbia chips themselves harbored great powers. The nut and the fruit that surrounded it were said to be poisonous. The gambling men so respected the powers of the chips that they did not even go near the tree to secure the nuts, instead sending women or children to get the nuts, which would then be split and carved. While nongamblers would occasionally wear the chips around their necks as a protective charm, the gamblers understood that the chips harbored such powerful forces, each based upon the carving, that they could not be stored in their own home. Instead, the chips were stored in a bag that would be suspended in a tree in the rain forest, "for the sack contained too malevolent a jumble of conflicting forces to be kept near people" (Reefe 1987, 63). Expert gamblers had many sets of chips and would choose which ones they felt were right based on the circumstances as well as what pattern they needed to have the chips make when they fell.

Gambling was certainly a means of commerce. Not only were the stakes that were wagered exchanged, but so, too, was debt incurred, which then meant that the loser had to "work" to repay the debt. This helps to explain, at least in part, why there is such a frequency of reports of human beings (usually women) being used as a gambler's stake. There was an understanding among the gamblers that the losses could be bought back with the proper amount of payment.

Gambling Then and Now

Gambling in general has been recorded to be a popular traditional pastime in many African populations. *Mancala* was called the "national game of Africa" by Stewart Culin, one of the world's best late nineteenth-century to early twentieth-century ethnographers (see Africa: Mancala). One aspect of its appeal was the gambling often associated with the play of the game, which allowed for wagers not only among the players but also those watching the game.

As mentioned, mothers have often (usually unsuccessfully) warned their sons about the dangers of gambling. Two instructive proverbs from northern Nigeria are "A gambler is not a man" and "Gambling soon estranges a person from his relatives" (Reefe 1987, 60).

But, as Reefe goes on to point out, most of the cultures in the rain forest, what he calls the *abbia zone*, lacked any type of centralized authority figure that had the power to enforce the antigambling sentiment. Therefore, the lure of a quick gain in economic prosperity—and thus prestige—was "open to all men who had or could beg, borrow or steal the stakes to play" (Reefe 1987, 60) In other areas of Africa, antigambling stances were able to be enforced, notably in the Ethiopian highlands which were self-governed by emperors.

One more modern example of a no-gambling stance was apartheid South Africa. Even then, gambling was not eliminated. Instead, it flourished for both the black nationals and the ruling white class inside the small areas called "independent homelands," allotted to the huge black population where white South African law did not apply. When the racist apartheid laws were broken down, gambling became a legalized and government-backed source of economic growth. Since legislation was passed in 1996 to allow up to 40 casinos throughout the country, 21 had been built by the end of the year 2000, many in the Las Vegas style. Up to 14 percent of South Africa's provincial government revenues were from gambling in the year 2000. Now the government fears that people are gambling beyond their means, with a study indicating that one gambler in seven borrows beyond his or her means in order to bet.

Sources

Basden, G. T. 1938. *Niger Ibos*, 1966 edition. New York: Barnes and Noble.
Reefe, Thomas Q. 1987. "The Biggest Game of All: Gambling in Traditional Africa." In *Sport in Africa: Essays in Social History*, edited by William J. Baker and James A. Mangan. New York: Africana.
Singer, Rena. 2000. "A Casino Quandary in Africa." *Christian Science Monitor*, November 27, Vol. 93, Issue 2, p. 1.

"A Tuscan Village in South Africa." 2001. *Economist*, April 7, Vol. 359, Issue 8216, p. 49.

▦ Mancala

Mancala is a counting and strategy game played around the world, with its densest penetration in Africa, Asia, and the Caribbean. Though there is some question as to its place of origin, it is often referred to as "The African Game" and in all likelihood originated on that continent around the time of Christ.

There are many different names for mancala, depending on where and how it is played. Despite the many variations, there is also the overriding commonality of this board game. The board has at least two rows of indentations, often referred to as holes or pockets; the game is typically played by two people; and each player starts with a like number of counters. After the counters have been distributed into the holes, the central theme of the game is initiated. A player chooses one hole, picks the counting pieces out of the hole, and then distributes them in a counterclockwise fashion putting one counter in each successive hole. The object is to end up with more counters than one's opponent. Counters can be almost anything: small seeds, pebbles or stones, nuts, maize, chickpeas. Modern boards often come with smoothed, somewhat flat pieces of brightly colored glass.

The strength of the game is that it offers an interesting duality. The outcome of a move can be predicted due to the mathematical properties of counting involved. But, a counter move can turn what appeared to be a good sequence of events into a bad one very quickly. Further, when the game is played with a greater degree of counters, pockets, or even rows, it becomes increasingly complex.

Boards have been found in Africa in Zaire, Angola, and Ghana dating back to the sixth century or earlier. A board found in Ethiopia in 1959 dates to A.D. 6 or 7. There is also a smattering of evidence that boards were cut right into temple structures dating back another 1,400 or more years.

Mancala has been suggested as a tool to define ancestral heritage. There are remarkable similarities between the style of play in different parts of the world that have little specific contact with each other. For example, a two-row game known as *warri* (or *awari, owari, wari, avale*) is most popular in West Africa, but its manner of play is consistent with the style of mancala played in the Caribbean, Surinam, and parts of Brazil. That West African tendencies would be transported to the Caribbean can be explained, at least in part, by the slave trade routes that ended in the Americas.

In southern India and Ceylon the Tamil women favor *pallanguli*, which is played with seven holes and six seeds starting in each hole. This game features a unique component. Four seeds in any hole is called a cow and can be immediately lifted by the owner of that hole even as play is continuing.

The four-row, eight-hole configuration known as *bao* is most popular among Swahili-speaking people in the East African countries of Tanzania, Ethiopia, Kenya, Zambia, and Zanzibar. *Bao* is played with 64 seeds, and the board includes two characteristic square holes in the center for captured seeds (counters). Unlike other mancala games, the counters are immediately reentered in the game, meaning there is never a letup in the game's complexity. Bao masters compete in worldwide tournaments, and many East African cities have cafés where playing bao is the main attraction. It has been noted that once someone becomes adept at bao, he is less likely to want to do anything else. As the old Swahili saying goes, "Bao is a leg of the devil" (de Voogt 1998a).

The monster of mancala games is *owela*, a four-row, 16-hole game that is popular in Namibia, Angola, and South Africa. A board would be large and unwieldy. Therefore, owela is usually played outdoors with holes dug in the sand and often by teams of players. While perhaps with not as many rows, playing the game outdoors with natural devices indicates that the game could be much older than any other board game that will ever be found, since it figures that the board was made to fit the existing game, rather than the other way around.

Mancala in the Americas seems to have gained a greater degree of ritualistic value after its cross-Atlantic migration. Awari, as played in the West Indies, is essentially the same as warri of West African style. Awari is played in a house of mourning to amuse the spirit of the dead, but this is done only during daytime because if the game was played at night, then the ghosts would join living players and could potentially carry off the spirits. Boards are made in two types—straight top and a curved, banana-top shape. The villages keep one of each on hand so when they have mourning games they can avoid using the style favored by the dead person, thereby lessening the chance of ghosts joining in the game. (Bell 1979, 122).

Mancala is usually a man's game when it is played in Africa and a game for women and children when played in Asia. There are exceptions. In Ethiopia, the game called *guebeta* in the native tongue of Amharic is popular with adults and adolescents of both sexes.

The specific rules for when a turn is concluded, when seeds are put into a storage hole, and how many seeds or counters are placed in a hole to start a game are quite varied. The key aspect is that both players agree on the rules beforehand. It's also important that they keep a close watch on their opponent. Skilled players purposely try to dispense their counters in exceedingly rapid fashion to create confusion, and "cheating is not unheard of" (de Voogt 1998a).

Suggestions for Modern Play

Unlike so many ancient sports and games, mancala is extremely accessible and can be played today just as it was probably played when some nomadic herdsman first decided to scoop out handfuls of dirt to make a row of holes and toss some seeds in. A 1995 article in *U.S. News & World Report* (1995) remarks how mancala had become a "low-tech" craze despite no one's actively marketing the game. As the article said, the reason for its longevity, cross-cultural play, and, more recently, its popularity in the United States is really not difficult to understand. "It's elementary: Folks of all ages have fun playing. A six-year-old can master the easy rules, an adult can devise devious moves" (1995, 59). Mancala games and basic instructions are readily available in toy stores, catalogs, and (for higher-quality boards) specialty shops. They have also become popular in classrooms as a tool for teaching mathematic principles. If buying a mancala board, make sure that the stones are easy to handle and that as many as 15 can actually fit in the holes. One game designed for young children has "stones" shaped like different types of fruit. Fewer than six pieces of fruit fit in a hole and because they are different shapes they are difficult to scoop and distribute.

Sources

Bell, R. C. 1979. *Board and Table Games from Many Civilizations*. Rev. double ed. New York: Dover.

De Voogt, Alex. 1998a. "Seeded Players." *Natural History*, February, Vol. 107, Issue 1, p. 18.

———. 1998b. "Going Full Circle." *Geographical Magazine*, December, Vol. 70, Issue 12, p. 22.

U.S. News & World Report. 1995. July 3, Vol. 119, Issue 1, p. 57.

Senet

Senet (also senat) is one of the oldest recorded tabletop games known to man, though exactly how it was played in ancient Egypt is still a matter of debate.

Boards consisting of three rows of 10 spaces each have been found extensively in Egyptian archaeological sites. The oldest known representation of senet is in a painting from the tomb of Hesy (Third Dynasty ca. 2686–2613 B.C.E.). Because of the configuration, the Egyptians also called senet the game of thirty squares. Also found have been 3×12 boards and 3 × 6 boards. Some of the senet boards have had a different

Along with the more popular game of senet, which used a 30-square board, many ancient Egyptians also played a game using a 20-square board, like this piece dated to the Eighteenth or Nineteenth Dynasties (ca. 1570–1185 B.C.). The game has a similarity in design to the ancient Sumerian game board found in the royal tombs of Ur and could be a descendant of that game. (Courtesy of Oriental Institute of the University of Chicago)

configuration on the back, apparently for a game known as the game of twenty squares.

Senet is regarded to have been a race game and an ancestor of modern backgammon. Some of the archaeological finds have included pawns and sticks or knucklebones (dice) in good condition. There are also many visual depictions of Egyptians playing board games, including the likes of the Pharaoh Ramses III in a drawing from his funerary temple at Medinet Habu.

While the high elite of Egypt enjoyed the game, senet was by no means reserved for the upper class. This is indicated by the variety of boards that have been found. Some of the playing surfaces were simply scratches of 30 squares in a flat stone. Boards made of clay were common. Others were completely manufactured. It was not unusual for the more elaborate boards to contain a drawer for holding the pawns and dice and also to have the 20-square game inscribed on the underside. The pawns also ranged from the strictly functional (one set spindle-shaped, the other shaped more like a bowling pin), to the ornamental where the playing pieces were shaped like animal and human heads.

Senet's popularity is demonstrated by the number of actual artifacts uncovered, the visual representations, and the written inscriptions, one of which attests to the relaxed process of playing the game: "You sit in the hall; you play the Senet board game; you have wine; you have beer" (E. B. Pusch, 1979 in Decker 1992).

The pawns were used to move about the board. Seven pawns are shown in the oldest visual depictions. At a later time, games with both five and seven pawns are represented: some instances show ten. Four flat sticks (and later a pair of knucklebones) were used as the dice. The use of sticks with two flat sides as a game piece is also seen in several traditional Native American games. In both locations, they were used much as we would the flip of a coin, with a marked side and an unmarked side. (The concept of two-sided dice, be they sticks, shells, chips of wood, and so on, was a common device for gambling or games throughout the world in antiquity. See Africa: Abbia for more on two-sided gaming pieces in Africa.)

The senet board had six squares marked with special symbols. The 15th square (or middle square) has been referred to as the Square of Rebirth. In squares 26 to 30, there were symbols that have been interpreted as both beneficial and negative. Square 26 is considered to be a positive square, sometimes called the Beautiful House or the House of Happiness. The 27th square, which represented water, was to be avoided. Chances are pawns would be sent back to the Square of Rebirth when they landed on one of the negative squares near the end of the game. Assuming the game was a precursor to backgammon, as most scholars do, then it is reasonable to believe that all pawns had to be cleared from the board. It has been hypothesized that a player could not land on a space already occupied. Since with four sticks the highest roll of the dice would probably have been five (given when all marked sides were up), it might have been possible for players to have "blocked" their opponent from advancing if they could keep their own group of pawns in a sequential pack. Other theories agree that a spot could not be occupied by two pawns at the same time but contend that if a roll forced a pawn onto an occupied space, then the positions of the pawns would be reversed.

There is reason to suspect that the game began to take on a ritualistic meaning, particularly as part of the funereal process. Early depictions show two players contesting the game. Later depictions are usually of one player competing against an invisible opponent. Decker makes a similar contention when he says that "it probably had a symbolic significance related to the resurrection of the dead" (Decker 1992, 6).

The path was probably that of a reversed capital S, with the first positioning being in the upper left corner of the three stacked rows and the finish being in the bottom right (See Figure 1.1). This is essentially the

1	2	3	4	5	6	7	8	9	10
20	19	18	17	16	15	14	13	12	11
21	22	23	24	25	26	27	28	29	30

Figure 1.1: Senet was a popular ancient Egyptian game featuring a thirty-square board and considered to have been played in a backgammon style. Several squares had special qualities and the direction of play can be described as a "reverse-*S*" pattern. (Illustration by Gary Harrison)

tack that Timothy Kendall takes. Bell takes a dramatically different—and much more complex—approach to the game, from starting at the specially marked squares (as opposed to finishing there), to having the game end with the pawns arranged on the board in either even or odd squares. Bell's description indicates that players don't know whether they are to place their pawns on even or odd squares until after the first pawn reaches the Number 1 square. In a civilization that spawned the almighty pharaoh and unquestioned devotion to that ruler, the notion of playing a game that has inherent ambiguity to its objective seems unnatural.

To actually play the game, Kendall's descriptions have been chosen, primarily because they are simpler and because they clearly define the objective before the game begins. It is important to note that there has never been a formal description of the rules of senet on either papyrus or tomb walls. Therefore, the detailed description for how to play the game is conjecture.

To play senet, take a large, rectangular piece of paper and mark off 30 squares in three rows of 10. The middle row is counted from right to left from 11 to 20. Use seven pawns of each color from a chess set and four Popsicle sticks with a mark on one side only. Use the following summary of Kendall's proposed rules for senet, which illustrate the specially marked squares and how to play the game.

1. At the beginning of the game the seven pawns per player alternate along the 14 first squares. The starting square is counted as the 15th. In the oldest games this square featured an *ankh*, a "life" symbol. The pawns move according to the throw of four sticks or, later, one or two knucklebones. When using the sticks, the points seemed to have been counted from 1 to 5: 1 point for each side without a mark and 5 points if the four marked sides were present together.

2. When a pawn reached a square already occupied by an opponent pawn, they have to exchange their positions.

3. The special squares have the following effects on play: *Square 15*: House of Rebirth, starting square and the return square for the pawns reaching square number 27; *Square 26*: House of Happiness, a mandatory square for all the pawns; *Square 27*: House of Water, a square that can be reached by the pawns located on squares 28 to 30, which moved back when their throws did not allow them to exit the board. They have to restart from square 15; *Square 28*: House of the Three Truths, on which a pawn may leave only when a 3 is thrown; *Square 29*: House of the Re-Atoum, on which a pawn may leave only when a 2 is thrown.

4. The winner is the first to move all of his or her pawns off the board.

Sources

Bell, R. C. 1979. *Board and Table Games from Many Civilizations*. Vols. 1 and 2. New York: Dover.

Decker, Wolfgang. 1992. *Sports and Games of Ancient Egypt*. Translated by Allen Guttmann. New Haven, Conn.: Yale University Press.

Kendall, Timothy. 1978. *Passing Through the Netherworld: The Meaning and Play of Senat, an Ancient Egyptian Funerary Game*. Belmont: The Kirk Game Company.

Soubeyrand, Catherine. "The Game of Senet." *The Game Cabinet* (Internet magazine), www.gamecabinet.com/history/

⣿ ASIA

INTRODUCTION

Sports and games have long histories on the rich and diverse Asian continent, and ancient scholars and artists have left many records of these games and why they were viewed as popular or, at times, unpopular. There is a sense of balance to the way that ancient Asians seemed to approach their physical activities. They, like all ancient cultures, had sports that were born from the activities of being a warrior or soldier, but these were often tempered with a philosophical approach that tried to humanize the sport—be it archery, wrestling, or sword-and-stick fighting—in such a way that it took on elements of an art form. To be good at such sports might protect a warrior's health on the battlefield, but it could also make him healthier away from the battle. Less emphasis was placed in victory in sports competitions in China, which can be considered the cultural heart of Asia, than was the case at relatively parallel times in Greece, the standard-bearer for athletics in Europe. Further, there were activities that were designed purely for overall fitness with no thought toward competition at all.

Of course, Asia does not start and stop with China. Even in ancient times there were many Asian nations, and those nations consisted of several subcultures or ethnic groups, many with long-standing traditions that include styles of play or sports. In fact, China itself is a perfect example of how there is no singly defined "Asian" prototype. The degree of ethnic diversity is represented in traditional games that are still played in their local areas of origin in China but have never reached widespread or mainstream acceptance. Among the examples are *boyikuo*, a game resembling modern hockey played among the Daurs of northeastern China; *kalo*, which involves skipping between bamboo poles in double Dutch style and is a favorite of the Li people of Hainan Island; and a stick-and-ball game played by the Gaoshan of Fujian. Wrestling techniques that date to the eleventh century B.C. still thrive in Yunnan Province, where the fiercely independent Mongolian tribes, often the Chinese emperors' greatest threat, still live in large numbers.

While some sports have stayed primarily a local endeavor, the centuries of interaction—both peaceful and military in nature—between the peoples of Asia have also had the opposite effect of diffusing some sports, games, and physical activities across the continent. This is particularly true in the area of the martial arts, which are, in some form, practiced in virtually every corner of Asia and are prolific in the Far East areas that include China, Korea, and Japan. Here the problem becomes at times sorting out where a particular variant of a martial art really began and how it has changed. Kung fu, for example, is generally considered by Westerners to be the oldest and best known of the martial arts and is indelibly associated with China. In actuality, this style of self-defense and fighting is not a wholly Chinese invention but was an amalgamation of fighting styles that drew heavily on techniques learned from Buddhist monks who had emigrated to China around the sixth century A.D. from India.

India is something of a fountain of games and play. In addition to its long history with the martial arts, India can lay claim to several forms of board games that remain popular, including pachisi and snakes and ladders, though neither is old enough to be included in this text. India also gives us two very distinct sports that are discussed in this chapter, *kabaddi* and *gilli danda*, which are still actively played today but have never become popular beyond the Indian subcontinent.

The areas of Asia that came under the influence of Confucian thought and theory also experienced lengthy periods of state- and scholar-supported disapproval of physically aggressive sporting activities, meaning that some traditional sports—notably, wrestling, martial arts, and archery—have gone through periods of great fluctuation in terms of their overall acceptability. Some martial arts styles have begun to be recognized only within the past 100 years. This does not necessarily mean that they are new derivatives. Some were purposely kept secret by followers, in part due to the periods in Asian history when publicly being associated with a martial art could result in persecution.

The following examples of sports, play, and games have been chosen because they represent a cross-section of activities. Some were widespread practices that were shaped by input from many different cultures. Others began locally and thousands of years later have stayed local. There are activities that were undertaken with the utmost solemnity and others that seem to have been invented with free-spirited fun firmly in mind. What can also be recognized by the topics chosen for more in-depth discussion is that very few have innate characteristics that effec-tively limit participation to only the young and strong. Because the martial arts were about much more than just subduing someone in a prearranged fight, even the very old could and did practice their craft. Such was also the case with archery, kite flying, and the indoor games of go and *tou hu*.

Sources

Holcombe, Charles. 1990. "Theater of Combat: A Critical Look at the Chinese Martial Arts." *Historian*, May, Vol. 52, Issue 3, p. 411.

Levinson, David, and Karen Christensen. 1996. *Encyclopedia of World Sport*. Vols. 1–3. Santa Barbara, Calif.: ABC-CLIO.

Riordan, James, and Robin Jones, eds. 1999. *Sport and Physical Education in China*. London: E & FN Spon.

Rizak, Gene. 1989. "Sport in the People's Republic of China." In *Sport in Asia and Africa: A Comparative Handbook*, edited by Eric A. Wagner. Westport, Conn.: Greenwood Press.

Sasajima, Kohsuke. 1973. "Early Chinese Physical Education and Sports." In *A History of Sport and Physical Education to 1900*, edited by Earle F. Ziegler. Champaign, Ill.: Stipes.

SPORTS

⊞ Archery

Archery predates any of the great Ancient civilizations and was known to all of them—Egyptian, Greek, Chinese, Olmec, and Mayan. "Either by diffusion, or independent discovery, archery occurred in every part of the world except in Australia and some parts of Oceania" (Burke 1957, 11).

Like wrestling, archery is an athletic endeavor that grew from survi-valist roots and was strengthened through military applications. While some cultures utilized it, others developed it, and still others embraced the bow as a tenet of life itself.

Nowhere was a philosophy of "archer as man," more prevalent than in the Asian steppes of grasslands that separate Mediterranean Europe (the lands of ancient Greece, Rome, and their predecessors) from China. Here a variety of people utilized the bow as their primary weapon in both war and hunting. Nomadic herders, who lived with relatively few possessions, they were great horsemen. They are also remembered and recorded throughout history as viciously effective enemies.

The first of these groups was the Scythians. Less a nation than an interconnected group of similar, but often warring, tribes, the Scythians were raised to be riders and archers from birth. They traveled light and covered huge areas. From the seventh to the third centuries B.C. they dominated the European steppes and were the superior force from the Carpathian Mountains in Europe to Mongolia, 4,000 miles away. They rode better than their opponents (who sometimes didn't even employ a cavalry), they were better bowmen, and they were certainly more accustomed to hardship and living on the land because of their nomadic way of life.

The Scythians sound a great deal like the bands of marauders led by the likes of Attila (fifth century) and Genghis Khan (thirteenth century). They lived, breathed, and bred their way of life into the region. While it took superior leadership to mobilize enough of the many factions to create a terrifying and thus historic adversary to European and Chinese culture, the core ingredients of skilled archers and brilliant horsemanship never left what is often referred to as Central Asia. "Like the Huns and the Mongols who thundered across the same open grasslands centuries later, the Scythians lived in the saddle and traveled light." (Stewart 2000).

As Burke contends, the arrow took its highest flight, tied to the domestication of the horse and the evolution of a recurved, composite bow. "The archery of Central Asia was the best in the world" (Burke 1957, 15), thanks to the advancements of using different materials (composite) for added strength and turning up the ends (recurved), which added more tautness to the string and also made it easier to shoot while astride a horse.

The urban, cultured Greeks avoided the first of these horse-borne nomads until Alexander the Great came along, and by that time the Scythians' had acquired wealth that had altered their defining lifestyle. They had begun to erect permanent settlements.

The Scythians did, however, trade with the Greeks and utilized Greek artisans who lived in cities along the northern borders of the Black Sea. In this region, in what is now Ukraine, the Royal Scythians, as the Greeks called them, lived, controlling the rich soils between the Danube and the Don Rivers.

Because of some rather crude tendencies (scalping, wearing ornate, but extremely gaudy, gold jewelry, drinking too much wine, and sometimes drinking it out of gilded skulls of vanquished opponents), the Scythians were given rude treatment by the Greek writers of the day. They were, in essence, viewed as barbarians and looked down upon. But fifth-century B.C. historian Herodotus, prone to exaggeration and "legend mongering," as a Greek contemporary put it, certainly was not about to question their might: "A people without fortified towns . . . accustomed one and all to fight on horseback with bows and arrows . . . how can such a people fail to defeat the attempt of an invader not only to subdue them, but even to make contact with them?" (Stewart 2000).

As is the case with virtually any discussion of archery in ancient times, it is difficult to separate the bow and arrow from its military purposes in Asia. Certainly, though, to become proficient enough to defeat vast armies, the bow and arrow must have been used on a regular basis. That would mean that people like the Scythians practiced, and if they practiced, it would stand to reason that they would create competitions to test both their range and accuracy.

Many centuries later, in the thirteenth century, when Genghis Khan was coming as close as any man ever has to ruling the world there is direct evidence of competitions in archery. A *stela* (tribute statue) using Mongolian text was raised in approximately 1226 A.D. to honor Khan's nephew, who, during a traditional festival to celebrate a military triumph, hit a target with an arrow from 536 meters. While hitting a target from 500 meters is considered pure luck in modern archery, there are repeated references to archers from the thirteenth century who could hit a target from "500 bows," with a bow roughly equaling a meter.

Was Genghis Khan's nephew really able to strike such long-range targets? Or is this a case of exaggeration, like the famously unique 55-foot-long jump from ancient Greece (See Europe: Olympic Games)? It's certainly easier to put more stock in the claim of the Mongolian archer. After all, he was a product of literally centuries of archery emphasis, part of a vast generational lineage of warriors who learned to shoot and ride from the earliest age and born of a region, Central Asia, where "archery reached its climax" (Burke 1957, 86).

The Scythians metaphorically strung the bow for the Mongols. But, because the Scythians did not have a written language (another reason for Greek scorn), and the only lasting monuments are burial sites, their history is a bit sketchy and mostly related to military pursuits. They are pertinent for a couple of basic innovations that have often been copied. They routinely carried a variety of arrowheads, ranging from small points designed to take down a bird in flight, to heavily barbed affairs designed to inflict as much damage when pulled out as when they went in. They also invented a quiver that held both the bow and arrows (up to 200 when entering battle), called the *gorytos* (or its Greek version *korybos*, as worn by Heracles in some artistic representations of the mythical man-god's labors).

The Scythians were one of the first groups of people to emphasize archery in conjunction with horsemanship (as opposed to the Hyksos, the mysterious chariot driver/archers who invaded and eventually subjugated the Egyptians during the fifteenth and sixteenth Dynasties, around 1600 B.C.). Horsemen with bows proved a powerful combination, that would repeatedly strike justified fear into city-bound settlers throughout Eastern Europe and Asia, as it would much later in the American Wild West.

The geographic range of these early archer-equestrians is shown in their burial sites. Extravagant, ornamental gold pieces have been found along the Dnieper River, which runs through the Ukraine and into the Black Sea. More than 3,600 miles to the east, burial sites near Lake Baikal in Siberia have given other hints of these fearsome nomads—including the intriguing find of women buried with recurved bows in their graves. Herodotus popularized the notion of Amazons, a race of warrior women. Usually taken as typical Herodotian exaggeration, perhaps his claims did have some validity.

Archery in China may actually predate that of the nomadic tribes, but it never trumped it. Archaeologists have found a specific area for arrow smiths adjacent to the ruins of the royal palace of the ancient capital in the Shang Kingdom (1766–1122 B.C.). While the archer was important, he was not a solitary force. Like other ancient kingdoms, China's approach to battle employed the archer as part of a group of three: chariot driver, lancer, and archer. In China, archery was viewed as both ritual and rite of passage. A bow would be hung on the door and arrows shot into the sky when a boy was born. In the Chou dynasty (1,100 to 256 B.C.) it was a vital part of education for the noble class and was taught from the age of 15. There was an aspect of godliness to archery. Men who could hit a target were viewed as fit to participate in religious festivals because they were able and virtuous. The practice of passing down archery skills from master to student foreshadowed the practice routinely taken by the secretive martial artists societies centuries later.

Learning from a master is a common theme in archery annals. In India's epic tale "Ramayana," the two main characters, Rama and Lakshmana, receive archery training from Vashista and then perfect it from tutelage by Viswamitra. Another common archery theme is that of the superbow, so powerful that only a hero or god can use it. India joins the list in the epic "Mahabharata." The hero Arjuna is able to string such a bow and hit a target on the other side of a spinning wheel with five consecutive arrows. His risk? His life. His reward? He may marry the lovely princess Draupadi.

Archery is still very popular as a sporting activity in Asian countries. In Mongolia the heartbeat of the ancient nomads is not only heard but also emulated by nearly half of the country's population. This heritage is emphasized with the annual *naamad*, a festival celebration of the three "manly" sports of the Mongols—wrestling, horse racing, and archery. They may be considered manly, but modern archery champions are often women.

The Japanese discipline of *kyudo* is a peaceful, modern derivative of the martial art of *kyujutsu* (jutsu implies an intent to kill), which was a formidable part of the samurai's arsenal. Kyudo is linked very closely to Zen Buddhism philosophy, with greater importance placed on the archer's state of mind when the arrow is released than on the practical

During the annual Naadam competition among the Mongolian people, the traditional "manly" sports of archery, wrestling, and horsemanship are celebrated. While once the domain solely of men, Mongolian women have in recent years asserted themselves as top-flight archers. Note the dramatic recurved shape of the bow and that it is a composite of several materials, signs of the craftsmanship that helped make the ancient Asian archer a superior shot. (Photo: © Jeannine Davis-Kimball)

application of being able to hit a bull's-eye or target. The respect for archery and its powers created a Japanese version of Robin Hood, known as Nasu no Yoichi, who inspired his clan against an attacking force by shooting a fan off a ship's mast from a distance of over 400 feet. It so disquieted the attackers that Yoichi's clan of samurais were able to crush them completely. Practiced today by half a million Japanese, kyudo is quite popular with women as a means to enhance grace and manners.

Suggestions for Modern Play

As the Japanese and the Mongolians have shown, archery is no longer a male-only sport. In fact, it is one of the few sports where men and women can compete on equal ground, though in international competitions they are separated by gender. Archery is taught in many physical education classes. Female participation can be encouraged by relating how the Mongolian women often beat their brothers, husbands, and fathers in their own "manly" sport and how in Japan, women see archery as a means to heightening their elegance.

Sources

Burke, Edmund. 1957. *The History of Archery*. New York: William Morrow.
Corcoran, John, and Emil Farkas. 1983. *Martial Arts: Traditions, History, People*. New York: Gallery Books.
Holcombe, Charles. 1990. "Theater of Combat: A Critical Look at the Chinese Martial Arts." *Historian*, May, Vol. 52, Issue 3, p. 411.
"Latin America, Africa, Asia (Journal Survey)." 1995. *Journal of Sport History*, Vol. 22, No. 2, p. 183–85.
Lewis, Peter. 1985. *Martial Arts of the Orient*. New York: Gallery Books.
Lhagvasuren, Gongor. 1997. "The Stele of Ghengis Khan." *Olympic Review*, Vol. 26, No. 13, pp. 9–10.
Sasajima, Kohsuke. 1973. "Early Chinese Physical Education and Sports." In *A History of Sport and Physical Education to 1900*, edited by Earle F. Ziegler. Champaign, Ill.: Stipes.
Stewart, Doug. 2000. "Scythian Gold." *Smithsonian*, March, Vol. 30, Issue 12, p. 88.

:::: Kabaddi

A traditional team pursuit game played among the many linguistic groups that make up India, *kabaddi* has become very formalized and well organized under the governing authority of the Amateur Kabaddi Federation of India. The game is also played in Pakistan, Burma, Ceylon, and China.

It is a game that would be remarkably easy to adapt to any schoolyard, since there is virtually no equipment required. Essentially, kabaddi is a well-organized game of team tag. No bats, balls, hoops, or even special shoes are required. All that is needed is a marked-out playing field that has a standardized size of 13 meters by 10 meters (roughly 43 feet by 33 feet) (see Figure 2.1).

The two sides stay on either side of the centerline and then send one player at a time, known as a "raider," into the other team's territory. It is the raider's task to try to tag or touch, with any part of his body, as many of his opponents as possible.

What makes the game both interesting and difficult is the aspect that

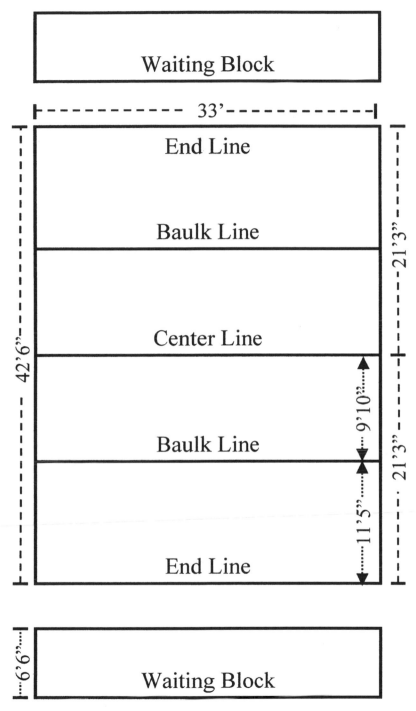

Figure 2.1: Kabaddi is an ancient game of team tag that is now played under formalized rules with a field of specific dimensions. Most popular in India, it has begun to be played sporadically in countries like England and Canada. (Illustration by Gary Harrison)

the raider must accomplish his or her (this is a game also played by women) tags without taking a breath. To ensure that raiders are not breathing, they must continually say loudly and clearly the word *kabaddi*. This process is known as the "cant." Three other factors make life difficult for the raiders: (1) for a tag to be counted, raiders must pass into enemy territory far enough to cross what is known as the "baulk line," which is three meters from the centerline, (2) raiders must return to their own territory before losing their cant, and (3) the enemy, known as the antiraiders or "antis," can physically try to detain the raiders and not allow them to return, though they cannot purposely shove them out of bounds or cover their mouth to willfully stop the cant (since the antiraiders do not want to be touched by the raider if they have not already been tagged, this is done by dodging, trapping, or blocking maneuvers).

If the raider can complete all three steps, he or she stays in the game, and any antiraider who was touched is confined to a "waiting area." A point is awarded to the team for each player whom the raider can put out. Players can be revived and returned to the game from the waiting area when one of their teammates puts out an opponent, with players returning in the order of when they were exited. The raider is allowed to come back to his or her own half of the court without touching or tagging anyone without penalty as long as he or she maintained the cant.

This process is continued until a time limit is reached. Games are usually played in two 20-minute halves with a five-minute interval, and there are scorekeepers and trained officials on hand to judge both how many tags have occurred and what the score is.

The refinement of the game has taken place primarily since 1923, when an organized set of rules was handed down by the Hind Vijay Gymkhana Baroda, which were eventually adopted for the whole subcontinent in 1944 by the Indian Olympic Association. The autonomous Amateur Kabaddi Federation was formed six years later and now organizes tournaments at the town, school, university, and state level as well as national tournaments for both men and women.

While now standardized, this indigenous game was once known by many different names, owing to the fact that India has long been a multilingual area. This is also the primary reason to suggest that it is valid to consider kabaddi a traditional, if not necessarily ancient, game to India. It has also been called *hututu, kapati, do-do-do, chedu-gudu,* and *kabardee* in different areas of the subcontinent.

In the 1990s, the game began to get increased exposure in both England and Canada. In England there was actually a weekly half-hour television show featuring kabaddi matches, while in Canada as many as 15,000 spectators showed up for the Kabaddi Canada Cup, which featured teams from India and Canada.

The Canadian version differed in two significant ways. The field was a circle 75 feet in diameter, and instead of the seemingly defining breath-holding characteristic, a 30-second time limit was used to limit the raiders' forays. There was also some renewed talk among enthusiasts of possible Olympic inclusion, although considering that it has been over 65 years since it was a demonstration sport at the 1936 Olympics, it does not seem likely that there is enough impetus behind that movement.

Suggestions for Modern Play

To adapt the game for play in the United States, here's a few more of the standard rules. Teams consist of 12 players, but only 7 are active at one time. The reserves stay in the waiting areas, which are demarcated boxes located at either end of the field. The game could be played either indoors or out, but since raiders are allowed to lunge, roll, or throw their bodies onto their half of the court upon their return, the softer landing area of a grassy field is better suited (and more traditional). Sportsmanship and fair play must be stressed so that players admit to being tagged. A respected official or final arbiter might be of value to resolve any disagreements, especially in regard to whether the raider has paused his or her cant long enough to take an additional breath. Also, it is custom that players closely crop their fingernails and that they are not allowed to wear any slippery, greasy substances. For first-time players, it might be advisable to limit the game to a pair of five-minute halves.

Sources

Arlott, John, ed. 1975. *The Oxford Companion to World Sports and Games*, London: Oxford University Press.
"On Wings of Gold." 1992. *Economist*, July 25, Vol. 324, Issue 7769, p. 8.
"Quick Wits, Good Lungs" 1992. *Macleans*, June 22, Vol. 105, Issue 25, p. 12.
Trillin, Calvin. 1996. "Kabaddikabaddikabaddi." *Time*, July 22, Vol. 148, Issue 5, p. 24.

⊞ Martial Arts of China

The martial arts in China are secretive, powerful, and often misunderstood. The origins of China's history of martial arts are an area ripe with intrigue and deception, making it difficult to tell what is myth and what is fact. Part of the problem of unraveling China's martial arts heritage is that the training and practice of the martial arts were almost always kept a secret, were often outlawed, and were usually practiced by lower-class men who did not possess the ability to read and write.

In ancient China, martial artists were "almost by definition members of the illiterate lower class and unable to leave written records of their own accounts" (Holcombe 1990). Even if they could write, because they were bound by strict codes of secrecy, they were not prone to do so.

The formative stage of Chinese martial arts goes back many centuries. Historical artifacts, including bronze work, depicting apparently martial exercises include one as old as 1,000 B.C. The Confucian thinker and author Moncius (ca. 372–289 B.C.) notes how archery skills were transferred from master to student in a way that seems similar to modern martial arts instruction. Other historical references that help to demonstrate that martial arts were known and practiced in ancient China include a fifth-century A.D. text called "Hou-Han shu," which describes the practice of striking down a projectile with the fist as commonplace. In the much later Ch'ing dynasty (1644–1911/1912), the last of the imperial regimes in this ancient land, a law stipulated that manslaughter by use of the foot, hand, metal weapon or any other instrument was subject to the death penalty. While this law does not offer direct evidence of martial arts practices, particularly in ancient China, it does suggest that by the seventeenth century, using the foot as a deadly instrument was known to happen often enough to stipulate the practice in law.

The word *wushu* is generally translated to mean martial arts. It comes from the Chinese words *wu* (war) and *shu* (skill). By the Chou dynasty (ca. 1122?–256 B.C.), it had already reached a relatively advanced stage.

This earlier date for the origins of the Chinese martial arts contradicts the legend of an Indian monk named Bodhidharma, who has often been referred to as both the "father of Chinese martial arts" and the founder of Zen Buddhism. Bodhidharma is refuted to have emigrated to China and established what became the famed Shao-lin Temple in A.D. 520, where he taught what is often referred to as Chinese boxing, which gave rise to the style of self-defense called kung fu. Bodhidharma now appears to be merely a fictional creation of historians writing many centuries later. The story was repeated so many times that it became accepted as truth. There is little certainty about the connection between the modern kung fu discipline and the Shao-lin Temple in the Sung-Shan Mountains of Honan Province. Still, some things are known. There was, and is, a temple inhabited by monks, and they did possess a fierce fighting ability. Exactly when it was founded and by whom are questionable. It is likely that from the sixth century through to the eighteenth century the monks were called upon and used by emperors for protection from threats to their kingdom but were never completely trusted to be loyal to the emperor.

Kung fu and the Shao-lin Temple became part of American pop culture with the 1970s television show called *Kung Fu*, starring David Carradine. Hollywood has also used martial arts as its primary vehicle for numerous movies, including those starring the late Bruce Lee and continuing today with the likes of Chuck Norris and Jackie Chan. Surprisingly, the connection between martial arts and entertainment is actually quite ancient and has taken the form of the ludicrous (head-butting wearing cow's horns), to the elegant, dancelike displays, both with and without weapons.

Religion and spiritual growth have long been intertwined with the practice of martial arts. During Confucian times, when the upper class did not regard physical prowess highly, martial artists were often viewed with a mix of fear and scorn and were often typecast as criminals and practitioners of the occult. In that type of environment, the temples provided one of the few safe havens for preserving the wushu traditions. It also heightened the secrecy of the practice, which is one reason that today there are a few hundred known Chinese styles of martial arts and probably many more substyles that are yet to be characterized.

As with most martial arts, the Chinese methods create a paradoxical mix of purposes: self-defense, better health through physical training and breathing techniques, and a more acute self-awareness. Today, the notion that having the ability to defend against attackers (and, if necessary, destroy them) can lead the student to a state of supreme peacefulness and serenity is generally accepted.

As an old Chinese proverb puts it: "He who overcomes others is strong. He who overcomes himself is mighty."

Sources

Corcoran, John, and Emil Farkas. 1983. *Martial Arts: Traditions, History, People.* New York: Gallery Books.

Holcombe, Charles. 1990. "Theater of Combat: A Critical Look at the Chinese Martial Arts." *Historian*, May, Vol. 52, Issue 3, p. 411.

Levinson, David, and Karen Christensen, ed. 1999. *Encyclopedia of World Sport.* Oxford: Oxford University Press.

Lewis, Peter. 1985. *Martial Arts of the Orient.* New York: Gallery Books.

⊞ Martial Arts of Other Asian Nations

Virtually every country in Asia boasts its own unique style of martial arts. Some put heavy emphasis on weapon use, like kendo in Japan, which is comparable to both modern fencing and ancient Egyptian stick fighting. Others, like judo or sumo, are essentially stylized and standardized forms of wrestling, which is itself a martial art. Some, like karate, are actually quite modern derivatives of ancient forms and therefore are not discussed here.

It is important to note that in China alone there are a few hundred styles of "martial arts." This section offers focus on four countries where unique martial arts styles with ancient histories have developed.

The martial arts in India may actually predate those practiced in China and later spread and assimilated into Japanese culture. (Essentially, the Japanese history of martial arts did not begin until the seventh century

A.D., when formal relations with China began a great incorporation of Chinese customs and habits by the Japanese.) In India, tales of warriors, princes, and gods performing remarkable, bare-handed battlefield deeds abound. In works of arts, especially in ancient Buddhist temples, warriors are depicted in positions "strongly provocative of modern karate kata (formal exercises)" (Corcoran and Farkas 1983, 191). A warrior class known as the Kshatriya was the dominant class in India, antedated the rise of Buddhism, and played the leading role in Indian culture until the rise of the Brahman (ca. 300 B.C.). As well as in art, bare-handed fighting is attested to in ancient Buddhist chronicles like the *Lotus Sutra*.

Korea, a peninsula on the southern coast of China, has long been a land and people who have battled for its own identity. Today, separated into North and South Korea in a tenuous, though possibly softening, stand-off, the Korean peoples share the history of tae kwon do, which loosely translated means "the way of kicking and striking."

Tae kwon do can be traced to the Silla dynasty (ca. 50 B.C.). Warriors, known as the Hwarang, spread traditional martial arts known as *tae kyon* (foot-hand) throughout Korea. Practiced in villages as a community form of exercise and military preparedness at least as early as the sixth century, tae kyon was outlawed during times of Japanese occupation.

Tae kwon do is distinguished from other martial arts by its emphasis on powerful kicking techniques. It also became one of the most widely practiced forms of Asian martial arts in the United States beginning in the 1950s. Exposed to tae kwon do during the Korean War, American military personnel were quite impressed with the style of self-defense and fighting they had witnessed. Many of them began practicing and then teaching the art upon their return to the point where today a tae kwon do studio—or *dojo*—can be found in virtually any town with an open storefront and a practitioner who has a bit of entrepreneurial spirit.

Thailand has its own form of martial arts—and a violent one at that. Thailand, formerly called Siam, has the unique honor of being the only Asian country never to have been under foreign control, even though this Southeast Asian peninsula has no shortage of aggressor neighbors. Thai boxing, or *muay thai* as it is correctly known, is a 2,000-year-old art stemming from the spirit of a people who would not submit. A characteristic of muay thai is that the combatants stand fully facing each other. When done correctly, this enables an easier way of blocking kicks and punches by simply raising one leg. Another characteristic is its lethal nature.

Today, muay thai, is a sanctioned sport in Thailand, though the combatants have accepted some modern means by donning gloves and foot pads instead of fighting bare-fisted. It is still extremely dangerous, and Thai boxers are perhaps the most feared of all martial artists. "Most masters of any of the martial arts concede that the best of the muay thai are the most dangerous simply because they are professional and hardened by repeated tests" (Lewis 1985, 124).

In Japan, the two oldest martial arts both deal with weapon use. One of those is defense with archery, known traditionally by the name *kyujutsu* and now practiced as a peaceful derivative known as *kyudo* (see Asia: Archery). However, it is the martial art of kendo that is most closely related to the ancient samurai warriors. Kendo dates back at least 1,500 years, making it one of the oldest of the Japanese martial arts, and it is also perhaps the truest to its original form, as opposed to judo and karate, which have evolved considerably in just the past 100–120 years. Kendo is now practiced with a bamboo pole called a *shinai* made up of four, even-length strips of bamboo that are tied together for stability. More advanced students might train and spar with a *bokken*, a wooden imitation of a real samurai sword, which is known as a *katana*.

Sources

Arlott, John, ed. 1975. *The Oxford Companion to World Sports and Games.* London: Oxford University Press.

Baker, Michael. 1999. "Korean Martial Art Kicks Its Way Back to Popularity." *Christian Science Monitor*, April 6, Vol. 91, Issue 90, p. 7.

Corcoran, John, and Emil Farkas. 1983. *Martial Arts: Traditions, History, People.* New York: Gallery Books.

Levinson, David, and Karen Christensen, ed. 1999. *Encyclopedia of World Sport.* Oxford: Oxford University Press.

Lewis, Peter. 1985. *Martial Arts of the Orient.* New York: Gallery Books.

Parney, Lisa Leigh. 2000. "Sports 101." *Christian Science Monitor*, August 11, Vol. 92, Issue 183, p. 12.

▦ T'su Chu (Chinese Football)

Claims can be made to rudimentary forms of soccer the world over. Most historians do not try to stake a claim for one particular culture as the originator of soccer. They leave that to the millions of partisan fans. One reason for the hesitancy is trying to decide what constitutes the beginning of modern soccer and what is simply kicking a ball.

China, however, does hold clear evidence of a fairly regimented game of football called *t'su chu* (also, *cuju, cuji*, or *taju*) and sometimes referred to as king ball. Evidence points to a foot-striking ball game being played as far back as 770 B.C. By the time of the early Han dynasty (206 B.C. to 8 A.D.) a game played by two teams and utilizing six goals and a ball made of animal skin stuffed with hair had been relatively standardized. Unlike the ancient ball games in Mesoamerica or the early forms of Irish hurling, the Chinese did not attribute any particular social, religious, or mystical meaning to their ball games. It wasn't until the game was transported to the Japanese and then adapted that it was assigned a fertility image aspect.

Instead, the Chinese viewed t'su chu with simple practicality: It was a valid form of fitness training for military warriors. Little emphasis was apparently placed on which team won. Instead, the notions of fair play, making good decisions under pressure, and a dignified acceptance of the outcome were stressed. It has been compared to a form of "military art," an abstraction that is perhaps a bit easier to understand by remembering that practices of hand-to-hand combat and defense were known as the martial arts.

As with almost any sport or athletic pursuit in this era of China's development, t'su chu was the domain of male members of the military and the aristocracy. Little emphasis or time was allowed for the peasantry to engage in recreational activities, especially anything that involved a team concept.

That was not necessarily the case during the early parts of the Chou dynasty (approximately 1100–256 B.C.), when physical education was very popular in schools. Also, to be in the noble class meant being a government official in times of peace and in the military services during war. Six distinct codes of conduct and learning were viewed as required elements of noble character in the Chou dynasty: (1) playing a musical instrument, (2) shooting with a bow, (3) riding horseback, (4) writing, (5) excellent ability in mathematics, and (6) mastery of civility and ceremony. This shows that physical health and skill were valued in conjunction with cultural pursuits, mental aptitude, and a level of obedience to tradition. In a way it is similar to the well-rounded man that Aristotle felt Greeks should aspire to become, creating a balance by not neglecting or overemphasizing physical prowess.

That viewpoint would begin to change in the years of the Han dynasty as the Confucian teachings began to gain a much firmer grip on official doctrine. Mental growth and quiet intellectualism as practiced in the Buddhist, Taoist, and Confucian traditions were valued at the expense of nurturing the muscles and stamina of the body. Athletics in schools ceased to exist. Civil servants were separated from the military class. Therefore, only the aristocracy and other wealthy people could utilize the military training to play t'su chu and participate in other sports, with archery probably the most popular.

As physical education in general became de-emphasized, some sports, notably the martial arts, became secretive endeavors and developed cultish sects to keep their practice alive. That was not the case with t'su chu. By the time of the Ch'ing dynasty (1644–1911), the last of the dynastic eras, ball games ceased to exist.

Suggestions for Modern Play

While the rules of the six-goal version of t'su chu are unknown, there is reference to its being called "football around a field," which might give a hint as to how the game could be played. It is possible that each team defended three goals. For modern play, it would be appropriate to have 11 players on each team, with 3 of those designated as goalies. Put two balls in play, preferably of different color. The objective would be to drive your team's ball into each of the three defended goals in a specific pattern (clockwise or counterclockwise) while at the same time defending your own goals.

Changing the shape of the field or the positioning of the goals would also impact the game. If a standard, rectangular field is used, place one goal at each end and two at equal distances from the end lines on both sides. Start with each team defending the three goals in one-half of the field. Then try it with a single team defending one end-line goal and the two furthest sideline goals. Goals could also be set up in a large circle with a team defending either three consecutive nets or every other goal.

Remember, this was a military exercise, so strategy—both offensive and defensive—would have been stressed. The task would be finding out what works best. Should you make an all-out offensive onslaught on one goal? Maybe a division of forces trying to attack in two or three areas at once works better. Or is a defensive posture of protection-first with an emphasis on counterattacks a sounder plan? Further, how do changes in the terrain (the positioning of the goals) alter a game plan?

Sources

Knuttgen, Howard G., Ma Qiuei, and Wu Zhongyuan. 1990. *Sport in China*. Champaign, Ill.: Human Kinetics Books.

Sasajima, Kohsuke. 1973. "Early Chinese Physical Education and Sport." *A History of Sport and Physical Education to 1900*, edited by Earle F. Zeigler. Champaign, Ill.: Stipes.

Umminger, Walter. 1963. *Supermen, Heroes and Gods*. London: Thames and Hudson.

▦ Wrestling: Varying Styles, Different Purposes

Sumo, perhaps the best known, though least practiced style of wrestling in the world, dates back to A.D. 23. Very ritualized in training and competition, sumo is known for the huge mass of the top wrestlers (no weight limits, à la the ancient Greeks at Olympia) and their scanty clothing (a thick belt with a diaper-like cloth to cover their genitals but not their posterior). Like two huge bull seals, the wrestlers slam together in a relatively small, circular ring 15 feet in diameter, defined by heavy

Recorded sumo wrestling matches date back nearly 2,000 years in Japanese history. In the past century top professional sumo wrestlers have been elevated to celebrity status. Sumo is one of a wide variety of wrestling styles known to Asia. (Library of Congress, Prints and Photographs Division [LC-USZ62–120838])

ropes. The object is simple: move your opponent out of the circle. Matches usually last only seconds, with the preliminary rituals taking much longer.

The wrestlers live in a closed society, almost feudal in nature, where they live, eat, and train together under the direction of coach-trainers called stable masters. There are different levels of expertise, and titles are accredited to each stage. The top-level sumo are called *Yokozuna* and are regarded as "virtual gods," (O'Brien and McCallum 1994) by the Japanese. Considerably fewer than 100 *sumotori* have achieved this status in the 2,000-year history of the sport.

While considered by fans, historians, and myth as the distillation of pure Japanese spirit, in recent times there has been considerable influx of foreigners to competition. In the late 1990s, a full 10 percent (about 90) of the sumo wrestlers were foreign-born.

Sumo is almost always represented as purely a male sport, but there have been frequent instances of women's sumo, dating back as far as the eighth century. Banned at various points over the past twelve centuries, women's sumo is virtually nonexistent today. Women's sumo usually served one of four purposes: as a rainmaking ritual, as entertainment accompanied with a show of strength, as a means of celebrating a special occasion, and as an erotic show. Women's sumo had its greatest significance when used as part of a rainmaking ritual in some rural Japanese communities. The bouts were held in a temporary ring inside a holy Shinto shrine. The contention was that this unclean act by women would anger the gods to such a degree that rain would fall.

The practice of housing and training wrestlers separated from mainstream society was also practiced in India, where the forms of wrestling known as *Pahalwani* or *Mallavidya* have been practiced since A.D. 11 as both a physical and a religious pursuit in temple-gyms known as *akharas*. It is deeply intertwined with the Hindu faith. The training philosophy is more akin to Oriental martial arts than to wrestling instruction in ancient Greece or the nomadic herdsmen of, say, Mongolia (discussed later). The objective is to teach self-discipline and to sharpen a man's soul and spirit through rigid training of his body. Very similar theories about wrestling and physical structures for the purpose of wrestling are seen in Iran (see Middle East: Wrestling).

Akharas are equipped with fine-grit, dirt floors, saturated with oils. A noted component of Indian wrestling is the use of one's own body for strength training through exercises like *yogi* (posture stretches), *bethak* (squats), *dand* (push-ups), and massage. They also routinely swung weighted balls, maces, and clubs. Indian males did not have to be part of the temple-gym, however, to enjoy and cherish wrestling as a sport worth practicing.

The Thadou-Kuki, an Assam people of northeastern India, saw wrestling as a pure and highly regarded sport for youth. They also picked an unusual time for a group wrestling match—weddings. The opposition was defined as soon as the engagement was announced. Following the wedding ceremony the male kin of the bride would square off against the male relatives of the groom. Victory did not result in any sort of material rewards. Rather, the contest was held for the sheer joy of the sport and honor. In time, a superior wrestler could receive a degree if he won seven such wedding matches. The practice remained relatively unchanged for centuries, providing kinship unity and a bit of a reminder of bride-capturing by show of strength.

In Mongolia, the men have participated for centuries in what they consider the "three manly sports" of archery, equestrian races, and wrestling. This traditional gathering is still practiced in the area that the Xinhua News Agency called "north China's Inner Mongolia Autonomous Region." Each year hundreds of thousands gather to recapture and replenish the spirit of their past in colorful *naadams*, gatherings for sporting activities. The wrestling matches are as popular as baseball games in the United States. The wrestlers wear an interesting ensemble that could be linked in a fashion sense to the modern professional wrestler's attire: open-fronted, long-sleeved vest, sporting shorts, and high boots. They wrestle standing up, with the winner being the person who can throw his opponent off-balance, forcing him to touch either his knee, elbow, or back to the ground. While wrestling is still a male-only affair, women do compete in other naadam events (see Asia: Archery).

Korea is home to a style of wrestling that may be related to both sumo and the Mongolian style. Believed to be over 2,000 years old, *ssirium* is the native style of Korean wrestling. In South Korea it has grown steadily in popularity in recent years, particularly after a 36-year period of Japanese occupation ended following World War II.

In South Korea, which hosted the 1988 Summer Olympics in Seoul, there has been a resurgence of interest in traditional sports in general and ssirium in particular. In ancient times the wrestling matches for this male sport took place as part of special annual festivals. It was typical for the wrestling festivities to start with matches between very young wrestlers, with a gradual escalation in ages and experience until full-grown men competed against one another.

The matches are conducted in large sandpits. The wrestlers are garbed in a cloth belt that is tied to their waist and around their right thigh. The objective is to throw one's opponent on the ground so any part of his body touches other than his feet. Each match consists of three rounds, with a round ending when one wrestler has thrown another. In the case of neither wrestler's completing a throw, the round typically ends after three minutes. In terms of dress and the appearance of the wrestling ring there are similarities to Japanese sumo, but the objective is significantly different. Further, since the matches can last significantly longer than the typical sumo match (which often is over in a matter of seconds), the wrestlers do not gain the huge amounts of bulk that a sumo wrestler does since that would inhibit their endurance.

It has been speculated that sumo may have been a derivative of the Korean form and that ssirium actually stemmed from a Mongolian tradition (Knez 1960). Certainly, the Japanese have a long history of adopting Chinese cultural values as their own, so it is possible they might have been willing to borrow from Korea and adopted and adapted the ssirium style, though no evidence is presented by Knez to back up either lineage claim. What is known is that the Koreans have adapted one aspect of sumo to their own national style of wrestling: ssirium is now a professional sport in Korea, with top wrestlers being well paid and matches televised.

Whether highly ritualized, regimented, or conducted in a carnival atmosphere, wrestling always has at its core at least a trace of ego-driven desire to prove superiority or worthiness in front of the rest of the community. When external control influences like spectators (sumo/ssirium), religion (the Indian akharas), or family and festival (naadam) are eliminated, wrestling can betray its brutal base.

For the Chukchi, a reindeer-herding people who cover the expanse of northern Asia, wrestling is extremely fierce and usually involves multiple stages, including a freestyle and then an "attacker" versus "passive" stage, where it is incumbent on the attacker to be able to throw the passive subject. Wrestling tournaments are usually round-robin affairs and taken quite seriously. Postmatch shouting and physical confrontations are not uncommon because the Chukchi male prides himself on fierceness, endurance, and strength.

Women also wrestle, and their matches also tend to degenerate into postmatch scuffles. "The will to be fierce and the desire to win make a volatile combination" (Blanchard and Cheska 1985, 58).

Usually, the basic motivation behind a wrestling match is to prove one-on-one superiority. Sometimes a match is held to solve personal disputes. In the Philippines, the aspect of resolution is taken one formal step further. A wrestling match can become a legal solution in a land dispute.

The purpose and the location make the "trial by *bultong*" in the Philippines a most interesting example of traditional wrestling. This is an accepted means of settling the often-occurring boundary disputes in the rice paddies. If the boundary is not well marked, the question of ownership eventually comes up. Then comes the "trial by bultong or wrestling" (Barton 1919). These matches can range from being very friendly (when the disputants are kinsmen), to relatively serious if the two parties contesting the rice paddy boundary are not related.

The paddy owners can fight themselves or choose a champion to do their wrestling for them. The wrestling matches create a popular diversion, drawing spectators. What is unique is that the wrestling match takes place on the disputed boundary itself. It is understood that the ancestral spirits decide whether the plaintiff or the defendant is in the right and that the fall will take place exactly where the boundary is supposed to be. Since the paddies are often terraced, this can often be a very literal "fall" of 10 to 15 feet into the mud and water of the lower terrace.

In effect, the losing wrestler is viewed to have been in the wrong, and the new, undisputed boundary will be where the loser fell. For that reason the Ifuagos try desperately not to be driven backward into their own field since it would be better to lose the match near the dispute line than to take a chance on losing the match *and* a significant amount of a rice paddy, too.

To ensure that the ancestors make the right choice, the proper sacrifices need to be offered. If it's a friendly match, not much is wasted on the sacrificial altar other than some dried meat. For more serious matches numerous chickens and as many as three pigs might be sacrificed.

Sources

Barton, R. F. 1919. *Ifuago Law*. Berkeley: University of California Press.
Bergman, Sten. 1938. *In Korean Wilds and Villages*. Translated by Frederick Whyte. London: John Gifford.
Blanchard, Kendall, and Alyce Taylor Cheska. 1985. *The Anthropology of Sport*. South Hadley, Mass.: Bergin and Garvey.
Chase, Guy. 1999. "All in Wrestling, Submission Wrestling" (Web site), www.guychase.com, Multi-culture Martial Arts Academy.
Dumia, Mariano A. 1979. *The Ifuago World*. Edited by Jean Edades. Quezon City, Republic of the Philippines: New Day.
Gaouette, Nicole. 1998. "Weighing in on a Sumo Match." *Christian Science Monitor*, February 27, Vol. 90, Issue 64, p. 1.
Kaneda, Eiko. 1999. "Trends in Traditional Women's Sumo in Japan." *The International Journal of the History of Sport*, September, Vol. 16, No. 3. pp. 113–19.
Knez, Eugene Irving. 1960. *Sam Jong Dong: A South Korean Village*. Ann Arbor, Mich.: University Microfilms.
Mulling, Craig. 1989. "Sport in South Korea: Ssirium, the YMCA and the Olympic Games." In *Sport in Asia and Africa: A Comparative Handbook*, edited by Eric A. Wagner. Westport, Conn.: Greenwood Press.
"Nadam Festival Opens in Inner Mongolia." 2000. *Xinhua News Agency*, June 7.
O'Brien, Richard and Jack McCallum. 1994. "Weighty Concerns." *Sports Illustrated*, January 10, Vol. 80, Issue 1, p. 12.

PLAY

▓ Breathing Exercises

The practices of breathing exercises like *dao yin* in ancient China, *suryanamaskar* in India, and many other forms, most with roots in the meditative philosophies of Buddhism, are forms of physical and mental fitness regimens and are absolutely vital components to many Eastern civilizations. In both China and India, learning how to breathe properly was a daily practice that was fundamental to the highly valued qualities of overall fitness and mental well-being.

This section focuses primarily on the Chinese physical art of *dao yin*, which was seen as a means to create the balance between the opposite and sometimes contradictory forces in the universe known as the yin and the yang.

Dao yin is a traditional exercise that emphasizes the intake of breath *combined with* regimented physical motions. The exercise is undertaken with a calm demeanor. As with other physical exercises from the early era of China—notably, the martial arts forms that fall under the general category of *wushu*—dao yin imitates animal movements while emphasizing a harmony of motion, breathing, and the practitioner's mental state.

While wushu (see Asia: Martial Arts of China) generally emphasized the martial, or warlike, movements of animals (or was practiced as a form of entertainment), dao yin was the sanctuary of all men and women as they strove for one of the most honored goals in Chinese society, that of a long, healthy life.

This key objective in the practice of dao yin was to promote the positive and consistent flow of *qi* (pronounced *chee*). Translated, qi means air, but it meant much more than just a molecular combination of hydrogen and oxygen. Qi is a product of the philosophy known as Taoism, which contends that everything in the universe is interconnected. Qi is the element that both forms the human body and provides the mental and physical vitality to make that connection to the rest of the external world. To have a healthy qi required plenty of healthy breathing, done in a yin-yang manner of balancing the various pulls in life.

In a practical sense, dao yin became an imitation of those things in the universe that surrounded people—other animals, many of whom possessed traits (speed, strength, stamina, flight) that were superior to those of people. Each individual movement associated with the breathing exercise had—and still has—a specific purpose. A silk wall hanging discovered in 1973 at a tomb in Hunan Province and dating to the early Han dynasty (168 B.C.) has been particularly helpful in detailing some of the ancient mysteries of dao yin. The painting has several identifiable categories, including movements that specifically imitate animals, some designed to treat disease, and others done with a physical tool, like a staff.

As the Han dynasty waned around A.D. 200, China became a fractured country with little centralized government. This was not uncommon during the very long history of a land that we often mistakenly think of as being homogeneous in both terrain and population. In fact, China consists of many different types of geography and peoples. In its way, the history of the practice of dao yin is a classic example of how, for every force, there is an opposite, contradictory force (yin and yang). Buddhism became the focal spiritual linchpin of the region, and physical exercise became less important, though breathing exercises, now in the shape of the meditative and relatively sedentary yoga, were still important.

Dao yin did not disappear completely but became significantly less popular as there was a shift of faith toward medicinal cures for the body. There were long periods of time where the scholarly elite in China avoided any form of physical exercise because of the overriding belief, proposed by Confucius, that those who used their brain (the elite) were inherently superior to those who had to use their brawn (common laborers).

As China became united into 10 distinct and centrally reporting districts under the Sui and Tang dynasties, dao yin once again became a popular and prescribed means of dealing with everyday health.

Also in China, the Shao Lin priests practiced a more secretive method of breathing called *chi-gong* (also *qi gong*), which has been attributed by a few staunch believers as having the power to cure otherwise debilitating diseases. The practice of qi gong by the Falun Gong has become the subject of harsh rebuke and debate in modern China. In the summer of 1999 the Chinese government banned the Falun Gong, which emphasizes the breathing exercises as a means of tapping into the qi, or the body's vital energy, making rather modern claims that it can arrest the aging process and smooth wrinkles. The Chinese government claimed that the group's leader is a fraud.

As was mentioned, breathing exercises were not the sole domain of the Chinese. In addition to the ancient people of India, breathing exercises were practiced with some regularity in Korea, even though that country never embraced the Taoist philosophies (instead, remaining a primarily Buddhist country). In addition, the traditional training of Buddhist monks in the rural monasteries of central Thailand includes specific instruction from the elder monks on the proper way to breathe during meditation.

Suggestions for Modern Play

The idea of "practicing breathing" is not an innate notion in the West but is becoming increasingly prevalent in the United States, usually stemming from the study of yoga. Finding a yoga class offered by a private instructor or through local town recreation departments is not a difficult task in most areas of the country.

Also there are numerous self-help books about how proper breathing techniques can help people to combat such concerns as stress, fatigue, weight gain, and stamina loss. While many emphasize just one potential gain of proper breathing as opposed to the more Eastern "full mind and body" approach, they are an indication that people in Western civilizations are finally tapping into a source of good health that has been practiced in China and other Eastern countries for well over 2,000 years. As opposed to the Buddhist monks and experienced yogis of the East, in the United States there are now medical specialists called respiratory therapists who work primarily in hospitals, though most practice their craft in emergency situations or for patients with pronounced lung disorders.

Students who would like to try the refined combination of body movements and harmonious breathing that characterizes dao yin might instead look toward the martial arts. While many martial arts emphasize quick and strong physical thrusts, others are focused on improving overall flexibility and wellness, without an emphasis on musculature or the development of power. Tai chi (also *taiji* or *taijiquan)* is the martial art most closely linked to the meditative Taoist philosophy of improving overall health by promoting a healthy and balanced flow of qi through the body.

Sources

Bourland, Julia. 1998. "Breathing Lessons." *Women's Sports & Fitness*, November/December, p. 50.
Clark, Charles Allen. 1932. *Religions of Old Korea*. New York: Fleming H. Revell.
Mitchell, Tracey. 1999. "Respiratory Therapists Give the Breath of Life." *Career World*, January, Vol. 27, Issue 4, p. 20.
Reid, Craig D. 1994. "Cystic Fibrosis and Chi-Gong." *Nutrition Health Review: The Consumer's Medical Journal*, Issue 70, p. 11.
Riordan, James, and Robin Jones, eds. 1999. *Sport and Physical Education in China*. London: E & FN Spon.
Terwiel, B. J. 1975. *Monks and Magic: An Analysis of Religious Ceremonies in Central Thailand*. Lund, Sweden: Curzon Press.
Watts, Jonathan. 1999. "Chinese Government Clamps Down on Falun Gong Sect Members." *Lancet*, August 7, Vol. 354, Issue 9177, p. 495.

⊞ Gilli Danda

Gilli danda is one of the rare games that is extremely ancient (perhaps 5,000 years old), is still played but has not spread significantly from its point of origin.

It is played in India, Pakistan, and Sri Lanka, with only slight variations, and also goes by the names of *gulli danda* or *danda guli* in the two former countries, while known primarily as *gudu* in Sri Lanka.

The name stems from the two sticks that are the only real equipment. The *gilli* is about five inches long, and the *danda* is about two feet long. Both are cut from the same length of wood and should be about an inch in diameter. The shorter gilli is then sharpened to a dull point at each end, while the danda is pointed at only one end. The game is played in an open field and can be played by two equal-numbered teams (normally not to exceed seven per team) or two individuals.

The game begins after a small hole, roughly the size of the gilli, has been dug, the two teams have decided which team will be the first to field, and the orders of play have been defined.

The game begins by placing the gilli over the hole, called a *guchhi*. The first player then inserts his larger stick, the danda, underneath the shorter one and then flings it as far as he can, trying to send it away from his opponents. This is because if the gilli is caught, the player is out. Also, once the gilli is stopped or comes to rest, the fielding team then has a chance to retire the player by throwing the gilli back and hitting the danda, which by this time has been placed over the hole.

The word "danda" has an interesting background. Meaning "big stick," the term has some very specific connotations, especially related to ancient India. The term *danda-niti* meant the "law of the big stick," or the law of punishment. It asserted that the king had the right to use force (in a just way) to keep the social order, specifically to keep "the big fish from swallowing the little fish."

The real fun of the game starts when the player is not retired in either of these two ways. He then returns the gilli to its initial spot over the hole and is entitled to three attempts to hit the gilli. He initiates these contacts by giving the gilli a tap on one of its ends, which pops it into the air, and then striking it as hard as possible with the danda. The player then gets two more attempts, striking the gilli farther and farther away from the hole in the ground. After the third attempt, the player returns to the guchhi and places his danda across the hole. One of the fielders will then try to throw the gilli, again with the objective of hitting the danda or getting it to fall into the hole. Three well-struck hits can send the gilli several hundred feet from the guchhi, making the return throw very unlikely to be successful. Of course, if the player misses on one or more occasions while trying to impart the "law of the big stick" upon his gilli then the likelihood of being retired is greater.

While commonly played in northern India by boys in the streets, there is some strictness to the rules. There are standard turns for play, which could be termed innings, as would be the case in baseball or cricket. That one team is trying to "field" the gilli while the other team puts it into play is also similar to the bat-and-ball games of baseball and cricket.

Scoring is a bit of an elaborate barter system. The scoring system is based on a unit of measurement called the *anna* which is equivalent to the length of the danda. The team that is "up" requests a certain number of annas, which should be equal to the distance between the guchhi and the final resting place of the gilli after the fielding team's return throw. The fielding team can agree to that total, and it will be rewarded. They can also challenge the number of annas, and then a measurement will take place. If the requested amount proves to be too great on a challenge, then the player is out. A player can continue to be "up" until he is out.

Play continues until a predetermined number of innings has been completed, with the winning team being the team with the most annas.

Gilli danda is truly a folk game. There is no official organization or association that administers the game or organizes tournaments. Probably a creation of young boys in ancient times, they are still the game's lone keepers and rule-makers.

Suggestions for Modern Play

Little about the rules needs to be changed unless the teams of players decide to change them. That seems to be the most significant aspect of gilli danda—the children playing the game served as their own rule-makers, umpires, and arbiters in the case of disagreement. This used to be common practice among children across America even as few as 30 years ago, but increasingly any form of competitive play in the United States is now under the organizational guidance of adults. The beauty of this game is how the Indian children have taken the crudest of implements and established a complex game that is self-governed. The suggestion is to show the game to children, instruct them in the bare necessities of the rules, encourage them to give it a try, and then leave them alone. Let the children create their own peculiar ground rules, teach each other the best way to strike the gilli, develop their own scoring system, and, most importantly, learn to settle differences by themselves.

Sources

Arlott, John, ed. 1975. *The Oxford Companion to World Sports and Games*. London: Oxford University Press.
Jernigan, Sara Staff, and C. Lynn Vendien. 1972. *Playtime: A World Recreation Handbook*. New York: McGraw-Hill.
Kosambi, D. D. 1965 *Ancient India*. New York: Pantheon Books.

▦ Jacks-Style Games

Like children in almost every part of the world, the children of the many different people in Asia commonly played a type of game that can be considered similar to our modern game called jacks.

The biggest difference is that Asian children played not with a bouncing ball but usually with game pieces that were all the same and consisted of either smoothed, somewhat flat stones, small sacks filled with sand or grains, or, especially in ancient times, the knucklebones of sheep and occasionally humans.

The term knucklebones commonly crops up in literature of ancient activities. The games routinely had local variations. It is not known where the games were invented. Comparing jacks-style games to some other nearly universal activities (archery, wrestling), it is probable that they developed independently in many areas of the world. Since many of the games are played with natural objects (stones, bones) as opposed to something man-made, it seems reasonable to suspect that children all over the world would use their own ingenuity to make the simple, natural task of tossing and catching an object into a codified, rule-controlled game, with younger children learning from older siblings.

In Mary D. Lankford's well-researched children's book *Jacks around the World*, she discusses six variations of jacks played in Asian countries: *otedama* from Japan, *zhua san* from China, five stones from Singapore, *kong keui* from South Korea, *maakgep* from Thailand, and *abhadho* from the mountainous country of Tibet.

Otedama originated in the ninth century and is still played today, usually by two, three, or four girls. The word comes from *te*, meaning hand, and *dama*, meaning ball, but a ball is not used. Instead there are nine small, silk bags filled with rice or beads. One of them is usually made distinctive from the other by having a separate color and is called the chief or parent. The game starts by tossing all bags in the air but catching only the chief bag. Then the chief bag is tossed, and one bag is picked up. This is repeated until all bags are caught. In the second round, two bags are picked up on each toss. The third round has three bags picked up twice, then the remaining two. The fourth and final round calls for four bags to be picked up on successive tosses. Each round is accompanied by particular words or phrases, as is common in jacks games, to denote what stage a player is in. Completing all four rounds is a winning effort.

Zhua san is played with small stones. It can be played by many people, but three is the usual number of players. Each brings nine of his or her own stones, but all stones are used during play. Just deciding who starts first could test eye-hand coordination. All stones are held in the palm, tossed in the air, then caught on the back of the hand. The person who catches the most goes first. From that point, the object is to continue to toss all stones in the air but to catch a certain number—depending on the stage of the game—on the back of the hand. Too many caught means that one is "fed up to death" and loses one's turn. Too few caught, and the player is "starved to death" and also loses a turn. The players also try to sweep up stones in one smooth motion, with their opponents having the opportunity to place stones at certain times in a way that will make it difficult for them to be swept up. Play continues until all stones are won, and the player with the most stones wins.

Five stones as it is played in Singapore is actually played with small, triangular-shaped bags filled with rice, sand, or seed. It is an elaborate game of tossing, picking up, and then placing the "stones," at times utilizing both hands (unusual for Jacks-style games) within a small circle.

There are eight designated steps. Since Singapore is a melting pot of cultures—there are four official languages (Mandarin Chinese, Malay, Tamil, and English)—it is likely that the local game is an amalgamation of several different styles. "Since some steps in this game are almost like juggling, it takes practice, skill and good hand-eye coordination to play" (Lankford 1996).

Kong keui is a bit different from many jacks games because it is primarily the domain of boys. It has three stages called *al-nat-ki*, *al-hpoum-ki*, and *al-kka-ki*, which mean "laying the eggs," "setting the eggs," and "hatching the eggs." Using five stones, it starts like many other variations. One stone is tossed, and the other four are picked up one at a time. That's called laying the eggs. Next, while the tossed stone is airborne, one stone at a time is nudged under the other hand, which is palm side down on the ground forming a nest. This is setting the eggs. In the final stage, three "eggs" are left on the ground, one is used as the tossing stone, and the fifth is placed inside the curled little finger of the throwing hand. While the tossed stone is airborne, the little finger stone is used to tap the other stones on the ground, one at a time. This is hatching the eggs.

Thailand's maakgep game is played with five stones to a predetermined score, usually 20. The key in this game is consistency combined with the ability to catch as many stones as possible on the back of one's hand. It starts by picking up one stone at a time while a selected stone is tossed. When all four stones are picked up, then all five are placed in the palm, and tossed, and the number caught on the back of the hand is how many points that have been earned. The second round is the same, except that two stones are picked up, then three, and one on the next round, and four at a time in the fourth round.

Abhadho, the game from Tibet, also uses five stones and goes through the steps of tossing and picking, first one stone, then two, then three stones, then four stones. One difference is that in the third round, the other player chooses which three stones are to be picked up. The game is ended by tossing all five stones in the air and then catching them on the back of the hand. The Tibetans play variations that are similar to the "setting the eggs" stage of the Korean kong keui game. In one, the non-throwing hand is placed with the fingertips on the ground and the palm raised to form a bridge, and stones are placed under the bridge. In another, the fingertips are spread apart more to form a shape like the talons of a bird, and the stones have to be placed in the gaps between the fingers, one per gap. Lankford notes that the Tibetans, especially, play for fun, not to determine a winner. Another difference is that they still routinely use bones (usually from goats' knees) as playing pieces, which is not surprising considering they are, by and large, nomadic herders.

Source

Lankford, Mary D. 1996. *Jacks around the World*. New York: Morrow Junior Books.

⊞   Kite Flying and Kite Fighting

In China and other Asian countries the wind-borne kite has long been a popular item that at times has had very utilitarian uses. It is said that as many as 3,000 years ago the Chinese used huge kites to pull wheeled vehicles across the plains, letting the wind do the work that otherwise would have tired out several animals. They also were used as a military signaling device in China as early as the sixth century.

Kites have certainly evolved in size, shape, and popularity to dramatic proportions in the Orient. An offshoot of the interest in kite flying is the sporting pastime known as kite fighting, which is practiced in Japan, China, Thailand, and India and also has devotees as far away as South America. Exactly when kite fighting became a popular pursuit is difficult to define, although there are seventeenth-century references of using a kite to "fight" from both Thailand and Japan.

The Thai episode was an example of kite-versus-man battle, with the kite being used for a specific military purpose during the reign of King Pet Raju in the late seventeenth century. One of the king's generals was having a difficult time overcoming the strong defensive fortifications of a rebellious prince who was causing disharmony in the kingdom. Having met with no success in traditional offensive forays, the general decided to fly kites equipped with fuses and gunpowder over the defensive perimeter and directly into the prince's city. The resulting fire and confusion led to the fall of the city. Also significant is that this is the first time that references to Thai kites used the terms *chula*, meaning a large kite representing a male, and *pakpao*, meaning a smaller, female kite.

The first kite-versus-kite wars were possibly fought in Japan in the seventeenth century as a countermeasure taken by rice farmers in Shirone, a city still famous today for its kites. Kite flying had become so popular that the farmers became disgusted with the number of kites that crashed into their rice paddies and destroyed valuable crop. They took an offensive approach and launched their own kites to "attack" the interlopers in the airspace above the paddies.

While it might seem as if a downed kite would do minimal damage, it is important to recognize that some Asian kites were (and are) significantly larger and heavier than the standard-issue American kites bought each spring at a department store or oceanside convenience shop. First, remember the reference to kites' being able to haul heavy wagons across China. While their size is not reported, it is logical to surmise that they must have been quite large to be able to trap that much wind power. In modern Japan it is not unusual for a group of neighbors to join together

Kite flying has been an activity for all ages in Asia for centuries. These two young boys take part in a kite-flying contest in Japan as part of a New Year's Day celebration in the first quarter of the twentieth century. (Library of Congress, Prints and Photographs Division [LC-USZ62–91893])

to build a fighting kite that might cost the equivalent of $1,700 and be as large as 23 feet by 17 feet (nearly 400 square feet). In Yokaichi, a 300-year-old tradition is to hoist a huge kite weighing over a ton and measuring 39 feet by 42 feet. These huge, rectangular "monster" kites, known as *odako*, sometimes require an entire village to hoist them into the air.

As with so many other cultural and sportive aspects of life, the Japanese adopted their fascination with kites from the Chinese, roughly around the sixth and seventh centuries during a time of politically encouraged trade between the two countries. This was also the time period when kite flying as a leisure activity grew in popularity in China during the Sui and Tang dynasties (581–907).

While Japan emphasizes size, China, the most populous nation in the world, focuses on beauty in its kite making. Delicately painted silk is shaped into unique, three-dimensional shapes, a custom that began in the Tang dynasty. Kites were made into the forms of birds, insects, animals, and even humans.

No matter the beauty, shape, or size, all kites must be able to fly to actually be kites. Some fly exceptionally well, with the ability—in the hands of an experienced kite master—to perform elaborate tricks. This is the critical aspect of kite fighting, where kites duel to the "death."

While kite fighting itself cannot be considered an ancient sport, it is fascinating to see how an ancient, lighthearted form of play—flying a kite—has evolved into a dramatic and competitive sport. Different styles of kite fighting have evolved in different regions. In India the kites routinely reach a mile in height. They are usually equipped with two strings, one for controlling the kite and the other covered in powdered glass and used by the kite's operator to try to cut through the control string of the other kite.

Thailand has developed a "battle of the sexes" with its kites, and well-organized leagues have a five-month-long season. The larger, male kite—the chula—is a star-shaped version. Its maximum size was recently reduced to standard heights of 80 and 65.5 inches tall for competition. Formerly, kites as large as seven-and-a-half feet tall were common. The sizes were reduced because of concern for the safety of the kite operators. Even with the reduced size, it often takes as many as 10 people to control the chulas in battle: a chief operator who sits in a chairtype pulley, a second-in-command, and about eight boys as rope pulley pullers. This is usually the way a young boy gets his introduction to kite fighting.

The *chula* is always matched against the smaller, diamond-shaped *pakpao* (female) kite, which has a maximum vertical height of 28.5 inches and is manned by a single operator. The *chula* must make the first advancement into the *pakpao*'s territory. Because of its smaller size, the *pakpao* can dance around the larger *chula* and tries to wrap its string around a point of the star and in this way drag the big kite to the ground. The *chula* utilizes several bamboo slats attached to its string and with these tries to ensnare the string or the tail of the *pakpao* and drag it down to the ground and into the *chula*'s territory.

Sources

Anderson, Wanni Wibulswasdi. 1989. "Sport in Thailand." In *Sport in Asia and Africa: A Comparative Handbook*, edited by Eric A. Wagner. Westport, Conn: Greenwood Press.

Arlott, John, ed. 1975. *The Oxford Companion to World Sports and Games*. New York: Oxford University Press.

"Bid the Wind Blow." 1995. *Economist*, May 6, Vol. 335, Issue 7913, p. 88.

Delp, Laurel, and Peter Charlesworth. 1998. "Land of the Rising Kite." *Travel Holiday*, April, Vol. 181, Issue 3, p. 88.

"Killer Kites." 1996. *Civilization*, March/April, Vol. 3, Issue 2, p. 35.

▦ Swinging

The swing has a varied history in many ancient Asian countries, but its use has most importantly marked one of the rare opportunities for girls and women to participate in a physically demanding and exhilarating activity.

In Korea, swinging was a favorite exercise for girls that at times could be considered an acrobatic challenge of balance and nerves. Often swinging competitions were held, with the objective to see which girl could swing the highest on an extremely long swing (some stretching 80 feet). Heights were measured by touching a string that had been suspended.

Swing competitions were often held in conjunction with wrestling matches at the time of festival gatherings. In the Upper Han Hamlet, there was a special "Swing Day," which was used as a way of marking the coming of summer. Prior to the celebration, swings would be erected on hills or on the stream banks. In this instance it is reported that boys did play on the swings during the day, but at night they became female property. The swings were similar to the typical playground swing (except for their height). They used two ropes of equal length attached at opposite ends of a wooden plank that served as the seat. It was not uncommon for the Korean women to swing while standing upright, as opposed to being seated.

This was also true in other regions when on the fifth day of the fifth moon (roughly May 5), the holiday known as either Tan-O or Dan-oh was held. Regarded as a women's holiday, the women had the opportunity to demonstrate significant prowess on the swing, either solo or in pairs, while dressed in their prettiest clothing. Wagering on the winner of the swing competition was popular.

It was not a game without danger. "The Koreans are adventurous swingers, and accidents are not infrequent. The rough straw ropes break sooner or later, and someone gets a nasty fall, which terminates the sport for the season" (Hulbert 1906, 278).

In China's courts the swing was the favorite pastime for the imperial concubines in the Han dynasty (202 B.C. to A.D. 8) as well as later. Prior to taking on a sexual connection, it was a popular pastime, and considered to be the only "sport" for women, and was known as *chin ch'ien*, and may have been adopted from conquered barbarians to the north in the seventh century B.C.

The swing was a natural plaything in the jungles of Southeast Asia, and the aboriginal peoples of the Andaman Islands were observed partaking of the pleasures of the swing by means of 40- to 50-foot creeping vines that descended from the tree limbs. The use of the swing by children was also reported among the Toradja, who live in the mountainous region of central Celebes, which is now a part of Indonesia. The latter group would attach boards to the swing and then straddle the rope.

Sources

Bergman, Sten. 1938. *In Korean Wilds and Villages*. Translated by Frederick Whyte. London: John Gifford.

Han, Chungnim C. 1949. *Social Organization of Upper Han Hamlet in Korea*. 1970 copy. Ann Arbor, Mich.: University Microfilms.

Hulbert, Homer B. 1906. *The Passing of Korea*. New York: Doubleday, Page.

Man, Edward Horace. 1932 (1885). *On the Aboriginal Inhabitants of the Andaman Islands*. London: Royal Anthropological Institute of Great Britain and Ireland.

Sasajima, Kohsuke. 1973. "Early Chinese Physical Education and Sport." In *A History of Sport and Physical Education to 1900*, edited by Earle F. Ziegler. Champaign, Ill.: Stipes.

GAMES

Go

Go is a tabletop board game of strategic position usually played by two people. It is one of the few board games from antiquity that is still a popular pastime today *and* has not changed substantially in its rules of play.

It originated in China over 4,000 years ago, where it is known as *wei ch'i*. The game is also known as *baduk* in Korea. The game is known for a board with 19 parallel lines intersected by 19 evenly perpendicular lines and the black-and-white game pieces traditionally made from slate and clamshells. It is still intensely popular in the Asian countries of Japan, Korea, China, and Taiwan, where a relative resurgence of play has spawned professional tournaments offering large cash prizes and created an overall number of players that exceeds the number of chess players in the West.

Because the board is designed as 19 lines by 19 lines, there are 10 axis points from the center in all directions. This has led some observers to suggest that it was an early forerunner to the abacus, the ancient calculator and another Chinese invention. Because of the black-and-white stones, it has also been compared to a visual representation of the philosophical notion of yin and yang, meaning that everything in life is balanced by a countering object or emotion (earth and air, fire and water, passive and aggressive, etc.). A major emphasis in mastering the game is learning how to balance aggressive tactics with patience in order to gain territory without leaving oneself vulnerable.

One famous legend holds that an emperor created the game to improve the intelligence of a slow-thinking son. Whether that legend is nothing more than an explanatory myth or is really grounded in fact, it is known that by the time of Confucius (about 600 B.C.), go had become a significant part of the Chinese culture. At that time it was regarded as one of the "four acccomplishments" (along with brush painting, poetry, and music) that must be mastered by the Chinese gentleman. It was primarily a game for the noble class and was played by men and women.

Still, go's history in mainland China has not always been one of noble acceptance. Confucius himself held that the game was a waste of time. Because of that opinion, the game's development stalled. It wasn't until the game was taken to Japan A.D. 600–800 that it began to reach its full potential as a challenge. By this time, it had also been accepted into Korea as a popular pastime. In Japan it really began to thrive after the warlord Tokugawa unified Japan in 1602 and decreed that four schools of go would be established.

Each year the winner of a tournament consisting of representatives from the four schools would be appointed to a high-ranking position called minister of go. With such political clout behind it, go reached a new level of skill and popularity. After a period of decline in the late 1800s, go got another boost in the 1920s with the formation of the Japan Go Association and the concurrent support of major newspapers deciding to sponsor—and extensively cover—tournaments. Newspapers in Korea also have taken on the multipurpose role of sponsor, promoter, and analyst when it comes to Go, spawning a cross-cultural competitive culture that has turned some of the top go players into national celebrities.

Go's prominence in China has depended on who was in charge. In more recent times it's had a roller-coaster ride. Mao Zedong, the chairman of the Communist Party in China until his death in 1976, thought enough of the strategic elements of go to require all of his generals to study the game. As Mao's influence faded, and the Cultural Revolution swept through the country, not surprisingly, go was condemned. By the end of the twentieth century, top Chinese players were participating in the large international competitions in Korea and China.

Despite the ups and downs of "official" opinion, go has persisted, in large part, due to its simplicity and aesthetic beauty. There are 180 white stones and 181 black stones, with black always starting the game. While the intersecting lines do make squares, the stones are not placed in the squares, à la checkers or chess. Instead, they are placed on the intersection itself. Once a stone is placed, it cannot be moved. It will, however, be removed from the board when it is completely surrounded. A stone is surrounded when it is bordered on all of the closest intersections by the opposite color. In other words, all lines that touch the stone (or group of stones) are blocked because the opponent has covered each of them at the nearest possible intersection (see Figure 3a–3c).

A single stone can be "touched" by two, three, or four lines, depending on whether it is placed in one of the four corners (two lines), along the sides of the boards but not in a corner (three lines), or in the vast interior of the board (four lines). Players make alternating moves (usually be-

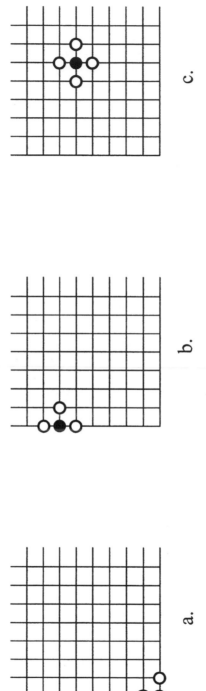

a. b. c.

Figure 2.2: The game of Go, or *wei ch'i*, as it is known in China, is a strategy game where the object is to surround an opponent's stone by blocking all of the lines that touch a stone (or group of stones). Figures a, b, and c show black stones that have been captured by the white stones. (Illustration by Gary Harrison)

tween 200 and 250 in a full game) until both agree that there are no more viable moves. The winner is the person who has surrounded, or gained, the most territory.

According to a Web page posted by the American Go Association,

The game rewards patience and balance over aggression and greed; the balance of influence and territory may shift many times in the course of a game, and a strong player must be prepared to be flexible but resolute.

Like the Eastern martial arts, Go can teach concentration, balance, and discipline. One cannot disguise one's personality on the Go board. ("What Is the Game of Go?" 1996)

Because of the few simple rules, the game can be learned in a matter of minutes. According to avid players, the trick is to understand the many, many possibilities. Getting a firm grip on these, as well as the often recurring situations, can take years of play.

One unique aspect of the game is that relative beginners can play experts in a competitive match through the use of a handicap system. The weaker player is allowed to place a certain number of stones on the board before play begins.

Go first interested Westerners in the early 1900s, when it came to the attention of a group of German mathematicians, including Otto Korschelt and Edward Lasker. The latter was a chess master and the cousin of legendary chess player Emanuel Lasker. Edward Lasker and Lee Hartman, the editor of *Harper's* magazine, formed the American Go Association (AGA) in New York in 1937. The AGA has about 1,500 members today. On its Web site, the AGA contends that go is a game that appeals to many different types of minds, from the likes of mathematicians to artists, from computer programmers to high-risk options traders. Like a foreign language, go is easiest to learn when young.

The full-sized Go game is available for purchase in the United States. The AGA's Web site (listed in Sources) has links to vendors. It is suggested, however, that beginners start with the basic rules but use a scaled-down, 9×9 board and a skills-based game that McAdams refers to as the "capturing game."

In the capturing game, the rules of go are applied, but the game ends when a player has captured, or surrounded, a single stone or a single group of stones. This obviously makes the game quicker but still teaches the essential elements of strategy necessary to both capture an opponent's space and ward off attempts to surround one's own stones.

Sources

McAdams, Mindy. 1995. "What Is Go?" Personal Web page, World Wide Web, well.com/user/mmcadams/gointro.html/

"What Is the Game of Go?" 1996. *American Go Association*. World Wide Web, usgo.org

▦ T'ou Hu

T'ou hu was one of the favorite recreational sports played in ancient China, according to the Book of Rites, known as "Li Chi," an ancient listing of ritual codes and principles of government compiled about the second century B.C.

It was a game played both indoors and outdoors and resembles a combination of the target-oriented games of hoop-and-pole as played by the North American native tribes and the modern-day game known as darts. The object is to throw an arrow from a fixed distance *into* a bottle placed on the ground.

According to the Li Chi, the dimensions of both arrow and bottles were quite well designated. If the game was played indoors, the arrow should be 40.3 centimeters (15 to 16 inches long) and should be increased to 72.57 centimeters (little more than 28 inches) if played outdoors. The target, or *hu*, should have a neck about 5 inches long and be just about 5 inches wide at the bases, with a good thickness.

While the Li Chi gives a great deal of accuracy to most of the measurements, it lacks two critical elements. We don't know how far away the players were from the bottle and how big the opening was of the bottle (though it can probably be assumed that a "bottle" would have a smaller opening than its base).

T'ou hu (or *touhu*) was developed during the Chou dynasty (eleventh century–771 B.C.) in part as a reaction to the changing way that archery was viewed and practiced. Archery had first and foremost been a military skill that was learned and practiced by aristocratic youth, along with the concepts of charioteering and, to a somewhat lesser extent, wrestling. Gradually, archery began to take on a more ritualistic nature. With archery increasingly reserved for ceremonies—combined with a limited amount of space—t'ou hu was developed as an alternative recreation. As the popularity increased, detailed rules were drawn up.

Red beans were placed in the bottle to prevent an arrow from entering the bottle but popping back out. The game was played by two people, each with four arrows. They took alternating turns, and the one who put more arrows in the bottle won that round of the game, which usually was part of a best-of-three match.

The Han dynasty period (206 B.C.–A.D. 220) was a time when sport and recreation thrived in China's imperial scene—despite the basic opposition of the two primary philosophical viewpoints of Taoism (ca. 500 B.C.) and Confucianism (ca. 100 B.C.). During this time, physical recreation took on more detailed or sophisticated forms when played in a social environment.

T'ou hu saw similar changes. It went from a replacement for archery because archery had become ritualized and ceremonial, into an event of great ceremony itself. It was mainly played by the upper classes, and its complex rules and rituals taught lessons in virtue, social skills, respect for elders, and deference, among other mannered traits, in part to make sure that both the winner and the loser could gain respect. By this point, t'ou hu had bowed to at least one edict of the philosophers: it was not a competitive event. Even the highly skilled players who were labeled as professionals "performed" as entertainment at festivals and courts—not as a means of winning a tournament.

We can see the rudimentary extrapolation of this game at carnivals and school fun fairs around the United States today. The object hasn't changed much: throw, toss, or drop a slender, spearlike object with enough accuracy to place it in a narrow target. A possible way to play would be to take a traditional glass bottle of the long-neck beer or half-liter soda variety and try dropping a pencil into it from a distance of four feet.

Sources

Riordan, James, and Robin Jones. 1999. *Sports and Physical Education in China.* London: E & FN Spon.

Sasajima, Kohsuke. 1973. "Early Chinese Physical Education and Sport." In a *History of Sport and Physical Education to 1900,* edited by Earle F. Zeigler. Champaign, Ill.: Stipes.

▦ EUROPE

INTRODUCTION

No other area of the world has had as much written about its sports history or seen as much time invested into the scholarly pursuit of its athletic antiquity as has Europe.

There can be no doubt that the ancient Olympic Games held every fourth year in Olympia, Greece, are the starting point for almost any discussion about sports that predate the modern professional era. Even when delving into the play habits of a tiny tribe in the New Guinea tropics half a world away, there is a temptation, even an inclination to compare their practices, no matter how similar or dissimilar, to those of the ancient Greeks. Did the group have organized festival games? Did they reward the winner? Was victory the primary purpose of an event? Did athletic accomplishment lead to greater prestige within the community? These are all standard questions asked when judging sports, play, or games in any indigenous culture. Each is rooted to a comparison to what was done at the ancient games in Greece.

This preoccupation with all things Grecian in the field of sports history can be detrimental to a fair, honest, and informed evaluation of the play practices of another culture. In truth, what the Greeks did with their games from 776 B.C. (the standardized date for the first Olympic victor) until well after the rise of the Roman empire had no bearing on the actual playing or development of ancient or traditional sport in the Americas, sub-Saharan Africa, or the thousands of islands that make up Oceania. The Greeks did have an impact on how the history of sport in these places has been interpreted, because the concept of the Greek Olympics is always going to be a standard to which another culture's athletic activities are measured.

The Greeks did not invent sports for the rest of the world. Nor is it likely that even the Greek games themselves were solely an Athenian creation (as has been suggested), since by the time of recorded victories there had already been a substantial amount of interaction, peaceful and not, between the various Greek city-states and between greater Greece and its neighbors around the Mediterranean. What the Greeks did do in large part, some 16 centuries after the ancient Olympics had ended, was to stir the passion for the modern Olympics and, in so doing, initiate a run of research and writing on the original.

E. Norman Gardiner (*Athletics of the Ancient World*, 1930), H. A. Harris (*Greek Athletes and Athletics*, 1964; *Sport in Greece and Rome*, 1972), and numerous others who wrote in their native languages about the Greek Olympics and athletic society created the whole notion of "sports history." There is an increasing effort in the scholarly world of sports history to break away from the Greeks and to give the rest of the world its due. But without the Gardiners and Harrises telling the exciting and detailed story of the Greeks first, it is unlikely that there would now be significant interest in seeing what other cultures claim as sporting traditions.

This chapter on Europe is not solely about the Greeks. Irish hurling and Nordic skiing are included. Effort has been taken to include numerous non-Greek or Roman references on the subjects of boxing and wrestling. Escaping the shadow of Greece and its athletes, however, is difficult whenever discussing the traits of ancient sports in Europe. This is primarily because of the voluminous documentation surrounding not only the ancient Olympic Games but also everyday athletic life within the great city-states. The sources are also varied, helping to enlighten and cross-reference the history through poetic works, historical essays, art and the most visible of all, the ancient stadiums that dot the landscape of Greece and the rest of the Mediterranean.

While it is generally considered that the Greeks were the first to hold standardized, spectator-attended "games" in honor of a god, there is research that points to a contrary opinion. Within the European boundaries it has been hypothesized that the rugged Vikings of the north held festival contests that pre-date the Olympic Games (Goulstone 1980). Others have proposed that festival games had their origin among the Phoenicians (see Boutros 1977 and several later articles in *Olympic Review*) and were copied by the Greeks. It is known that the ancient Hawaiians held their own lengthy, well-planned, and royally supported *Makahiki* Games on an annual basis (see Oceania: Introduction, Canoe Racing, and Surfing).

Where each of these alternative "First Games" fail to compare to the

Greeks is in their recorded legacy. For over 1,000 years the Greeks organized, held, and recorded who won at Olympia. Along the way, the ancient Olympics spawned numerous other festival games in the immediate and distant Panhellenic world. Athletics became an avocation to pursue and athletes became well-known figures. It is possible that the Greeks weren't the first great "athletes" and their Olympics certainly had its share of flaws and idiosyncrasies. They were however, undisputedly, the forefathers of sports history.

WHAT IS "ANCIENT" IN EUROPE?

In other sections of this book the notion of what is ancient is rather ambiguous. Since the indigenous people in Oceania, the Americas, and much of Africa did not have written language, there has to be a little leeway in those areas when assigning "ancient" status to sports and games. In Europe the attempt has clearly been made to define a chronological cutoff time when ancient turned medieval. For the purposes of this book and the entire "Sports and Games through History" series, that date is the year A.D. 470. That explains, in part, why some games that are very old and/or were traditional parts of a European culture have not been included. Notable among this list are the Highland Games of Scotland, European derivatives of field hockey (though there is scanty evidence that a type of stick-and-ball game was played in ancient times), the *pelota* games of the Basque, and real tennis. While rowing as a group was done in ancient times, it was essentially the domain of slaves forced to row and a long way from being a sport.

Sources

Arlott, John, ed. 1975. *The Oxford Companion to World Sports and Games*. London: Oxford University Press.

Baker, William J. 1988. *Sports in the Western World*. Rev. ed. Urbana, Ill.: Illini Books.

Boutros, Labib. 1977. "The Phoenician Stadium of Amrit." *Olympic Review*, No. 112, pp. 114–20.

Golden, Mark. 1998. *Sport and Society in Ancient Greece*. Cambridge: Cambridge University Press.

Goulstone, John. 1980. "The Northern Origins of the Olympic Games." *Olympic Review*, No. 152–53, p. 336–39.

Harris, H. A. 1972. *Sport in Greece and Rome*. London: Thames and Hudson.

Levinson, David, and Karen Christensen. 1996. *Encyclopedia of World Sport*. Vols. 1–3. Santa Barbara, Calif.: ABC-CLIO.

SPORTS

▦   Boxing

Boxing was one of the primary "heavy" sports of the Olympic Games of Greece. As with the wrestling and the extremely rough combination of boxing and wrestling called the *pankration*, there were few rules, no time limit, and no ring per se. Most importantly, there was no weight limit. In other words, a 125-pound man could be pitted against someone twice his size. (As with other Olympic events, there were age limits.) Since it was usually a significant advantage to be larger, which translates into more power, although sometimes at a loss of speed and quickness, the notion of "heavy" events is easy to understand. Simply put, most of the competitors and especially most of the winners were heavy.

Boxing was added to the Olympic program in 688 B.C., 88 years after the first recorded Olympic victor in the *stadion* (approximately 200 meter-) race, which is typically considered the beginning of the ancient Olympics. The heavy events took place on the fourth day of the five-day Olympic festival and were crowd favorites.

Greek boxers wound heavy strips of leather around their hands and wrists, with the fingers left free. As with other sports in the Greek games, they boxed without clothing and would oil their bodies, then rub dust on themselves in a manner prescribed as a nod toward hygiene. When the day's activities were done, boxers, like pentathletes, wrestlers, and virtually any athlete at the Greek games, would use a metal strip called a *stirgil* to wipe themselves clean of dust, oil, and perspiration. The stirgil acted like a modern squeegee. A similar device is commonly used today for horses to rid the animal of excess sweat and grime after a workout or water after a bath.

Once a bout started, the Olympic boxer did not waste much time, energy, or attention on trying to land punches to the body. The attention was given to the head or neck. Sometimes an open fist slap was used in an effort to distract or cut the opponent. This was not a bout that could be won—or lost—by a judge's decision. There was no benefit in being stylish, as there is in modern boxing in which boxers are judged on a point basis per round, and a fighter can win a bout without ever inflicting serious damage to his opponent. In the ancient Greek games, there weren't even rounds, and there was almost always damage. By the end of his career, a Greek boxer was almost certain to sport the telltale signs of cauliflower ears, broken teeth, and a generally scarred face. As with modern boxing, there was a serious threat of long-term injury to the skull and brain. The fight went on without a break until a fighter was too exhausted to continue or was knocked out, or until one raised his right hand as a signal of defeat. This last point leads to an interesting irony of history.

No contestant from Sparta ever participated in Olympic boxing, even though the rigidly militaristic Spartans prided themselves on the fitness and strength of their bodies. In some circles, boxing is even credited as being invented in Sparta. In the mythical days of early Sparta the queen Helen, who is known to us more commonly as Helen of Troy, had two athletic twin brothers named Castor and Polydeuces (or Pollux). The latter was said to be the originator of boxing, with his brother his natural first foil. In fact, in its rigid training of young boys to be warriors for the military state, Spartans found it quite acceptable, even desirable for boys to pummel one another. (As a society, Sparta also supported ritualistic flagellation that was to be suffered without moan or whimper.)

So why didn't the Spartans go to Olympia or the other national games (Pythian, Nemean, Isthmian)? Because before there could be a winner, usually someone had to *admit* defeat. That he might fall into the latter category was a risk that a Spartan would not take. As Forbes puts it: "[N]ow a Spartan might accept a ruling which declared that he was defeated, but his code did not permit him publicly and of his own free will to acknowledge defeat" (Zeigler 1973, 136).

Boxing remained a staple of the Olympic Games until the Games dwindled from favor and eventually came to their unceremonious end in A.D. 396.

By no means were the Greeks the only people of Europe to engage in boxing. It is a sport that is almost as universal as wrestling, at least in the basic sense of someone trying to defend himself from danger. Artifacts from archaeological findings in Crete, dating from the Minoan Bronze Age of 3,000 to 1,200 B.C., often represented boxing.

The Greeks, as with their other athletics, actually went to the extent of teaching boxing in the gymnasiums and eventually ascribing it enough importance (and attendant fan interest) that a man could, in effect, become a professional boxer. As with other Greek sports, the shift from elite participant to professional athlete proceeded gradually from the fourth century to the second century B.C.

At the same time as the Olympic Games were first beginning to grow and flourish, boxing was also being practiced by the Etruscans, the people of central Italy who flourished from the eighth to the fourth century B.C. The Etruscans are often credited (or discredited) with creating the gladiatorial contests that helped to define the Roman Empire. In their boxing the Etruscans had two distinct types: shadow and contest. The former was more of an art form or dance and was often accompanied by the double flute. Contest was the more serious.

When the Romans took to public displays of boxing as their influence widened, it should come as no surprise that they felt compelled to upgrade the gore factor. If a boxing match was held for public entertainment in one of the many stadiums of Roman rule, then a "piece of metal (was) secured on the fists under the leather thongs . . . to ensure brutality and the abundant flow of blood" (Baker 1988, 32)

Suggestions for Modern Play

Whether boxing, in its modern form, is a good thing to participate in for young people is a matter of personal taste and family influence. Its emphasis on training, endurance, and agility can be very beneficial. Because it is an acceptable release for aggression and a means of building self-confidence, boxing can also aid a person's mental health. If a young person intends to try boxing, he or she should stick to modern practice: use protective headgear and big, padded gloves and spar against someone of equal size. Leave the leather straps and bouts without time limits or weight limits in antiquity.

Sources

Baker, William J. 1988. *Sports in the Western World*. Rev. ed. Urbana, Ill.: Illini Books.
Forbes, Clarence A. 1973. "The Spartan Agoge." In *A History of Sport and Physical Education to 1900*, edited by Earle F. Zeigler. Champaign, Ill.: Stipes.
Harris, H. A. 1972. *Sport in Greece and Rome*. London: Thames and Hudson.

⊞ Irish Hurling

There is some debate over exactly when and even where this game, which has been described as an airborne form of field hockey, was first played. What is definite is that it was embraced anew in Ireland in the late 1800s as a quintessential Irish sport. Hurling has been called the fastest and fiercest of team sports (Levinson and Christensen 1999), and the Irish's devotion to the sport is legendary.

The first reference to hurling in the Irish annals is in a description of the Battle of Moytura (1272 b.c.). The invaders apparently defeated the residents in a game of hurling and then duplicated the victory on the battlefield. More than 3,000 years later the connection between hurling and military prowess was still commonplace, according to a story from the infant days of the Irish army after independence was gained in the 1920s. A soldier looking at a promotion board spat in disgust as he spotted the name of one particular new corporal: "God help us. . . . The man never held a hurley in his whole bloody life" (*Economist* 1993).

The oldest known legal code in Ireland, the Brehon Laws, mentions that compensation should be rewarded for any person injured during a hurling match. Strong evidence (law codes, annals, and hero tales) suggests that Irish hurling as well as its sister sport, *shinty* in Scotland, are "unquestionably pre-Roman" and that it is likely that shinty is an offshoot of hurling, as suggested by the common name for the stick in both sports, *caman* (Baker 1988).

While some factions think that hurling was actually introduced to Ireland by the English in the fourteenth century, what is more likely is that the ancient Irish game matriculated to England and then made its way back around when English landowners encouraged the playing of hurling as a stabilizing and binding influence for their dominion.

In the early days of hurling there were two basic forms of play. One is very similar to the modern game, with teams aiming their attack toward defined goals in a playing field. The other has a cross-country quality akin to the intertribal games of lacrosse at times played by the indigenous peoples of North America. This form of the Irish national game was called "hurling home" and was played by a large group of parishioners who aimed to move the ball across country between two parishes to a determined place.

British rule and the famines of the 1840s combined to nearly wipe out hurling as a sport in Ireland. It was restored due to a concerted effort from the Gaelic Athletic Association, founded in 1884 for "the preservation and cultivation of (Ireland's) national pastimes," and other pro-Gaelic organizations that feared that the whole of Irish culture was on the verge of being lost due to anglicization.

The modern rules are fairly simple. The ball, known as a slitter, cannot be thrown with the hand; when the ball passes below and between a football- or rugby-style goalpost, it is worth three points, and it is worth just one point when it goes above the crossbar but between the posts. Fifteen players are used per side, with one of them being a goalie. The field is large, usually 150 yards long by 90 yards wide.

The game is incredibly fast, and because the ball cannot be carried in the hand (it can be caught), the player must learn and excel at the skill of bouncing the ball on the wide-set blade of his hurley (also called a *caman*), a curved stick made of ash, as he runs—with others trying to dislodge him from the ball.

Because of the unique and difficult-to-learn skill, the game is played at a skillful level only in Ireland, and then really only in the southern counties, including Kilkenny, Tipperary, Limerick, Wexford, and Cork. In 1993 it was estimated that there were only about 50,000 hurling players in all of Ireland, including all levels of play. While immensely popular in its native country—the all-Ireland final, the culmination of a series of matches that begin between club teams at the county level, is watched with great fanaticism on television and routinely fills a 70,000-seat stadium—it is still an amateur sport. That the players are not paid professionals may, in part, speak to why the rough-and-tumble game is also known as an honor-bound sport. Blows are forgiven, and generally the play is clean.

Hurling is played by men, but women have their own game, which is very similar. It is called *camogie* and also employs the hurley stick and the slitter ball.

Suggestions for Modern Play

An American student who wanted to get a taste of hurling or camogie could try taking a golf ball or other small, hard ball, bouncing it on the blade of a hockey stick or, better yet, a field hockey stick, and then running with it. Create two 15-person teams, each running across a large field trying to possess and advance the ball.

There are certainly similarities to field hockey but with one big difference. By allowing the ball to be struck into the air—and top players can strike the slitter with their hurley up to 100 yards—the game is exceedingly fast and does offer a bit more danger from the ball's potentially striking someone's head.

Sources

Baker, William J. 1988. *Sports in the Western World* Rev. ed. Urbana, Ill.: Illini Books.

Economist. 1993. July 10, Vol. 328, Issue 7819, p. 87

Levinson, David, and Karen Christensen, ed. 1999. *Encyclopedia of World Sport*, (paperback) Oxford: Oxford University Press.

⊞ Olympic Games

No sporting event in antiquity or perhaps even to this day connects itself to its country and its populace as resolutely as the original Olympic Games did to ancient Greece. Contested at Olympia, which was essentially a small village existing for the purpose of hosting the most prestigious of all Greek games once every four years, the winners received a traditional olive wreath as their only physical token of superiority.

The games at Olympia, in honor of Zeus, however, were far from the only so-called Festival Games in Greece. They were part of a classical circuit often referred to as the Crown Games for their habit of awarding botanical wreaths to the winners. They included the Pythian Games of Delphi, which were sacred to Apollo and awarded laurel wreaths every four years; the Isthmian Games, held every two years, paying tribute to Poseidon and held on the Isthmus of Corinth, which awarded a pine wreath; and the Nemean Games, also held in alternate years again to honor Zeus, supreme deity, and contested first in Nemea and later at nearby Argos.

Gradually, more and more festival games were held. Some were smaller, localized games, which in their way served as tune-ups for the top athletes and gauges of ability for younger ones, while the sponsors of the games (even smaller festivals could be costly affairs to organize and run) gained civic recognition. Others were, as the Crown Games became, Panhellenic affairs, meaning that they were open to any competitor. These usually can be contrasted with the Crown Games because they offered valuable prizes to the winners (and perhaps even appearance fees) as inducements to encourage participation. By the second century A.D. there were almost 300 different athletic festivals, spreading to the farthest reaches of the Greek world: Marseilles, Africa, even the Black Sea.

The Olympic Games, however, stand alone as the longest running event and one that offered a virtually unchanging program for nearly 1,000 years. The usual starting date of the games at Olympus is given as 776 B.C., because this is the first date for which a winner has been recorded. It is reasonable to assume, however, that such games were held prior to that date in Greece (almost certainly) and even at Olympia (probably). Certainly, the general populace was known to test each other's skill, strength, and stamina, as Homer depicts with his funeral games in the *Illiad* and with the tests undertaken by his epic hero Odysseus in the *Odyssey*. Still, 776 is a convenient date to start from. After that point we can chart the growth of the games' program, their peaks in popularity, and their eventual popular decline through the times of the Roman Empire and ultimately their disappearance.

The Olympics survived Roman occupation until gradually it lost its financial support and the interest of the Roman public, which had acquired the taste for bloody gladiator sports, which had spread from the floor of the Colosseum to the far reaches of the empire. "There seem to have been no protests when the Olympic Games were brought to an end in 396" (Harris 1972, 42).

In their heyday the Olympic Games were a happening that was worth the financial costs and hardships of travel to the remote site for both athletes and spectators. Once there (athletes and trainers were required to stay for 30 days, even though the events took only 5 to complete), living conditions were squalid since the Olympics were contested in the heat of the summer, and there were virtually no accommodations. For an athlete, to win an olive wreath symbolized superiority and a sense of immortality, since victors were allowed to commission statues, poems, and songs commemorating their victorious moment. Initially, the contests were for Greek-born males only, but as the scope of Greece's dominion increased, so did the hometowns of the competitors. One thing that did not change, at least for several centuries, was that no women were allowed even as spectators.

Women did have their chance to compete, however. They held the Heraean Games. Though there is some evidence that the Heraean Games actually predate the Olympics, little has been recorded of their events.

This small bronze figure of a running girl was found in the Serbian town of Prizren but is considered Greek in origin and dates from 520–500 B.C. and was possibly made in or near Sparta, the one city-state in ancient Greece above all others that actively encouraged women to participate in athletic competitions. (© The British Museum)

Some theories hold that the competitions were cultish in nature and that the races were related to fertility, initiation into womanhood, and marriage. It does seem certain that, especially in Athens, the role of women in ancient Greece was to be chaste, obedient housekeepers who bore children and as much as possible stayed out of the public eye. The one city-state that was a definite exception was Sparta. At an early age both boys and girls were sent to separate schools, and physical exertion and exercise were very much a part of the prescribed training for young women. Numerous references in plays and literature attest that Spartan women continued to exhibit athletic tendencies that were well-known customs but not accepted as typical behavior in other city-states (Spears 1984). While there is no clear evidence that women ever directly competed with men at Olympia, there are recorded instances where women owned winning chariot teams. Since the owners were declared the champions (not the driver), it is accurate, albeit a bit deceiving, to state there were female champions in the ancient Olympics.

In comparison to the modern Olympics, the menu of events was extremely sparse. No team handball or beach volleyball on this athletic card. Neither were there any aquatic sports, a somewhat surprising omission since the Greeks were shipgoing colonizers who valued the ability to swim as a sign of civilized education and a trait that separated them from the "barbarian" peoples with whom they came in contact.

By 520 B.C. the schedule of events had been set for the men's events and would remain unchanged (though some additional chariot races were added along with some events for boys). The first event for which a victor has been recorded is the *stadion*, a footrace of approximately 200 meters, which was one length of the field. A *diaulos*, or 400-meter race that included a turn around a pole, and the *dolikhos*, or long race, possibly as much as 2,000 meters, were added within the first 15 Olympiads. By 648 B.C., nearly 120 years later (which is longer than the current modern Olympic period), the program of events was up to a whopping eight: the stadion, diaulos, and dolikhos for running events; the five-event, one-afternoon test called *pentathlon*; wrestling; boxing; the four-horse chariot race; and *pankration*, which was a virtually no-holds-barred combination of wrestling and boxing. The last significant event added, which some have suggested was done as much for comic relief as anything else, was the *hoplites* race, which was a race in full armor, in 520 (see Table 3.1).

Some of the individual events warrant discussion in their own specific segment (see boxing, pentathlon, and wrestling).

Certainly, the huge spectator base added to the drama of the games, and the audience's support and derision of various athletes added to the excitement. The two events that prompted the greatest interest were also the ones that possessed an element of danger. The chariot race is considered by some scholars to have been the most prestigious of all the events to win. At the very least, it was the most costly and therefore was limited in its participation to only the elite. The pankration was another fan favorite. It was a brutal combination of boxing, wrestling, and judo. Strangleholds were not only allowed, but encouraged, since the object was to gain an admission of submission from one's opponent. Apparently, the only things not allowed were gouging of eyes and biting. One famous practitioner, a Sikyonian named Sostrates, was nicknamed the Fingerman because he would bend the fingers of opponents until they surrendered. His tactic was effective enough to win 17 Panhellenic games, including 3 at Olympia.

The Greeks' enduring fascination, focus, and expenditure of energy and finances on producing athletic champions have several viable sources, for example, Aristotle's call to exercise both body and mind to become a fully developed man. Public gymnasiums were commonplace, often accompanied by a *palaestra*, or wrestling school, in Greek cities and towns. The popularity and pervasive nature of sport in Greek culture are emphasized by its constant inclusion in poetry, not just when

Table 3.1
The Olympic Program and the Traditional Date When Each Event Was Added

Event	Date
stadion, 200-m race	776 B.C.E.
diaulos, 400-m race	724 B.C.E.
dolikhos, long race	720 B.C.E.
pentathlon	708 B.C.E.
wrestling	708 B.C.E.
boxing	688 B.C.E.
tethrippon, 4-horse chariot race	680 B.C.E.
pankration	648 B.C.E.
keles, horse race	648 B.C.E.
stadion for boys	632 B.C.E.
wrestling for boys	632 B.C.E.
pentathlon for boys	628 B.C.E. (dropped immediately)
boxing for boys	616 B.C.E.
hoplites, race in armor	520 B.C.E.
apene, mule-car race	500 B.C.E. (dropped in 444 B.C.E.)
kalpe, mares' race	496 B.C.E.) (dropped in 444 B.C.E.)
sunoris, two-horse chariot race	408 B.C.E.
salpinktes, trumpeters	396 B.C.E.
kerukes, heralds	396 B.C.E.
tethrippon for foals	384 B.C.E.
sunoris for foals	264 B.C.E.
keles for foals	256 B.C.E.
pankration for boys	200 B.C.E.

Source: Golden, Mark. 1998. *Sport and Society in Ancient Greece.* Cambridge: Cambridge University Press.

specifically directed to athletic contests or prowess but also by the common use of sports terms and themes as metaphors and analogies to other aspects of Greek life. One reason that the Greeks had such enthusiasm for the games is the spectators, "practised at home the sports that they watched at Olympia" (Umminger 1963, 25). Victory also brought fame and honor not only to the athlete but also to the city from which he hailed. Research of Olympic victors indicates that some cities were either predisposed or preoccupied with churning out quality athletes.

Consensus opinion is that the games were initially open only to free-born Hellenes, meaning Greek citizens. Throughout the history of the Festival Games there were also age divisions, which served to separate those too young or too inexperienced from the elite athletes. At Olympia, there were only two divisions: boys and open. Other festivals used multiple age divisions. At the outset the games were, for the most part, the domain of the wealthy, for they were the only ones able to afford both the cost of travel as well as the time away from other pursuits needed to diligently train. Exceptions would have likely come in the footraces, where a poorer competitor might have the natural speed needed to overcome his lack of tutelage from a paid trainer. Whether poor or rich, though, the goal was the same: to win. It is plausible that there was some honor in simply participating, but it was nowhere near the same level that we associate with making an Olympic team in modern times. There were no prizes for second or third place, no silver or bronze medals, offered at Olympia. This did not mean that there was honor in a tainted victory, one earned from cheating. Rather, the victor alone received the praise and prizes.

Gradually, the socioeconomic makeup of the contestants began to change. In a word, the athletes became professionals. Usually subsidized by their communities, these professionals would routinely make the circuit of the Crown Games and also attend several other prize-offering festivals, which at times were quite generous with their rewards. Growing spectator interest in the games, not unlike the fanaticism that we associate with our modern professional sports teams, helped drive many wealthy "amateurs" out of the competitions as the demand for highly skilled athletes increased.

The increase in professionalism led to some significant intellectual debate among the philosophers of the time as to the worthiness of a life spent solely in the pursuit of athletic victory and the spoils that went with it. Milo of Croton is known to us as perhaps the greatest of all the "heavy" athletes, the term that the Greeks applied to those who participated in the body contact sports of boxing, wrestling, and pankration. He was also routinely ridiculed for the excesses of his diet as well as his relative lack of intellect. Apparently, though, the intellectuals' derisive comments did not completely reflect the opinion of the masses because the pankration winner was often awarded the most lucrative prizes at the non-Crown Games festivals.

Two other characteristics make the ancient Olympics uniquely different from the modern Olympiads, which pretend to pattern themselves after the originals. First is the often-noted aspect that the athletes competed in the nude. Harris says that this practice started about 720 B.C. after a competitor's shorts fell off in a footrace. Several stories of the initial disrobing offer two basic and divergent paths: (1) he won the race, so everyone copied him, or (2) he tripped over his trunks and lost (perhaps even died), so it was determined that running without clothes was the smarter, swifter choice. Another possible explanation is that the games at Olympia were originally held to honor the warrior-athlete hero Heracles (or Hercules, as he is known in the Latin version of his name). Heracles is generally considered and depicted as a nude hero (Mouratidis 1985).

Interestingly, the Greeks felt that their willingness to strip in public actually separated them from, and made them superior to, the barbarian tribes that surrounded them, quite the opposite of our post-Victorian moralists who have decried the recent trend of Olympic athletes, male and female, to model in the nude, albeit these acts have been done as a means of self- or team-promotion.

The other aspect worth noting is that for all the mention of victors over the span of a millennium, there are no known mention of how far anyone threw the javelin or discus and just two questionable references to long jumps covering the hard-to-believe distances of 55 and 52 feet. The Greeks certainly had the knowledge and the tools to record distances. Apparently, they did not care to. The object was not to set a record but to be victorious on that day against that day's competition. There may also have been a desire to preserve family pride. Without a record to contest, combined with the age divisions and the relatively short span of an athletic career, there was almost no chance that a son could ever compete, directly or indirectly, with his own father.

Sources

Golden, Mark. 1998. *Sport and Society in Ancient Greece*. Cambridge: Cambridge University Press.

Harris, H. A. 1972. *Sport in Greece and Rome*. London: Thames and Hudson.

Miller, S. G. 1991. *Arete: Greek Sports from Ancient Sources*. 2nd ed. Berkeley: University of California Press.

Mouratidis, John. 1985. "The Origin of Nudity in Greek Athletics." *Journal of Sport History*, Vol. 12, No. 3, pp. 213–232.

Poliakoff, Michael. 1984. "Introduction. The Significance of Sport: Ancient Athletics and Ancient Society." *Journal of Sport History*, Vol. 11, No. 2, pp. 5–7.

Scanlon, Thomas F. 1982. "The Origin of Women's Athletics in Greece." *North American Society for Sport History* (proceedings and letters), pp. 33–35.

Spears, Betty. 1984. "A Perspective of the History of Women's Sports in Ancient Greece." *Journal of Sport History*, Vol. 11, No. 2, pp. 32–47.

Umminger, Walter. 1963. *Supermen, Heroes and Gods*. English ed. London: Thames and Hudson.

▦ Pentathlon

The pentathlon was a five-event competition that was a staple of the Olympic Games as well as the other Crown Games and Panhellenic athletic festivals of Greece. It consisted of three events that were not competed as separate events, namely, the discus, javelin, and long jump, along with a footrace and wrestling. The latter two events were also stand-alone competitions at the Greek festival games.

The concept of a multidiscipline sporting event is very prevalent today. There is, of course, the decathlon, a 10-event activity, and the women's version called the heptathlon (seven events). There are also the triathlon, which includes swimming, bicycling, and running and has recently been added to the modern Olympic Games schedule as a full-medal sport, and the modern pentathlon (equestrian, fencing, shooting, swimming, and a footrace), which belies its name a bit by including pursuits that stem in origin from nineteenth-century and early twentieth-century military exercises. For the winter sports enthusiasts there are the biathlon (cross-country skiing and marksmanship) and the Nordic combined (cross-country skiing and ski jumping). All of these modern events are rigidly timed and measured. In the cases of the decathlon and heptathlon, elaborate performance tables are then employed to distribute points based on an athlete's performance in each event, with the greatest number of points determining the winner.

Exactly how the Greeks determined their winners in the pentathlon is a long-running debate among scholars and has still not been exactly determined. In fact, there is even debate about the order of the events. The consensus is that the three nonspecialist sports (discus, javelin, jump) were contested first, followed by a 200-meter race and then the wrestling. H. A. Harris, one of the foremost scholars of Greek and Roman athletics, postulates that it is quite likely, given the Greeks' emphasis on winning, as opposed to being competitive, that the first athlete to win three events would win the pentathlon. In other words, if he excelled in the field events, he would never have to run or wrestle, having been a "victor in the first triad" (Harris 1972, 34). In the statuary commemorating winners there are clues to suggest the validity of this statement. Some won the pentathlon in *akoniti* fashion, meaning without having to raise dust, that is, without wrestling.

Harris also suggests a strategy for what would happen if there were multiple winners in the first three events. If one person had won two events and a second the third, then they would race. If at that point one of the contestants could claim three victories, then the pentathlon would be over. If each had two victories, then they would wrestle to settle the issue.

If after the field events there were three winners, then they would race. The winner of the race would advance to the final of the wrestling, and the other two would hold what would amount to a semifinal wrestling bout. While watching as one's future foe was having to beat someone else first seems like an unfair advantage, it is by no means uncommon in current wrestling tournaments. Further, in both the individual wrestling and the pentathlon, winners were noted to have won the tournament either with or without *ephedros*, which meant to stand by.

Harris' evaluation has come under critical review in the nearly 30 years since he published. Kyle, in 1990, came to essentially the same conclusion as Harris with a relatively minor difference. He postulates that instead of a semifinal wrestling bout stemming from the situation where there were three winners after the three field events, the two runners-up in the run then had a second run, with the winner advancing to the wrestling final. Kyle bases this on the assumption that a second run would have been less tiring than a second wrestling match, thus lessening the advantage of the person waiting to wrestle.

One thing is clear: whatever the means were for determining a winner, it worked. There is no record of squabbling or debate, and since all the athletes competed in the nude (thus, no numbers or uniforms), and there were no elaborate scoreboards, the method for advancement must have been easy to understand not just for the athletes but also for the several thousand fans in attendance.

Unique aspects to the technique in both the javelin and the jump are different from today's methods. The javelin was thrown with a thong that wrapped around the shaft of the spear and looped over the fingers of the throwing hand, creating a sort of short, attached slingshot mechanism. This added acceleration at the point of release and also created a spin that perhaps gave the javelin truer flight.

The jump was considered the most technically difficult of the competitions, according to ancient writer Philostratas, who wrote "On Gymnastiks," ca. A.D. 230. This is possibly because the feet had to land in precisely the right way to afford measurement and also because the athletes used jumping weights.

The pentathlete was much admired by poets and artists for his well-balanced muscularity. No lesser authority than Aristotle said that "pentathletes are the most beautiful" of all the competitors at Olympia. It was not, however, the most popular event for spectators. Many Greeks viewed the pentathletes with a trace of scorn because they assumed that the reason they entered a multiple-sport event was that they were not good enough to stand as an Olympic champion against event specialists. This corresponds to the Greeks' emphasis in sport and life in general on success being the most important criterion for judging performance. An example is that Hellenistic scholar Eratosthenes was somewhat mockingly called "beta" and "pentathlete" because he was only second best in every field of study.

It's also instructive to note that at the Panhellenic games, where prizes, usually ampulars of olive oil, were awarded to victors, the winners of the *pankration*, wrestling, and usually the *stadion*, or sprint race, garnered

The discus was one of the five events in the pentathlon competition in the ancient Olympics. The athletes
who competed in the pentathlon were often the subjects of praise from poets, writers, and artists for the
symmetry and balance of their physiques, even
though the pentathlon was not a favorite event of the
spectators. This particular statue is a Roman copy of
a bronze original and hails from Hadrian's villa in
Tivoli, Lazio, Italy. Perhaps it is indicative of the Romans' relative lack of interest in the ancient Olympics
that the position of the discus thrower's head is incorrect. He should be looking at the discus. (© The
British Museum)

greater awards than those given to the winner of the pentathlon (Golden
1998).

In this way we see another parallel between the ancient games and
our own modern Olympics. While even the casual fan will recognize the

names of Maurice Green and Marion Jones as sprint champions from the 2000 Olympiad in Sydney, Australia, few can name the most recent winner of the decathlon.

Sources

Golden, Mark. 1998. *Sport and Society in Ancient Greece*. Cambridge: Cambridge University Press.
Harris, H. A. 1972. *Sport in Greece and Rome*. London: Thames and Hudson.
Kyle, Donald G. 1990. "Winning and Watching the Greek Pentathlon." *Journal of Sports History*, Vol. 17, No. 3, pp. 291–305.

▦   Wrestling

We do not know how wrestling began. We do know, however, that the famous cave drawings of France, which are 15,000 years old, include scenes of wrestling (along with archery). We also know that wrestling, in a variety of forms, exists in every corner of the world and was practiced in ancient times by the tribes that can be considered "primitive" in regard to the degree of tool and animal usage compared to that of ancient groups considered highly civilized. It has been suggested by anthropologists that "play" is an innate human condition. Wrestling is certainly one of the simplest, most natural forms of play and one that seems to be innate to almost any animal, human or otherwise.

It is recorded in the archaeological history of Egypt and Babylonia as far back as 3,000 B.C. It is described in the ancient Sumerian epic of Gilgamesh. Chinese and Japanese societies have long emphasized it. In Asia, Europe, and Africa, some tribes or civilizations of people erected specific structures to allow wrestlers to train and live in a monklike existence apart from the rest of society.

When it comes to wrestling's history in Europe, its grandest interpretation is in ancient Greece, where wrestling became a central part of the ancient Olympic Games and the rest of the Panhellenic contests that spread across Greece and its holdings.

One of the earliest descriptions of Greek wrestling indicates that the idea was to throw one's opponent on the ground, rather than wrestling on the ground to produce a submission hold, or a "pin," as is the purpose of modern freestyle wrestling. In Homer's *Illiad*, a ninth-century account of the Trojan War, wrestling was part of the famous funeral games held to honor Patroklos by his close friend Achilles. The wrestling match is declared a draw when neither Odysseus nor Ajax can throw the other.

Greek wrestlers competed without clothes on (as did all the rest of the Greek Olympians), but with their bodies slippery and slimy due to the use of olive oil. Wrestling became a standard part of the ancient Olympics in 708 B.C. (although some later scholars, notably Guttmann, have dismissed the accepted growth of the Olympic schedule and have suggested that the games started with at least five events around 600 B.C.). Wrestlers and the other heavy athletes had a standard equipment "kit" that included a container to hold their olive oil and one or usually two *stirgils*, a device that can be compared to a sweat scraper, used to wipe water and perspiration off horses. The stirgil was usually made of bronze and had a concave blade that was designed to scrape the body clean of oil and dirt.

Other notable aspects of Greek wrestling matches included the lack of restrictions. There were no defined ring or circle, no time limit, and, especially significant, no weight limit. Wrestlers won when they scored three falls, making their opponent touch the ground with their knees. Emphasis was placed on upper-body holds in conjunction with tripping techniques. The most famous Olympic wrestler—and also one who was openly derided by contemporary literary types—was Milo of Croton. He was the Olympic boys champion in 540 B.C. and then won six successive Olympic titles and over two dozen other crowns in the other Greek Crown Games (Isthmian, Nemean, Pythian). His only defeat came when a younger opponent evaded and dodged Milo's attempts so successfully that Milo withdrew from pure fatigue.

Wrestling Greeks also produced a combination of wrestling and boxing called the *pankration*, a brutal form of combat that allowed virtually everything but biting and eye-gouging and went on until someone gave up.

By no means were the Greeks the sole practitioners of the basic test of strength, stamina, and agility of being able to subdue or throw another man. Some accounts place ancient forms of European wrestling in the British Isles as far back as 1829 B.C. (Chase 1999). At the very least, wrestling is mentioned in Gaelic lands in the description of the Games of Tailtinn in 632 B.C.—less than a century after wrestling was incorporated into the Olympic menu.

Here's a sampling of three styles of wrestling that arose in European areas that were not heavily influenced by the Greco-Roman traditions.

Glima

The Vikings in northern Europe contested each other in a form of wrestling known as glima, which is now the national sport of Iceland, which is the only Scandinavian country that puts much stock in the sport. It is one of several types of European wrestling that fall into the "back-hold" category, meaning that the opponents gripped each other around the waist, torso, or chest and then clasped their hands at the back of their opponent.

There are similarities to Japanese sumo in that the wrestlers wear specialized clothing that affords the opponent to get a grip (usually the

This Panathenaic prize amphora was probably filled with olive oil and awarded to a victor in one of the "heavy" sports in the Greek games. Made in Athens about 367–366 B.C., it was discovered in modern Libya, attesting to the fact that Greek-style festival games were held throughout the Mediterranean area. The two men are possibly competing in the violent *pankration*, a combination of wrestling and boxing. The man on the left is probably either a judge or a trainer, while the man standing to the right is possibly waiting to take on the winner. (© The British Museum)

trousers in nonsanctioned or folk bouts), there are standardized moves, and the match is finished with one fall. Unlike sumo, the object is not to push the opponent out of a circle but rather to put him to the floor. Also, the specialized clothing affords a higher level of modesty since it covers significantly more of the wrestler than the scant "diaper" on the huge *sumotori*.

In 1908, Icelandic wrestling champion Johannes Josephsson wrote a small manual on the sport of glima and the basic holds and throwing techniques. He also made it clear that both wrestlers start from the same, specified, point, which—from his description—must have looked a bit as if the opponents were getting ready to waltz, not wrestle:

The game is commenced, after shaking hands, by taking the grips, each having his right hand on the left hip of his opponent and the left hand on his right thigh. This is the only lawful grip. Both must stand erect, and the feet must not be too far apart nor yet together, about ten to twelve inches is sufficient, the right foot being a little in front of the left, and the right shoulder turned a little towards the opponent, the head facing his right shoulder. This is the only position allowable. (Josephsson 1908)

Glima fell from favor in most of Scandinavia because the priests at the end of the Viking age viewed it as a pagan activity and de-emphasized it. The people of Iceland took the opposite approach, considering glima to be good for moral development and discipline. Practiced by both sexes, there is a legendary tale of a match between a man and a woman lasting several days.

Glima Variants Among the Saami

The Saami are the reindeer-herding people who populate the northern regions of Norway, Sweden, and Finland along with the Kola Peninsula in Russia.

They have several varieties of wrestling, but the most common are two styles that are similar to the glima of Iceland. One is referred to as waist wrestling, where both wrestlers face each other and take a grip around their opponent's waist. The objective is to try to twist the opponent onto his back and then keep him there until he acknowledges defeat. These matches often take place on bare ground while the men of various groups are out searching for their reindeer that have been allowed to roam free during the summer. Should a wrestler defeat his partner in three consecutive matches, the defeated wrestler accepts that he has "lost for one year ahead" (Itkonen 1948).

Back wrestling among the Saami groups is similar in that the object is to throw the opponent to the ground and to hold him for a significant amount of time. The difference here is that the wrestler in back is the obvious aggressor while the person in front tries to resist being thrown or to escape but is not attempting a throw. For this reason, it is understood that the wrestlers will each get two turns in the back position. A loser is determined if one person cannot throw his opponent on both occasions.

Rapa das bestas

Not all wrestling is man-against-man (or woman-against-woman, as is the case in some exceptions). In the village of Sabucedo in the Spanish province of Galicia there still exists today the outgrowth of an ancient form of sport that also produced goods for commerce and provided a test of a man's character and worth that could elevate him to the upper ranks of society. It is the process of wrestling horses to a standstill, without the use of ropes, until the mane and tail are sheared. Today it is a three-day festival involving most of the men of the village and a herd of 600 horses, including stallions, mares, and foals. The festival is called *rapa das bestas*, meaning "the reaping of the horses."

While the horse hair is used in brushes and mattresses, the primary purpose of the festival has always been to declare the village's independence and virility. The notion of man against beast is by no means an isolated case. Consider the fascination with bulls in the Minoan culture of the island of Crete, the modern rodeo, and Spanish mainstays of bullfighting and the famous running of the bulls through the crowded streets of Pamplona. But the sheer chaos of the rapa das bestas, and its uniqueness to Sabucedo make this test of bravery, skill, and heritage something completely different. The Spanish writer Borobo "claims that the running of the bulls in Pamplona is a game for children compared to the *rapa das bestas* of Sabucedo" (Winn 1998).

There was also a wide variety of techniques and styles used in what is now modern Ireland, England, and Scotland that eventually evolved into forms that we recognize today in the fast-paced format of freestyle amateur wrestling.

Suggestions for Modern Play

Almost every person, unless physically unable, has some experience with wrestling. Taking a toss and turn at glima is worth a try. Determine what type of body shape has an advantage. Is strength most important, or is technique the key? Use Josephsson's description of the starting position as a guide.

Sources

Baker, William J. 1988. *Sports in the Western World*. (Rev. ed.) Urbana, and Chicago, Ill.: Illini Books.

Chase, Guy. 1999. "All in Wrestling, Submission Wrestling." www.guychase. com, 1999, *Multi-cultural Martial Arts Academy*.

Einarsson, Thorsteinn. 1988. *Glima—The Icelandic Wrestling*. Self-published.

Guttmann, Allen. 1992. "Old Sports." *Natural History*, July, Vol. 101, Issue 7, pp. 50–57.

Itkonen, Toivo Immanuel. 1948. *The Lapps in Finland up to 1945*. Vol. 2. Helsinki: Porvoo (translated from Finnish).

Josephsson, Johannes. 1908. *Icelandic Wrestling*.

Scothack, Cinaet. 1999. *Wrestling in Gaelic Culture*. The Clannada na Gadelica.

Winn, Jasper. 1998. "Running Wild." *Geographical Magazine*, July, Vol. 70, Issue 7, p. 12.

PLAY

⊞ Episkyros

A ball game played by the Greeks, the central theme of *episkyros* was for one team to drive another, by means of the flight of a thrown ball, across a boundary. Ball play was not a game for the serious Greek athlete. Instead, it was a means of light to moderate physical activity and something to be played by "women, children and old men but not by serious athletes" (Baker 1988, 21).

The ball games were often a part of a young man's early military training, with the emphasis on teamwork and fitness. Pollux in the second century A.D. offers this account of the game episkyros, also spelled *episkuros*:

This is played by teams of equal numbers standing opposite one another. They mark out a line between them with stone chips; this is the *skuros* on which the ball is placed. They then mark out two other lines, one behind each team. The team which secures possession of the ball throws it over their opponents who then try to get hold of the ball and throw it back, until one side pushes the other over the line behind them. The game might be called a Ball Battle. (translation, Harris 1972, 86)

It is likely that the ball was large and light, similar in size and weight to a child's plastic ball commonly purchased in a supermarket. In that way the very first throw could not drive a team immediately over its back boundary line.

Like so many forms of ball play, there were peculiarities of location. Organized ball play was especially important in Sparta, the paramilitary city-state where even young girls and women participated in mandated and state-run physical exercises and games. In Sparta a form of episkyros was played during an annual city festival that included five teams of 14 players each, all trying to use a thrown ball to push opposing teams over a barrier.

In Roman times, as the traditional Greek Olympic-style contests fell out of favor with the elite, ball play grew in interest. It was often seen as a vital preliminary to warm the blood before bathing. As Roman soldiers expanded the empire to ever more northern locales, baths were often built as quickly and with as much detail as were fortifications. This may have led to the introduction of some forms of ball play to indigenous peoples of France, Germany, and the British Isles. Some forms of ball play were certainly introduced by the Romans, but it would appear that the native customs of ball play were undoubtedly introduced *to* the Romans as well. Episkyros appears to have enjoyed its greatest peak in popularity prior to Roman control of Greece.

Suggestions for Modern Play

The relatively scant historical evidence concerning episkyros actually makes it easily adaptable for a modern game. There is very little to debate about the peculiarities of the rules, which appear to be quite simple. No player crosses the centerline, made of small stones (chalk would do just as well). The ball can be passed among teammates to produce a better angle for throwing over the opposing player's heads. If the ball is dropped—either from a teammate's or an opponent's throw—then the ball would be returned to the other side, and they can begin play at their discretion. If the back boundary is too easily cleared, just extend the boundaries. For formal play, take the Spartan example of 14 players per side. If fewer players are used, the boundaries should probably be reduced. The only real question is how the game was begun. We'd suggest a neutral observer to bounce the ball at the centerline, or *skyros*, as high as possible and for players to joust for it as they do a center tap in basketball.

Sources

Baker, William J. 1988. *Sport in the Western World*. Rev. ed. Urbana, Ill.: Illini Books.

Golden, Mark. 1998. *Sport and Society in Ancient Greece*. Cambridge: Cambridge University Press.

Harris, H. A. 1972. *Sport in Greece and Rome*. London: Thames and Hudson.

▦   Harpastum

Harpastum is a word of Greek origin meaning "snatch." Greek literature is sparse in regard to ball play. Harpastum is a social ball game that was popular in the time of the Roman Empire, with roots dating back centuries earlier. It is also referred to as the "small ball game." The game's name was derived from the ball with which it was played.

The game consisted of a group of players, probably not fewer than five but sometimes with teams of many more. Exactly how it was played has been interpreted in a variety of ways by different historians. Some see it as a forerunner to modern rugby. Others describe it as a group exercise of keepaway, or what many English-speaking Americans might have called "monkey in the middle" in their youth. Both viewpoints agree that one participant was in the middle of two rows of players.

Alexander the Great was an avid ballplayer, and during and after his life games played with a variety of balls in different sizes and weights are more frequently mentioned. A generation after Alexander the first mention of *sphairisterion*, a place specially dedicated to ball play, is found in Greek literature. Still, Greeks viewed being a ballplayer as akin to being a social juggler, someone who is adept enough to keep the rhythm and speed of the game moving at a solid and cooperative pace. It was not a spectator sport.

The relatively infrequent references to ball games by the Greeks themselves can partly be attributed to the approach that the Greeks took to this activity. Unlike the more famous Greek sports of the Olympic variety (wrestling, running, boxing, *pankration*, and the pentathlon), ball games were not seen as matters to be won or lost. They were played to encourage cooperation, coordination, and a measure of fitness. High-quality players were determined by their skill and grace.

The Romans, however, seem to have embraced the notion of ball play, particularly as a means for the wealthy to keep fit. The Roman elite was greatly inclined to distance itself from actual participation in the Greek festival sports, preferring to view them as spectators and leave the performances to professional athletes. They latinized the name sphairisterion to *sphaeristerium*. Ball courts became common inclusions in the public baths and were seen as a necessary facility for the wealthy. Whether the game was harpastum or its stripped-down cousin *trigon*, which was a three-person game, the object was to keep the game moving at a pace fast enough to exert some energy but not to the point of exhaustion. Some of the ancient literature describes ball games in general as being the best form of exercise because they worked the total body and not just a certain area. While spectators in the truest sense were still not part of the ball game culture, it was quite common for a small circle of fellow players to form around a game to watch, critique, and praise.

As in most pursuits that have their roots in Greece, it was important for practitioners to justify their purpose. This allies with the common theme of exercising both mind and body. Several centuries later, a court physician for Marcus Aurelius, a Greek named Galen, wrote a medical treatise called "Exercise with the Small Ball." The game that he describes appears to be harpastum because of its emphasis on intercepting or snatching the ball. Galen contends that ball play is not only beneficial but also pleasant because of its relatively low cost, the limited time that it takes from serious pursuits compared to other sports of the wealthy like hunting, and that, depending on how a group wants to play, it can be either vigorous or gentle exercise. This is also true of many of our modern forms of ball play. Playing in an organized game of five-on-five basketball is extremely taxing due to the size of the court, the amount of running, and the ever-increasing amount of contact allowed under the baskets. On the other hand, two people can enjoyably shoot baskets at a hoop atop the garage for hours.

Harpastum, according to H. A. Harris' interpretation of ancient literature in his work *Sport in Greece and Rome*, is "a game in which a player, standing between two lines of opponents, tries to intercept the catches as they throw to one another. This accounts for the name Harpastum, 'Snatch.'" (Harris 1972, 89). There is evidence that at least by the fifth century A.D. the game included an element where the interceptor also could be a target. Therefore, if he felt that he could not "snatch" the ball, then he must dodge it and be quick to twist his neck and his body about to be alert to the next throw coming from behind him. A common tactic was the faint or fake, similar to modern basketball's no-look pass, called the *phaininda*, which was essentially to look toward one player but to throw the ball to another with the intent of deceiving the interceptor.

Other researchers have looked at some of the ancient writings and have decided that the game had a marked resemblance to rugby and American football. This is due, in large part, to the words of Athenaeus, who says he is quoting Antiphanes, a fourth-century B.C. author of comedy who reportedly described *phaininda*, as the game was called in Greece, this way: "He caught the ball and passed it triumphantly to one player, while he dodged another, knocked it out of another's hands and picked up yet another player" (Harris 1972, 89, from Deipnosophistai I, 14). Several later historians and researchers have scoffed at Harris' contention that the game was not like rugby, especially since Harris said that there was no evidence of anyone's using his feet to knock the ball around. Thus, in his opinion, it could not be rugby. Of course, large parts of modern rugby are played without kicking the ball. What neither viewpoint explains adequately is how the interceptor was selected or how that person was replaced.

Suggestions for Modern Play

Modern harpastum players would be wise to keep the teams to 11 players or less. Pick the first interceptor by coin flip to see which team has to put someone out there. When he catches a pass, the person who threw it sits down. If the interceptor goes for a catch and misses or is struck by the ball, the interceptor joins his teammates and is replaced in the middle by a player from the opposing team. In this way, an interceptor is encouraged to be aggressive without the fear that if he misses, he will be immediately dispelled from the game. Harpastum continues until one side no longer has any players. This version of the game corresponds more to Harris' "no-body-contact" interpretation.

Sources

Golden, Mark. 1998. *Sport and Society in Ancient Greece*. Cambridge: Cambridge University Press.
Harris, H. A. 1972. *Sport in Greece and Rome*. London: Thames and Hudson.

Hoop Bowling

Anyone who has ever tried to roll a spare tire can appreciate the innocent fun and fascination of rolling a hoop. In the early 1900s it was a common practice among children of the world, in part due to the abundance of iron wheels and barrel hoops before the onset of rubber tires and plastic storage containers. Adult Native Americans played a variety of hoop games, many of which included the practice of trying to throw a spear, stick, or stone at or through the rolling hoop or to aim a projectile at the anticipated spot where the hoop would teeter to the ground (see North America: Hoop-and-pole).

The Greeks and the Romans were also fond of bowling hoops around their streets, much as the nineteenth- and early twentieth-century children would. The one difference appears to be that it was not viewed as solely the preserve of children and was, in fact, seen as valid exercise for men. Ovid, writing about a century after the formation of the Roman Empire, includes hoops, javelins, weapons, and horsemanship as valid activities for "tough young men" compared "with their female counterparts" (Harris 1972, 135).

The rolling of the hoop was done by pushing and steering the wheel-like structure with some form of stick or shaft. A piece of iron was often used. Most hoops in Roman times included attached jingling rings. This served the purpose of forewarning oncoming traffic to clear a path for the hoop. Martial, an especially helpful ancient author when it comes to the particulars of sports during the empire, wrote: "Why do tinkling rings wander around the large rim? So that the crowd who block the path may make way for the clanging hoops" (translated in Harris 1972, 136).

The hoop was relatively large, usually standing at mid-chest level to the bowler. When one was particularly adept at rolling the hoop, it was not enough to simply roll it in a straight line. It was also important to be able to turn the hoop and, as a real sign of expertise, to be able to jump and run through the hoop while it was in motion. This helps explain why a hoop needed to be so large.

The benefit of hoop bowling was similar to that ascribed to popular Roman ball games like *harpastum*, the three-person game often played with two balls called *trigon,* and the varieties of *episkyros.* It required the stamina and strength training of running but because of the nimbleness, agility, and eye-to-hand coordination involved, it lessened both the mental and physical monotony of just running alone.

Suggestions for Modern Play

Modern applications are easy to imagine. Take a hula hoop and any old stick and see if you can keep it rolling in a relatively straight line. Once that's mastered, work on turning the hoop while keeping it upright. The featherweight construction of a hula hoop won't require any degree of strength but will test agility, hand-to-eye coordination, and stamina. The rules are simple. Keep the hoop rolling. This is not a game to win as much as it is a game to master, adding difficulty to the task by changing the terrain and the path. As for trying to jump through a rolling hula hoop, it is feasible but would best be done on soft grass as opposed to asphalt.

Sources

Harris, H. A. 1972. *Sport in Greece and Rome.* London: Thames and Hudson.
Levinson, David, and Karen Christensen, eds., 1999. *Encyclopedia of World Sport* (paperback). Oxford: Oxford University Press.

▦   Nordic Skiing

Nordic skiing is believed by some to be a refinement of snowshoeing, appearing for the first time around 3,000 B.C. in Scandinavia as a more efficient means of getting over the snow-encrusted terrain. A ski from Kalvatrask ca. 3200 B.C. is one of the oldest preserved artifacts from that part of the world.

As with so many activities that evolved into sporting recreations, Nordic skiing, or cross-country skiing, as it is commonly called in the United States, has its roots in man's instincts to provide for his family and to survive nature's harsh conditions. When several feet of snow are on the ground, it is immensely tiring to trudge through the white stuff. But if you can literally overcome the snow, to stride atop it, then it not only eases your travel but actually, with practice, expedites it. Thus, it is not surprising that one of the earliest visual representations of skiing in a rock carving north of Norway at Rodoy, Tjotta, depicts men on skis hunting elk.

The early skiing maestros were the Saami, who populated the northern areas of Scandinavia. Their exploits were given literary credence in the sixth century by Procopius and again down through the next 700 years by other historians. Along the way, a princess weighed in on the subject. The daughter of a tenth-century Norwegian king named Gunhild is said to have claimed that the Saami were such good skiers that they could not be outrun by beasts or humans. At first it was rather a crude adaptation of snowshoeing until people discovered that the use of poles to help push off the surface would create a gliding effect while strapped to the wooden boards.

In the 1500s, Finnish Lapp skiers were using 9- to 11-foot skis (half-again as long as most modern cross-country skis) and a single, long pushing pole. This single-staff style was also used in the area known as Slovenia and was referred to as Bloke skiing, so named for the Bloke Plateau, which is located south of the Slovenian capital, Ljubljana. A description of Slovenian skiing dates to a document printed in 1689, at a time when it was already over 300 years old.

Poles were developed to fit the individual needs. The Finnish pushing pole used by the Lapps worked well on relatively flat, crusted snow but not as well on deeper snow. Thus, the Norwegians developed the leathered basket at the end of the pole to keep it from penetrating too deeply.

Skiing eventually would become an integral part of warfare tactics and was utilized with great effectiveness by Allied forces in World War II. An early example of military use was the great snow escape of Gustavas Vasa in 1520, who skied 51 miles from Salan to Mora, Sweden, to lead his countrymen to freedom against the Danish king, Christian II. That famous trek is memorialized each year with the Vasaloppet Race, which follows the historical route that Vasa took. Interestingly, despite this royal and heroic jaunt, the Swedes—like virtually all of Europe—were slow to embrace skiing as a popular pastime. It seems that skiing for virtually all of its history was the domain of the Lapps, the Finns, and the Saami—the people who traversed the Arctic Circle, often as herdsmen.

It wasn't until two Saami explorers, Pava Lars Tuorda and Anders Rossa, wrote about their trek across Greenland on skis in 1883 that the consciousness of Europe and the world was raised to the idea of skiing as a sport. (At that time, skiing in the Alps was unheard of. It was, however, already a popular pastime in another future hot spot for the schussing and après-ski crowd. Both men and women in the gold-mining communities of California took part in regular skiing competitions in the mid- to late 1800s.)

Many people, both laymen and explorers, were skeptical of Tuorda and Rossa's claims that they had skied across the polar ice cap, covering 460 kilometers (roughly 275 miles) in 57 hours. A race was set up in Lapland the following year of a distance of 220 kilometers. Tuorda won, and enough other competitors finished to silence the skeptics. Less than 10 years later, Norwegian explorer Fridtjut Nansen published his journals on a cross-Greenland trek, and it was translated into several languages. Within a few years, ski clubs were popping up in the Alps and around Europe.

Today, cross-country skiing is a highly competitive sport dominated by the Scandinavian countries and Italy, as well as Russia and other former Soviet bloc nations. Another competitive offshoot is the biathlon, the combination of cross-country skiing and target shooting with a rifle. The biathlon originated in Norway as a training exercise for soldiers. The first known competition took place in 1767 between companies of guards who patrolled the border with Sweden. Late in the nineteenth-century, local rifle and ski clubs in Norway and other Scandinavian countries practiced the sport to keep their members prepared for combat. It would be fair to say that the biathlon is an outgrowth of a much earlier form of survival when man hunted (with bow and arrow, throwing stick, or spear) from atop skis.

Suggestions for Modern Play

For a modern-day school project, try to make cross-country skiing an interdisciplinary task from start to finish, incorporating woodworking and leather crafts to make skis from planks of wood and an old-fashioned binding. Let students choose their own woods. Will they wax them or not? What does it take to curve a ski's front to keep the tip from digging into a snowbank? Then incorporate some basic outdoor survival skills, like compass use and mapmaking to chart a new ski trail. Combine the ancient skill of archery to create your own old-fashioned biathlon (this is a burgeoning sport in itself that is being promoted by several archery clubs in the northeastern United States). Novice skiers will find that it's a pretty difficult task to stop skiing and still be able to control tired lungs and limbs well enough to notch an arrow and hit a target.

Sources

Rajtmajer, Dolfe. 1994. "The Slovenian Origins of European Skiing." *The International Journal of the History of Sport*, April, 1995. Vol. 11, No. 1, pp. 97–102.

Sörlin, Sverker. 1995. "Nature, Skiing and Swedish Nationalism." *The International Journal of the History of Sport*, August, Vol. 12, No. 2, pp. 147–163.

Umminger, Walter. 1963. *Supermen, Heroes and Gods*. English ed. London: Thames and Hudson.

▦ Quoits

Quoits is both the ancient forerunner to modern horseshoe pitching and now a modern, alternative to its better-known pitching relative.

Its origin is a debatable question. The most ancient references stem from the contention that quoit was synonymous with discus in ancient Greece. Some have speculated that quoits was part of the original pentathlon in the Greek games. If that was the case, then the question of whether it was a game involving pitching or hurling the heavy metal rings at a target—as in the game of quoits—or whether the quoit was thrown for distance—like the discus—is still unresolved.

Stepping back even further in ancient history, it has been noted that a Minoan boy-king of Knossos, ca. 2000 B.C., used the discus/quoit to strike down escaped slaves, which gives a bit of anecdotal credence to the theory that the quoit started out as a weapon of war.

An alternative explanation is still based in the military but is more mundane, that Roman soldiers, among the first to shod their horses, created a diversion out of the used iron horseshoes. When time and the availability of a blacksmith allowed, the shoes were reforged into a circle. (It may be worth noting that even today there are occasions when a horse is purposely shod with a full-circle shoe, usually as a corrective measure.) In this theory, quoits and what we commonly call horseshoes were developed simultaneously and really began to become a target-based sporting endeavor around the first century A.D. in the British Isles, where it can be supposed that the Roman armies had need for leisure diversions between repelling barbarian attacks and building public baths. In this case, the game of horseshoes was just the poor man's version of quoits.

Modern practitioners would probably agree with that synopsis, if for no other reason than that quoits is a trickier game. The iron stakes, called hobs, are pounded nearly flush or completely flush to the ground in a pit of mushy clay as opposed to the relatively tall target of horseshoes. Further, at least in some locales, the quoit is quite heavy, and the distance that it is thrown is considerable.

By the second millennium, evidence indicates that quoits was played quite regularly in England, in particular, in areas near mining communities. The quoits of the era were made from the leftover, poorer-quality metals from the forges. The object was much like horseshoes, but because the pin was embedded in the ground, the notion of a ringer was not as prevalent. Rather, the concept was to get as close to the pin as possible, with as many quoits as possible, while trying to flip or nudge opponents out of the way. In this sense, the game has some similarities to sliding-disc contests like curling and shuffleboard.

Quoits has survived as a minor interest in the United Kingdom, particularly in northern England, Scotland, and Wales, and also as a cruise ship diversion, with rings of rope having replaced the heavy iron circles. It is played in a few isolated pockets in the United States, notably, Pennsylvania and Trenton, New Jersey.

The quoits' weight makes the game unwieldy for many people. The Northern Game, played primarily in England, created a standardized set of rules in the late 1800s, which include the dimensions of an 11-yard field, with quoits measuring 5.5 inches in diameter and weighing 5.5 pounds. In the Long Game, favored in Scotland and Wales, strength is as important as skill, harking back to the Scots' Highland Games' mentality. The quoit weighs up to 11 pounds and is thrown a rather substantial distance of 18 yards. In the United States the game has been stripped down to a distance of 21 feet.

Both horseshoes and quoits were brought to colonial America by the English, but horseshoes has gained the greater foothold on this continent.

Suggestions for Modern Play

Quoits can be played today. Rules and equipment can be purchased from specialty distributors of traditional games. A simpler method, perhaps, would be to pound a stake almost all the way into the ground, leaving about an inch exposed, step off a predetermined distance (probably the Northern Game measure of 11 yards would be better suited for beginners), and then use some five-pound plates from a school's weight room.

Source

Masters, James 1997–2001. "Quoits—History and Useful Information." *The Online Guide to Traditional Games*, Web site address: eb.ukonline.co.uk/james.masters/TraditionalGames

GAMES

▦　Knucklebones

Just as the name implies, actual bones—both human and animal—were used to play this game, which had a number of variations in the ancient Grecian world and was also played by many different cultural groups all around Europe and the world.

One thing that is clear about knucklebones is their prevalence in daily life, as at an archaeological site or in a research library. Unfortunately, in the ancient writing and in the modern descriptions that follow, there is little about the *specifics* of knucklebones. They were sometimes used like dice as a means for gambling and were also a children's game, something akin to what we would call jacks.

According to Pollux, a writer in the second century, "the knucklebones are thrown up into the air, and an attempt is made to catch them on the back of the hand. If you are only partially successful, you have to pick up the knucklebones which have fallen on the ground without letting fall those already on the hand" (Beaumont 1994). This is similar to the way of determining which player will go first in many international versions of modern jacks. It also appears to be a partial description of the game fivestones, described in detail later.

Two women are depicted in the Hellenistic Greek style (ca. 330–300 B.C.) in a terra-cotta statue playing *astragalos*, or what is more commonly known as knucklebones. There were many varieties of games played with dice in ancient Greece and Rome. A popular game for women and girls was known as fivestones and can be compared to modern jacks games that are found in slightly different forms around the world. (© The British Museum)

The bones were sometimes real bones, but terra-cotta replicas were also used. They were particularly popular with girls, who played fivestones with them. The boys used them as dice, with the differently shaped faces representing different values.

Children playing knucklebones were a common sight in Athens, but it is not a native game, according to the Greek historian Herodotus (ca. 430 B.C.). He ascribed the invention of such games to the Lydians, who used them as a means of distraction during a legendary famine. The Lydians apparently recognized that they needed to ration what little provisions they had. As a means of doing this, they ate only every other day. To ward off feelings of hunger on the days when no food would be consumed, they amused themselves with games, like knucklebones, that took little energy.

Another theory holds that a nobleman named Palamedes taught the game, in the form of jacks, to Greek soldiers during the time of the Trojan War. It is quite possible that the game was not invented in the ancient Mediterranean but was imported. More likely is a scenario of concurrent invention of like games in different cultures. This would certainly appear to be the case with other sports and games (notably, archery).

The girls' version of knucklebones, referred to as fivestones, was a variant of what we would commonly call jacks. We know with a high degree of certainty that it was something enjoyed in the time of Roman rule as well and was known by the name of *tali*. In a marble frieze uncovered in Pompeii, the southern Italian city covered by the eruption of Mt. Vesuvius in A.D. 79, women are shown playing the game of jacks.

Suggestions for Modern Play

Most of us think of jacks as a game with six-pronged metal pieces and a bouncing rubber ball. Fivestones required much greater dexterity and did not include a ball. Today it is still a common activity for the school-children in Israel and is called *hamesh avanim*, with gold-colored cubes the size of dice used instead of knucklebones. Here's how it is played. As with virtually all games in the jacks family, the tasks are carried out with only one hand. Start with five stones. Select one and place it on your palm. While tossing the one stone from palm to the back of your hand, pick up as many stones as possible. Continue until all stones are picked up. In subsequent rounds, use two, then three, then four stones in the palm-to-back-of-your-hand trick. The player who can successfully complete all four rounds wins.

Sources

Beaumont, Lesley. 1994. "Child's Play in Classical Athens." *History Today*, August, Vol. 44, Issue 8, p. 30.
Lankford, Mary D. 1996. *Jacks around the World*. New York: Morrow Junior Books.

⊞ Tabula

Tabula was a popular tabletop game of the Romans that is markedly similar in its rules to modern backgammon. It is quite possibly a descendant in the history of tabletop games from the ancient Egyptian game called *senet*, which was also played by the Romans. Both are what were termed "race" games by the eminent games historian R. C. Bell, meaning that the players start with the same number of playing pieces, and the object is to race around a designated board in one direction—in this case counterclockwise—to a final destination. Usually, the pace of movement is determined by the means of throwing dice. In tabula, three six-sided dice (essentially like modern dice) were used. Rules were instituted to create obstacles for movement.

According to amateur historian and Roman game devotee W. J. Kowalski's description of the rules of tabula, anyone who has had an introduction to modern backgammon could play the game and play it on a backgammon board. Here are Kowalski's rules for tabula:

1. The board can be a backgammon board. Each player has 15 pieces.
2. All pieces enter from square 1 and travel counterclockwise.
3. Three dice are thrown, and the three numbers determine the moves of between 1 and 3 pieces.
4. Any part of a throw that could not be used is lost, but a player must use the whole value of the throw if it is possible.
5. If a player lands a piece on a point with one enemy piece, the enemy piece is removed from the board and has to reenter the game on the next throw.
6. If a player has two or more men on a point, this position is closed to the enemy, and these men cannot be captured.
7. No player may enter the second half of the board until all men have entered the board.
8. No player may exit the board until all pieces have entered the last quarter. This means that if a single man is hit, the remaining pieces may be frozen in the last quarter until he reenters and catches up with them again.

Tabula probably grew out of a game from Roman antiquity called twelve lines (*duodecim scriptorum*) and predates the heady days of the Roman Republic. A bronze mirror from about 200 B.C. depicts a young man and a young woman playing tabula. The woman is saying, "I believe I've won."

It was apparently a game enjoyed by emperors as well as soldiers and, if the mirror is indicative, by both sexes. Much of the knowledge of tabula's rules stems from a late fifth-century A.D. description of a game involving Emperor Zeno. In the game, Zeno found himself in a predicament when with one roll he went from an advantageous position to having to leave a single, uncovered playing piece in seven different spaces. This is related to the preceding fourth rule, that all rolls must be played to their full value if they can be. Since the object of the game is to keep at least two pieces on a space to protect them (rule 5) from capture, Zeno's roll was so horrendous that it warranted description. It is also known that tabula was the favorite game of Emperor Claudius (A.D. 50), who went so far as to have a board, called an *alveus*, equipped on his imperial carriage.

Because it was also a popular game with the far-flung legions of Roman soldiers, tabula helped to spawn a number of similar games around Europe and the Middle East, among them *ad elta stelpur* in Iceland, *taefle* and *fayles* in England (A.D. 1025), *six-ace* in Spain (A.D. 1251), and *tournecase* in France. The Arabian game *nard* appears to be a slightly modified version of tabula, perhaps incorporating aspects of Egyptian senet. The gaming pieces were usually made from severed pieces of bone, leaving them in flat discs.

Sources

Bell, R. C. 1979. *Board and Table Games from Many Civilizations* (revised double edition). New York: Dover.

Kowalski, W. J. 1997. *Roman Board Games*, World Wide Website, personal.psu.edu/users/w/x/wxk116/roma/rbgames.html

▦ LATIN AMERICA

INTRODUCTION

When it comes to sports, "Latin America is primarily a recipient region which, over the last century, has adopted sports mainly developed in other places" (Arbena 1986). Consequently, "older forms of sport and popular recreation were modified, reduced or even eliminated." That means that the most noteworthy of all the games of this region, generically referred to as the Mesoamerican ball game, has been all but extinguished despite a history that stretched back at least 1,500 years and had created an institution of the highest sporting, religious, and civic development when Cortés and his conquistadors first began the process of exploiting the land, its riches, and its people.

Though it is a nearly extinct game, the Mesoamerican ball game is the centerpiece for any study of ancient Latin American sports and games. It was a contest that modern sports can only hope to duplicate in terms of its significance to a mass population. The game itself was fast-paced and exciting; the players set to their craft with intensity and skill, utilizing probably the most ornamental of any ancient sporting arenas; and very much was riding on the outcome: personal monetary gain for players and fans, the socio-political stability of a ruling class, possibly the success or failure of a year's worth of crops. At times, even the ultimate fate of life or death hung on the outcome.

Latin America also included in its list of traditional sports and games a number of varieties of ball games, a strong affinity for the bow and arrow, pockets of intensive wrestling, and an affinity for gambling-oriented games.

The powerful Andean ruling elite known as the Incas will be only marginally mentioned in these entries. This is due to two primary factors. One is a strictly historical explanation. The Incas did not come to power until the twelfth century and really began to expand their empire by significant measures only in the final 100 years before the Spanish arrived in 1532. The empire was lost by 1535, meaning that the reign of the Incas, though glorious in some of its accomplishments, was relatively short-lived. The second factor has more to do with the way that the Incas ruled a territory that at its height stretched nearly the length of South America's western border and encompassed approximately 12 million people. Most of these people were not of Incan descent; rather, they were people who had succumbed to harsh control of the empire. Also, as the major currency was not money but a tax on labor, the Incas essentially had a socialistic state that put little emphasis on leisure. To paraphrase McIntyre, if there was no work to be done, work was invented to keep the people busy. Instead of emphasizing Inca contributions, this survey of Latin American sports goes to the deeper level of the smaller tribes that populated the Andean Mountains. In some cases they have preserved a good deal of their traditional cultures well into the twentieth century, as exemplified by the Mataco's stubborn refusal to give up their personal version of field hockey.

Gambling, as mentioned, was practiced and enjoyed by a wide variety of Latin American people. On the other hand, a large number of tribes in South America do not seem to have had any interest in gambling, nor did they practice the rudimentary play with dice or lots that is extremely common throughout the world. The major emphasis of those gambling cultures are explored in the section entitled "Games of Chance." In the interest of balance, it is appropriate to point out the following examples of ethnographic research that asserts that in other areas gambling was a nonfactor:

Gambling is unknown [for the Kuna]. (Marshall 1950)

Gambling has not been reported for the tribes of this region [of Colombia]. (Park 1949)

Gambling (among the Aymara) is unimportant, although small boys occasionally bet portions of their lunches while herding livestock. (Tschopik 1946)

No gambling is indulged in by any of the Fuegians. The elaborate games so common in North America are absent from Fuegian culture. (Cooper 1917)

An exception to the pervasive trend of nongamblers in South America comes from the Mataco region, where Karsten details extensively an elaborate dice game where "gambling is always connected with the *shuke* game and the stakes lost—whether it be a collar, a shirt, a pair of trousers

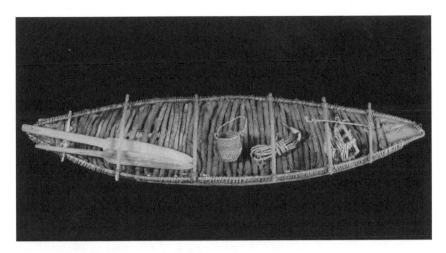

This intricate model canoe is a nineteenth-century work made by the Yahgan people, who lived on the island of Tierra del Fuego off the southernmost tip of South America. The Yahgan existed for centuries in a harsh climate, cultivating a physical lifestyle that stressed wrestling, archery, and fishing. They are one of the many tribes of South America that are now considered completely extinct. (© The British Museum)

or some other valuable object—are always scrupulously paid as real debts of honour" (Karsten 1932).

THE LOST TRIBES OF SOUTH AMERICA

It is estimated that the Amazon had a sprawling indigenous population of at least 6 million people before first European contact in the late fifteenth century. Only a quarter million indigenous people remain, and a third of the tribes known to exist in the Amazon in 1900 were considered extinct by 1992. In the following sections are repeated references to the tribes of the Tierra del Fuego, particularly the Ona and the Yahgan. They are instructive for the purpose of this book because of the extensive research on their traditional physical sports of wrestling, archery, and running, which were still relatively unaltered at the time the research was conducted. They are also instructive in a much broader and more significant sense, for they are both cultures that no longer exist, wiped out by the introduction of new diseases that they had no defenses against, despite the fact that they were conditioned from childhood to be able to withstand significant hardships in climate and daily toil. More horrendous is a history of deliberate campaigns of extermination against the Indians by white settlers. Today the problems of race extinction still are a very real worry, particularly in the Amazon basin, where many ethnic groups have already disappeared, and the indigenous population is ebbing away, partly due to acculturation with other groups but also due to the ever-shrinking rain forest.

Sources

Alvarsson, Jan-Ake. 1988. *The Mataco of the Gran Chaco: An Ethnographic Account of Change and Continuity in Mataco Socio-economic Organization.* Stockholm, Sweden: Almqvist and Wiskell International.

Arbena, Joseph L. 1986. "Sport and the Study of Latin American History: An Overview." *Journal of Sport History,* Vol. 13, No. 2, p. 87–96.

Bennett, Bradley C. 1992. "Plants and People of the Amazonian Rainforests." *Bioscience,* September, Vol. 42, Issue 8, p. 599.

Cooper, John M. 1917. "Analytical and Critical Bibliography of the Tribes of the Tierra del Fuego." *Bureau of American Ethnology 63.* Washington, DC: Government Printing Office.

Karsten, Rafael. 1932. *Indian Tribes of the Argentine and Bolivian Chaca: Ethnological Studies.* Helsingfors: Adademische Buchhandlung.

Kennedy, John W. 2000. "Out of the Ashes." *Christianity Today,* January 10, Vol. 44, Issue 1, p. 67.

Marshall, Donald Stanley 1950. "Cuna Folk." Thesis, Harvard University.

McIntyre, Loren 1975. *The Incredible Incas and Their Timeless Land.* Washington, DC: National Geographic Society/Special Publications Division.

Park, Willard Z. 1946–1949. "Tribes of the Sierra Nevada de Santa Marta, Colombia." In *Handbook of South American Indians.* Vol. 2, Washington, DC. Government Printing Office.

Tschopik Harry, Jr. 1946. "The Aymara." *Bureau of American Ethnology* No. 143, Vol. 2. Washington, DC: Smithsonian Institute.

SPORTS

■ Archery

The bow was an almost universal tool throughout Latin America among the traditional indigenous people, whether they chose to equip it with poison-dipped arrows, use it to secure fish in the murky Amazon River, or relegate it to the status of second-class weapon.

A wide range of poisons was known to be placed on arrowheads among South American tribes, with curare being the active ingredient in many of them. These poisons were designed more to ensure a successful hunt than to incapacitate a human enemy. Whether the poison itself was even particularly effective is questionable. What was important to the indigenous hunter were the magical attributes obtained by applying the concoction. A sense of how the bow and arrow has traditionally been entwined with magical properties can be gleaned from even the relatively modern practices of a Kuna medicine man in Panama. As part of his wide array of potions and items are miniature bows and arrows made from the black palm, which are used by placing them in a bath with the patient because the bow and arrow can combat demons. This is a representation of how the physical manifestation of the bow and the arrow, even without its archer and in miniature, possesses a magical power.

Since the "magic" of a bow is well known, many North American tribes place taboos on how a bow must be handled, the foremost one being that no woman is to touch a bow lest it lose its accuracy. This behavior is not as prevalent in South America, but the power of archery is respected. Among the Mataco of Argentina and Bolivia, a dead man's bow and arrows were burned along with all of the rest of his possessions, including his home, to make the dead spirit feel less welcome. Should the spirit still decide to linger, arrows were placed around the new dwelling of his kin because of their "effective protection against the malicious demon. . . . Arrows play an important part as charms and amulets among the South American Indians" (Karsten 1932, 194).

The quality of the arrows represented quite a range of craftsmanship and was often reflective of their intended use. Some of the most rudimentary arrows were those used by Costa Ricans, who simply shot a reed shaft without fletchings, a bowstring nock, or even a head. At the other end of both the technological and the geographic spectrum, the Ona of Tierra del Fuego had very good fletching, and, despite their generally simple technology, their "bow and arrow were of consummate workmanship" (Cooper 1946, 125). The Xingu of Amazonia were known to specifically plant a reed called *uba* to ensure that they would have an adequate supply of arrow shafts.

The bows, by most accounts, shared the general characteristic of being made of a single piece of wood and being quite large, averaging over six feet in length, with the Tauapuery of the Rio Negro area in Brazil topping the charts with a bow nearly 11 feet long. References to long bows of over six feet come from all regions of the continent. The large bow was also a staple of the Bororo of Brazil and was outfitted by spearlike arrows that could be as long as five feet and usually included three separate pieces of wood for the head, shaft, and arrow nock. The heads, or points, would vary depending on the purpose, which is not an unusual trait among people who use the bow extensively. The Bororo had one harpoon point especially designed for fishing, though it was not their sole—or even most effective—means of fishing.

One of the fiercest and most successful of all Native American archers were the Araucanians (also known as Araucano). They alone among all Amerindian tribes were able to resist the incessant flow of colonizing armies and white settlers and retain their ancestral land in southern Chile.

Significantly farther away were the Caribs, who probably hailed from

The use of the bow and arrow as a means of fishing was relatively common along the Amazon River. This photo, taken between 1890 and 1923, demonstrates a couple of common characteristics of many Latin American archers: the bow is quite long and made from a single piece of wood, while the arrow is extremely long, and the head is attached with a separate piece of wood from the rest of the shaft. (Library of Congress, Prints and Photographs Division [LC-USZ62–109129])

the basins of the Amazon but had migrated to what are now the Caribbean Islands, where they drove off most of the people who already lived there. Two early seventeenth-century Europeans—the Reverend Thomas Davies and a French Dominican, Jean Baptiste Labat—both wrote glowing praise for the Caribs' accuracy with the bow. Davies said that they could consistently hit a coin the size of a half dollar from 225 feet, while their young boys could hit small targets from approximately 36 feet up to 20 times in succession. Labat related that they were expert shots at birds and, with a fiber string attached to their arrow, were also adept at using their bow for fishing purposes. Further, they were extremely quick at getting off multiple shots.

Not all of the activities with bow and arrow were restricted to obtaining food or warfare. The Ona, who were excellent bow hunters, also encouraged games for boys that involved the bow and arrow, including regular target practice, shooting an arrow through a rolling grass ring, and shooting headless old arrows that had been lit with a flame. The Goajiro of north Colombia and Venezuela played at an archer's version of skeet shooting by taking aim at pieces of fruit or other round objects that were tossed into the air. Young boys of the Yanomamo tribe, spreading across Brazil and Venezuela, would make a game of hunting for lizards with their toy bows and featherless arrows. Particularly good fun for the boys was had when a lizard would be caught alive and then tied, by means of a string, to a stick in a village clearing. They then would try to shoot the lizard but invariably would miss since they were not yet well-trained shots, and lizards are quite quick. This usually ended when an older boy came by and showed off his skills with the adult bow, terminating both the lizard and the game. (Many South American people hunt lizards for either their meat, hide, or blood, which is viewed by some as a powerful medicinal tool. Most, however, would not taunt a lizard since the reptiles are so intricately interwoven into mythology, often representing dangerous spirits.)

An interesting aspect to the history of archery in South America is how some groups of people had the bow but opted not to use it with any regularity. The Maya, for all their advances compared to other Amerindian groups, preferred the obsidian sword and a throwing stick, called the *atlatl*, to the bow, although it is known that they had knowledge of it and were surrounded by people who used it.

In the high peaks of the Andean Mountains near Lake Titicaca, the Aymara Indians of the mid- to late nineteenth century could not recall ever seeing an adult use a bow and arrow as a weapon, even though they had terms for "bow" use in their language, and children made bows as toys. This apparent contradiction can, in part, be explained by the Aymara's widespread use of slings, which would hurl stones of various sizes. The people had become so adept with the slings that they could kill everything from birds to human enemies. The movement from bow to sling may have been a result of a lack of suitable wood for bow-making in the high plains. The island of the Tierra del Fuego is an interesting example of how tribes in relatively close proximity can make different choices about bow usage. About the only time that the Ona was separated from his bow was when, via messenger, he sent it to a woman as a physical proposal for marriage (if it was returned by messenger, it meant she refused; if she returned the bow, that meant acceptance). The Yahgan had the bow but saw it as a subordinate tool to the spear in hunting and never used it in warfare. Among the Alacaluf use of the bow depended on geographical location, with one group using it from earliest time, the latter adapting it to use only late in the nineteenth century.

Suggestions for Modern Play

With either a basic, store-bought bow or a hand-made effort, use blunt arrows and practice target shooting at small objects, like a pine cone on a bough, or an apple on a tree. Once the target begins to be hit with some regularity, try the bow-and-arrow version of "skeet" shooting by throwing a target into the air. Make sure all practice is done in an open space, with no people or animals within the shooting range. Archery clubs are also an option.

Sources:

Blanchard, Kendall. 1996. "Traditional Sports, North and South America." In *Encyclopedia of World Sport*, edited by David Levinson and Karen Christensen. Santa Barbara, Calif: ABC-CLIO, pp. 1075–1083.

Burke, Edmund. 1957. *The History of Archery*. New York: William Morrow.

Chagnon, Napoleon A. 1968. *Yanomamo: The Fierce People*. 1968, New York: Holt, Rinehart, and Winston.

Chapin, Norman Macpherson. 1983. *Curing among the San Blas Kuna of Panama*. Ann Arbor, Mich.: University Microfilms International.

Cook, William Azel. 1909. *Through the Wilderness of Brazil by Horse, Canoe and Float*. New York: American Tract Society.

Cooper, John M. 1917. "Analytical and Critical Bibliography of the Tribes of the Tierra del Fuego." *Bureau of American Ethnology* 63, Washington, D.C.: Government Printing Office.

———. 1946. "The Ona." In *The Marginal Tribes*, edited by Julian H. Steward. Washington, DC: Government Printing Office, pp. 107–125.

Karsten, Rafael. 1932. *Indian Tribes of the Argentine and Bolivian Chaco: Ethnological Studies*. Helsingfors: Akademische Buchhandlung.

La Barre, Weston. 1948. *The Aymra Indians of the Lake Titicaca Plateau*. Menasha, Wisc.: American Anthropological Association.

▦   Field Hockey

What modern sportsmen and sportswomen call field hockey is a derivative of a game and physical activity that seem to have had very few cultural boundaries, since early humans commonly carried a stick, club, or staff and would naturally want to use it to strike at objects.

There are pictorial representations in the Beni Hasan tombs of ancient Egypt (ca. 2000 B.C.) and then very similar depictions in an Athenian sculptural relief dated about 500 B.C. The Romans played a game called *paganica*, in which a small ball filled with feathers was batted about with a club. Continental Europe produced a number of similar games that led to the development of such sports as hurling and *shinty*. Golf is a more refined version because it has the added aspect of using finesse to push the small ball into a small hole (as opposed to a larger goal), and there is evidence that the Chinese (independently from the Scottish) developed a game called *chiuwan*, played mainly by the royalty, that was markedly similar to golf.

That the native North Americans had a variety of games involving both a stick and a ball—the most famous being lacrosse, with *shinny* being most closely related to field hockey—is well documented and accepted. What is not as well known is that games closely resembling field hockey were also played with great devotion and intensity among some people of South America. Sixteenth-century European explorers to Argentina discovered a refined field hockey game played by the Araucano Indians called *cheuca*. The name meant "the twisted one" and stemmed from the stick that was used because it had a twisted end. The Araucano used a stuffed ball encased in leather and played on fields that were usually 100 paces long and a relatively narrow 10 paces wide. Games would be between four, six, or eight players, with the smaller teams a function of a smaller field. The end lines served as the goals.

"The Araucanos considered *cheuca* to be an important feature of their lives because it kept them healthy and in good physical condition for war" (Arlott 1975, 482). In this way, cheuca served a purpose similar to lacrosse, the indigenous stick-and-ball game of most of the North American native populations.

Another variation of field hockey was played by the Mataco of the Gran Chaco, which is a dry forest that spreads from the foothills of the Andes in Bolivia into Argentina. Since the time of settlement in this area, which predates Spanish expeditions, the Mataco have resisted interaction with any type of colonization or other ethnic groups, a stance that they still pursue.

The *ha'la lhota'* or hockey was the only type of ball game played by the Mataco and was played by boys, adults, and even old men as both a diversion and a sport, with teams from 10 to 25 players evenly divided. The game was played with curved sticks and a wooden ball. The goals were unique; they were wood piles. A definite number of goals to produce a winning team was decided before the game began. These games took on a more sports-oriented direction when they pitted teams from two different villages, usually with prizes (a goat, attractive clothing).

While the fact that the Araucanos' game of cheuca served as physical training for warfare shows similarities to one purpose of the North American game of lacrosse, the Mataco's ballgame shared a slightly different approach that was at times also seen in lacrosse matches. The ha'la lhota' games could serve as a substitute for armed conflict between villages that had a recognized dispute or long-standing tension. Instead of waging a war, the battle would be decided on the hockey ground. Also, the hockey games demonstrated the relative strength of different villages. If one village continually lost at hockey, it had a vivid demonstration that its physical forces were probably not sufficient to engage the other village in an act of warfare. (For discussions of other games that served as substitutes for warfare, see Oceania: Prun; Latin America: Wrestling.)

One reason that the hockey games of the Mataco were such a good gauge of a village's fitness for war is the manner in which they were played. "In its brutality and fierceness each hockey party resembles a pitched battle. The Indians paint themselves and dress as if they were getting ready to face a real enemy. . . . The adversaries are frequently members of bands which are on unfriendly terms" (Métraux 1943, 207). That the players gambled large stakes on the outcome of the game only fueled any natural animosity between the two village teams and increased the intensity of the play.

The variations of field hockey in both the Araucano and the Mataco societies illustrate the pervasive nature of the ball game—in many variations—in indigenous American cultures.

Suggestions for Modern Play

While modern field hockey is a popular sport for girls at the junior high and high school level, boys in the United States seldom play it in an organized fashion. Try to emulate the Mataco (without the violent undertones and high-stakes gambling). Boys in two classes from the same grade begin the process by selecting their own hardwood sticks with a natural curve at one end and then carve them to the appropriate length (generally slightly higher than waist level). They should also make their own wooden ball. The test will be how quickly they adapt to the rough-hewn quality of the playing material and to understand the limits of their own passing skills. As the Mataco did, use two woodpiles as goals, set up at opposite ends of a relatively large, even patch of firm grass.

Sources

Alvarsson, Jan-Ake. 1988. *The Mataco of the Gran Chaco: An Ethnographic Account of Change and Continuity in Mataco Socio-economic Organization*. Stockholm, Sweden: Almqvist and Wiskell International.

Arlott, John, ed. 1975. *The Oxford Companion to World Sports and Games*. London: Oxford University Press.

Metraux, Alfred. 1943. "Suicide among the Matako of the Gran Chaco," *American Indigena*, Vol. 3, pp. 199–299.

⌗ Mesoamerican Ball Game

The Mesoamerican ball game has its roots in the ancient Olmec culture of Mexico and Central America at least 3,400 years ago and was one of the most significant social events of the ancient and highly developed civilizations of Central America. Utilizing a rubber ball and played on a court enclosed by stone walls and usually shaped in the manner of the capital letter *I*, it was a fast-paced game that was a spectacle for the masses and carried with it deep sociological and religious meanings. Essentially extinct today as a sport, the importance of this game is clearly evidenced by architectural ruins from as far north as Arizona, throughout modern Mexico and Central America, and even extending into South America.

Long before Spanish explorer Hernando Cortés and his conquistadors pushed inland to bring a European historical context to the continent, civilizations had been evolving, growing, and creating marvels of architecture and commerce in what is now Mexico and Central America.

The ruling peoples whom Cortés met and eventually betrayed and conquered in 1520–1521 were the Aztecs, the rulers of the last of the significant stages of pre-European political power in the region (Olmec, Mayan, Toltec, then Aztec). Among the wonders that Cortés and his men saw was an aggressively played court game using a rubber ball (which was unknown at the time in Europe) that was propelled by means of hip, buttocks, and occasionally shoulders but never by feet or hands. To the Aztecs the game was known as *tlachtli*. The Mayans called it *pok-ta-pok*, and it had other names in different eras and geographic locations.

It was a game rich in history and replete with social and religious meaning. "No other game in the world is so laden with ideology. It was philosophy, theology and cosmology rolled in one," contends Michael Coe, an anthropologist from Yale University (Blank 1999, 64).

There were many unique features to the game: its traditional *I*-shaped courts made of stone; the later addition of suspended stone rings (probably around A.D. 700), through which, with great expertise and some luck, the ball could be passed, bringing an immediate victory; elaborate equipment for both protection and pageantry; and ritualistic human sacrifice of players following the match.

Most significant—and essential—was the ball itself. For all the advancements and technological savvy of the ancient Egyptians, the Greeks, and the Chinese, none had a ball with the resiliency and elasticity of the rubber ball. The Europeans' disgust over the bloody sacrifices was almost matched by their amazement with the rubber ball itself.

The Olmec, the oldest major Mesoamerican civilization, left behind ball courts and rubber balls made around 1,500 B.C. Some balls still survive today, remarkable when you consider the average shelf life of a modern rubber ball. The Olmec had come to the discovery that combining the juice of the morning glory vine with the sap of the lowland rubber trees would form a pliable rubber ball.

The ball was large and heavy, weighing from five to perhaps as much as nine pounds and described by early missionaries as "somewhat smaller than a man's head." Because of the speed of play and the heft of the ball, injuries and sometimes deaths during the match were not uncommon. It is also why the players typically used some protective equipment. Hip belts made of leather or basketry were common. There is evidence of stone hip yokes, weighing approximately 60 pounds. While it is possible that these were used during the match, since substantial protection would have been nice due to the weight of the ball, it also seems reasonable that such a heavy piece of equipment would have made quick and agile moves very difficult. It's possible that the yokes were only ceremonial. Protection for hands and elbows and even primitive face masks have been discovered. Considering the unforgiving boundaries of the enclosed stone structure, such precautions make sense.

The rules for scoring are open for debate, though there are some commonly accepted theories, most of which stem from firsthand accounts by Spanish soldiers and missionaries. It's important to remember that what the Spaniards saw was essentially the final stage of a game that had been evolving for 3,000 years. Rules and scoring certainly would have been refined over such a long time period. Still, archaeological evidence indicates that the basic *I*-shaped court design and the equipment were used in the earliest stages of the Mesoamerican game.

Teams consisting of two to seven players were the norm, though sometimes the teams would include as many as 11 or 12 players depending on the size and configuration of the court. A goal of the game was to keep the ball constantly in play without allowing it to touch the ground. Probably points were gained when the ball (1) touched the ground on the opponent's side and was unable to be returned, (2) when the ball struck an opposing player's hands or feet, and (3) when the ball penetrated the end zone of the other team. As previously mentioned, many of the surviving courts have two stone rings attached to the side walls, which were usually encircled by carvings of the ancient gods who oversaw the ritualistic aspects of the game (light vs. darkness being a common theme). Since the opening of the rings was only slightly larger than the ball itself, it is easy to understand that scoring a "goal" by striking the ball with your hip would be extremely difficult. That's why, when the feat was accomplished, it was cause for immediate victory. It also was cause for an immediate redistribution of wealth, at least among the Hohokam people of what is now Arizona. Since scoring through the stone ring was so difficult, the scorer could claim the clothing and jewelry of the *spectators*.

As was common with even the most humble of sporting activities, the indigenous peoples of the Americas enjoyed gambling on the game's outcome. The size of the wagers, though, seemed to bespeak the ball games' social significance. It has been reported that gold, clothing, jewelry, slaves, and even the children of the players were wagered.

One of the best surviving examples of a ball-game court is located at the Mayan site Chichén Itzá in the northern Yucatan. Seven courts are located in the ruins. The largest measures 77×184 yards and must have been a wonder for the populace. "The great court at Chichén Itzá was probably the most extensive and complex sports facility constructed in the New World prior to the modern era and rivals the Roman Colosseum in the history of sports arenas." (Cox, Glassford, and Howell 1973).

Courts were located in urban centers to allow for spectators and because the cities typically could afford the cost of both supporting the athletes (usually warriors) and the idle time of those watching the matches. Further, such a complex and institutionalized game is an indicator of a technologically and politically advanced culture. Typically, one court was located near the priests' temples, and this is where the important, state-sanctioned matches were played. While there is increasing evidence that over time the rubber-ball games took on a recreational aspect due to their geographic spread and popularity (Cox, Glassford, and Howell 1973), that does not mean that the mythical and religious significance of the games lessened at the major courts. In these matches it is generally accepted that the ruling class participated, and this is when the stakes were the highest: the losing captain was beheaded, and later others were sacrificed. There is also evidence that sometimes the winning team made its way to the priests' sacrificial altars. While the practice of human sacrifice seems hideous to our modern sensibilities (as it also did to the almost equally barbaric conquistadors of Cortés), it is even more difficult to believe that any one would try to "win" a beheading. What is important to remember is that the religious tenor of the community saw sacrifice as both a vital and an honorable means to promote benevolence from the gods. The "ancient Mexicans accepted death on the altar without hesitation" (Umminger 1963, 73).

The game was much more than a simple athletic contest. It was a physical manifestation to explain and represent the creation of the world and the meaning of life. Aztec mythology says that it was played by the gods centuries before men were created, with the stars as the ball and the heavens as the playing field. Human sacrifice is by no means uncommon in ancient history. For the Mesoamerican people, the ball game was an appropriate means to choose who would be sacrificed to replenish the generous ancient gods. That it was done so often and the sacrifices glorified became significant factors in the games' demise.

In 1519 the soldiers of Cortés counted 136,000 human skulls on display at the major court of the Aztec capital, Tenochtitlan, the present-day site of Mexico City. When the Aztecs were conquered and the conquistadors replaced by missionaries, the ball courts were systematically eliminated, and the games were outlawed.

Suggestions for Modern Play

Could this game be simulated today? It is, in fact, played in a simplified version in northwestern Mexico with an outdoor court using lines for boundaries. Mark off a field in an *I*-shape. Adding a relatively small net (ice hockey goal or smaller) along either sideline could replace the concept of the stone rings. Place the goals on either side of the centerline, so if a shot on goal is missed, the ball will likely go to the opposing team's side. The ball should probably be the type used for kickball or four square as opposed to a soccer ball, because of its elastic characteristics. Remember, the ball can be advanced only by means of the hip, buttocks, and possibly shoulders. No hands *or feet* were allowed. Use an equal number of players on each team. Single points can be scored by driving the ball beyond the end boundaries. Award three points for a strike that goes into a net. Play to a predetermined score to determine the winning team. Though the *I*-shape design would be lost, playing in an alleyway or indoors on a racquetball court or a narrow hallway would help to re-create the speed and ricochet angles of the original.

In lieu of sacrifices, carry on a mild form of tradition and partake of some good-natured wagering, with the losing team having to perform some type of community service chosen by the winning team.

Sources

Arroyo, Raziel Garcia. 1969. *Five Mexican Sports*. Mexico: Publicaciones Internacionales.

Baker, William J. 1988. *Sports in the Western World*. (rev. ed.), Urbana, Ill.: Illini Books.

Blanchard, Kendall, and Alyce Taylor Cheska. 1985. *The Anthropology of Sport*. South Hadley, Mass.: Bergin and Garvey.

Blank, Jonah. 1999. "Playing Hoops—for Keeps." *U.S. News & World Reports*, June 28, Vol. 126, Issue 25, p. 64.

Cox, A. E., R. G. Glassford, and Maxwell L. Howell. 1973. "Rubber Ball Games of Central America." In *A History of Sport and Physical Education to 1900*, edited by Earle F. Zeigler. Champaign, Ill.: Stipes.

Levinson, David, and Karen Christensen, ed. 1999. *Encyclopedia of World Sport* (paperback). Oxford: Oxford University Press.

Stokstad, Eric. 1999. "How Aztecs Played Their Rubber Matches." *Science*, June 18, Vol. 284, Issue 5422, p. 1898.

Umminger, Walter. 1963. *From Supermen, Heroes and Gods*. (English ed.) London: Thames and Hudson.

Running

Perhaps the most famous runners of the ancient Latin American world are the postal messengers employed by the great Aztec and Incan Empires to traverse their extensive networks of roads. Cortés, the Spanish explorer who overthrew the Aztec Empire in 1521, lamented with a fair degree of respect in his personal writings that couriers had described his ships, guns, and troops to the Aztec ruler Montezuma within 24 hours of Cortés' landing, which took place 260 miles from the Aztec capital of Tenochtitlan (modern Mexico City).

In contrast, Pizarro conquered the vast Incan Empire with great rapidity, in large part due to the excellent system, known as the Capac Nan. This engineering marvel of some 14,000 miles allowed Pizarro relatively easy transport of his troops and, most importantly, his cavalry across what otherwise would have been often deadly terrain.

While these messengers are well known, they are not really representative of the aspect of running that could be called sport or even play. Instead, it was work. The Incan messengers, known as *chaquis*, would run their mile- or mile-and-a-half-route from one postal stop (*quinto*) to the next, then wait for some other message that would require them to run back to their base where they lived with their wife and children, along with another chaquis and his family.

Instead, the smaller indigenous tribes—those often referred to as "less civilized" but perhaps instead offering a more humane and less corporate and materialistic approach to life than the great empires—are the areas where running is best represented as a common sport and a recreation. Footraces were, in fact, so frequent—Blanchard contends that they were probably universal among the indigenous people of the Americas—that in much of Latin America they have been given scanty coverage as a traditional game because their commonality made them ordinary and rarely worth mentioning in early accounts.

Still, the Ona from the island of Tierra del Fuego and the Bororo of the Amazon region offer two different approaches to footraces that were important parts of both cultures. The now extinct tribe known as Ona were strong wrestlers and among the best marksmen with bow and arrow from the South American continent. In the matter of footraces they again serve as an example of a group of people who enjoyed a competitive event, prepared for it, and ascribed to exceptional runners titles of social merit and respect.

Champion runners were called *soijens*. This was a title usually reserved for the men who competed in more formal races, which took place on racing tracks and were judged by arbitrators, who were usually old men representing the different communities from which the racers hailed. The men would decorate their bodies with special paint for these races and would wear a bracelet of feathers.

The track itself was unique. The Ona would have a section of flat open space, some as long as 500 meters. Instead of the two athletes (usually these were match races) standing side by side, they would be at opposite ends of the track. In the center of the two footracers would be the old men serving as the judges, who would signal the start by simultaneously throwing down a leather ball. The men would then throw off their capes (the Ona competed and hunted in the nude) and would begin racing. They did not engage in an all-out sprint at the beginning but would gather speed. The object was to get to the centerline first.

While this was the standard approach for formal footraces, informal races were very common, and anyone could join in a race, though they seldom involved both genders. Race distances would usually be set by the competitors and would involve racing to a geographic spot.

The footraces served a purpose. Speed afoot made for more effective hunters. It has been said that the Ona could chase down a galloping guanaco (a close relative to the llama and alpaca) and that the Ona's powerful stride was nearly two meters (about six feet) long.

The Bororo's emphasis on running was less sportive in nature but was a vital part of the male initiation process, which took up to a full year. It is known via the oral tradition as the *ipare eregoddu*, or "the race of the young men." The young men are accompanied by some elders who lead them far away from the village and then during the course of the year lead them, like a modern army drill sergeant, through exercises in swimming and "forced running through the forests, going up hills, scaling craggy slopes. By force the body must be exercised, mortified, trained. They knew very well that it is not in slackness and in vice that bodies become robust" (Cobacchini and Albisetti 1942, 416). After this year they are returned to the village, and at this point they are considered to be part of the social life of the greater Bororo community.

Sources

Blanchard, Kendall. 1996. "Traditional Sports, North and South America." In *Encyclopedia of World Sport*, edited by, David Levinson and Karen Christensen. Santa Barbara, Calif: ABC-CLIO. pp. 1075–1083.

Chapman, Anne. 1982. *Drama and Power in a Hunting Society: The Selk'nam of Tierra del Fuego*. Cambridge: Cambridge University Press.

Cobacchini, P. Antonio, and P. Cesar Albisetti. 1942. *The Eastern Bororo Orarimogodogue of the Eastern Plateau of Mato Grosso*. Rio de Janiero: Companhia Editora Nacional (translated from Portuguese).

Johnson, R. W. 1992. "The Irony of the Capac Nan." *Social Studies*, January/February, Vol. 83, Issue 1, p. 21.

Nabokov, Peter. 1981. *Indian Running: Native American History and Traditions*. From Peabody Museum, Harvard College Web site: "Against the Winds: American Indian Running Traditions," posted 1999.

▦ Wrestling

Wrestling was a very serious sport among several distinct populations in South America and was often used as a way of judging the worthiness of a man within the tribe and, at times, of those who lived outside the tribe. The Caraja of central Brazil were especially fond of using wrestling as a tool to gauge any person or party that entered their camp. They would challenge recently arrived outsiders to a wrestling match. This was a common practice among other tribes in the region. It is not difficult to imagine the surprise of the first European visitors when they were introduced to this practice, especially since it was expected that the leader or chief of the visiting group would be the person inside the wrestling ring. The leader would then wrestle Caraja villagers in order to be accepted as an equal. The Caraja would routinely include wrestling in religious festivals and intervillage visits.

Wrestling was also a source of pride and honor for the now extinct Yahgan people, who referred to themselves as "Canoe Indians." Despite living in the inhospitable and chilly island called Tierra del Fuego at the southernmost tip of South America, these people were tough enough physically and mentally to live with virtually no clothing. Unfortunately, they had no defense for European disease, which wiped out their relatively small numbers in the first half of the twentieth century.

Wrestling was the Yahgan's most popular sport and was called *kalaka mulaka*. It was always man against man, with no women allowed. A wrestler chose his opponent by placing a small ball (*kalaka*) in front of him, and a match was won when the whole of an opponent's back was on the ground. Tripping was not permitted, but a swift kick to the shin was allowed, making the man easier to topple. Losses were taken hard and were an embarrassment, not just to the wrestler but also to his friends. This meant that one wrestling match inevitably would lead to more as a friend of the vanquished wrestler would immediately grab the kalaka and put it in front of the winner, starting the next match. Being a successful wrestler meant being a better marriage partner, and, not surprisingly, wrestling figured prominently in Yahgan mythology.

The Yahgan were not the only tribe of Tierra del Fuego. Also living on this island were the Ona (also called the Selk'nam) and the Alacaluf, which also met the similar fate of twentieth-century extinction due to disease and, at times, systematic elimination of their race by white settlers. While the Ona did not normally go about unclothed, these vigorous hunters, who emphasized the daily training of the body from early age, did disrobe when they intended to wrestle or hunt.

Wrestling was routinely practiced by Ona boys as a diversion, a good-natured sport, and a means of testing their strength and fitness. When Ona adult males wrestled, however, there were usually serious issues involved. Most wrestling matches took place as the result of a source of conflict between two men or because of communal concerns. "If a man had a grievance against another of a different *haruwen* (a family-occupied territorial unit) he could seek him out and challenge him to a bout" (Chapman 1982, 48). Matches routinely attracted male kin and friends of the two wrestlers and at times could even draw a crowd of spectators that included women and children from several unaffiliated territorial groups. Especially good matches would generate much discussion in the following days about the various rounds and even specific holds and grips that were applied.

Matches usually began with the two wrestlers locking their hands about the other's hips and gripping the lower back. The intent was to throw the opponent onto the ground, usually a dry, mossy area. As with the Yahgan, tripping was not allowed. In serious matches, the wrestlers would usually paint their bodies in specific patterns.

Further study of the Ona wrestling tradition reveals some striking similarities to the mock warfare of certain Australian Aboriginal people (see Oceania: Prun) in one set of circumstances, while at different times it bore more resemblance to the sport-style wrestling found among intertribal groups in Africa and in ancient Greece (see Africa: Wrestling, Europe: Wrestle/Olympics).

The Ona were known to formally organize wrestling matches between two groups that are opposed and seek some form of retribution. Like the Aboriginal Prun, this was a means of relieving group tensions in a controlled environment as opposed to succumbing to open warfare. Because certain rules were adhered to—as well as the presence of women and children—deadly results, though not unknown, were kept to a minimum. Still, it was a team battle. It would begin with several simultaneous matches, with a few of the strongest men from both groups waiting a bit to relieve a needy team member. Winners would take a short break and then match themselves with another opponent. The group match continued until all of the wrestlers on one side had been defeated. The losing team would typically ask for a rematch but not an immediate one.

There were times of peaceful gatherings among the Ona, however, known as *kuash-ketin*. These were a reunion of families from all parts of the island, and the purpose of the gathering was twofold: to exchange objects and to perform in shamanistic and sporting competitions. During the kuash-ketin wrestling had an air of Olympic ceremony to it. Champion wrestlers from different regions could challenge another region's champion, even though the two had neither met nor had any personal or group animosity as the motivation for the match. At stake in these matches were the individuals' reputations as great wrestlers and the attendant praise and status that they could achieve. "Champion wrestlers ... were men of great renown and since the title was a relatively rare achievement, they were famous throughout the island" (Chapman 1982, 49).

Wrestling was also practiced among the Bororo of the central Mato Grosso of Brazil, who emphasized tripping techniques and employed thrusts at the hollow of an opponent's knee, and among many other groups, including both the Caingang and the Ge from Brazil as well as the boys of the Tzeltals, who live in the Mexican state of Chiapas and are linguistically descended from the Maya.

Suggestions for Modern Play

The Onas' practice of having groupwide wrestling contests could be adopted by neighboring high school wrestling teams. Several wrestling mats should be placed together on one gymnasium floor. The wrestlers should begin the simultaneous matches—as the Ona did—by having one of the older leaders (a senior captain) begin the battle by choosing a like adversary. Then the wrestlers should pair up with opponents of like size and ability. Since tripping was not allowed by the Ona, moves should be limited to upper-body holds. Victories would be secured in one of two ways, either by putting an opponent to the floor by means of a throw or by pushing the opponent backward over a predetermined and marked line. The Ona did use the latter method at times. Once a wrestler has suffered a defeat he or she cannot reenter the fray. Winning wrestlers should be allowed a predetermined rest period before beginning another bout, probably 60 to 90 seconds. Coaches would need to be alert to anyone's using illegal moves or resting too long and be even quicker to disqualify one of their own wrestlers for an infraction than they are for an opponent's. The purpose of this exercise would be twofold: to increase stamina and to build team spirit. Positive side effects (as long as fairness and sportsmanship are maintained) could be an increased mutual respect among opponents and the development of sparring-partner relationships that could be utilized in the postseason and the off-season.

Sources

Blanchard, Kendall. 1996. "Traditional Sports, North and South America." In *Encyclopedia of World Sport*, edited by David Levinson and Karen Christensen. Santa Barbara, Calif: ABC-CLIO. pp. 1075–1083.

Blanchard, Kendall, and Alyce Taylor Cheska. 1985. *The Anthropology of Sport*. South Hadley, Mass.: Bergin and Garvey.

Chapman, Anne. 1982. *Drama and Power in a Hunting Society: The Selk'nam of Tierra del Fuego*. Cambridge: Cambridge University Press.

Cooper, John M. 1917. "Analytical and Critical Bibliography of the Tribes of the Tierra del Fuego." *Bureau of American Ethnology* 63. Washington, DC: Government Printing Office, p. 223.

Gusinade, Martin. 1995. *The Fireland Indian*. Vol. 1: *The Selk'nam, on the Life and Thought of a Hunting People of the Great Island of Tierra del Fuego*. 1931. New Haven, Conn. HRAF (translated from German).

Kramer-Mandeau, Wolf. 1992. "Games and Festivals in Latin America, 1500–1900." *The International Journal of the History of Sport*, April, Vol. 9, No. 1, pp. 63–82.

PLAY

▦ The Log Run

The log run of the Timbira in central Brazil is an example of a team race that is made especially difficult by the aspect of having to carry a large object. The primary purpose of this event and others similar to it is to hold an annual, community-wide exercise that promotes teamwork and continuity. At its core, the log run of the Timbira has a simple, but grueling, concept. A team of villagers—both men's and women's teams— take a log weighing up to 100 kilograms (approximately 220 pounds) and carry it a significant distance, ranging from three to over seven miles.

It is a special example of sporting activity for a number of reasons. Chief among them is that it is one of the relatively few traditional sports in Latin America that have survived the widespread European and Anglo-American influx of sports (soccer, baseball) to remain unchanged. Also, it has a duality of purpose. It is a race, but it is more a reflection and reaffirmation of the communal structure that emphasizes "cooperative teamwork as well as competition within the tribal community" (Kramer-Mandeau 1992, 73). The log run as a competition is also known among the Ge-speaking people of Brazil, who typically hold their contests as relay races.

William Cook, a Protestant missionary, witnessed an interesting variation on the log run in the early 1900s among the Bororo, one of the Ge-speaking tribes of Amazonia. It was at a time when the Bororo were still practicing most of their traditional culture but had already seen nearly 100 years of outside interaction, which would ultimately lead to a decimation of the people from a group estimated to be about 15,000 individuals at the time of first contact in the late 1700s to as low as 500 in the 1960s. In the mid-1990s there were an estimated 700 Bororo still living in a traditional manner.

The race started with the preparation of the heavy object that would be carried. In this case it was not a single log but a large number of the spongy stalks of a small banana plant known as *mano*. The process began by cutting the stalks and then ferrying them down the river from the groves to the starting spot of the race—about 700 yards from the village. There, two divisions of the village lashed together their separate piles of mano stalks into what Cook termed "a huge roll, or wheel" that is tightly bound. Once both divisions were finished, they put the wheels in an upright position. At this point a formal process took place where both divisions, with the aid of a representative from the other division, introduced each man to the wheel one by one.

Now the race was ready to begin. Despite having constructed a fibrous wheel, the Bororo did not roll it. Instead, they grasped it and heaved it up and then ran, "pell-mell, yelling wildly in a mad race for the village. The spectacle suggested strongly a swarm of ants that had seized a huge living worm and were running frantically with it for their dark galleries" (Cook 1909, 383). The best way to run was with the wheel in an upright position, but apparently that was not an easy task. In the particular race Cook wrote about, as the divisions neared the finish in the center of the village, one wheel crashed "through the wall of one of the residences and into the sitting-room." The two divisions on the day that Cook witnessed the mano race threw down their bundles at the same time, and all were acclaimed by the entire village. The men quickly went to a large, communal hut for a big feast while the women and children tore up the wheels to use the mano stalks in small bundles for pillows.

What Cook saw proved the Bororo capable of a planned, community-wide endeavor that was physically taxing and required a high degree of cooperation and intensity. Winning the race was apparently not as important as the act of competing. Cook suggests that it was simply a large-scale production of the Bororo's acute ability to imitate nature (hence, the reference to looking like a swarm of ants). This would appear to simplify the meaning behind the process.

This type of strenuous activity has its cousins in other parts of the Americas, particularly with the ball races of the Tarahumara of northern Mexico and the Zuni and Hopi in the southwestern United States (see North America: Running). Given that the act of flipping a ball forward is significantly less taxing on the body than carrying a 220-pound log, the ball races of the Tarahumara are always much longer, as long as 200 miles in traditional 48-hour tests of will. Both, however, are running events that incorporate a static object (log/ball) that must be propelled in some way along the course. Only if the runner moves the object the full distance can the team be declared victorious.

As with the Tarahumara, once the race was finished, it was cause for feasting and relaxing and probably a time of significant storytelling about previous races and the details of the just-completed race.

Suggestions for Modern Play

Log runs are still used today as a training exercise by military groups. The concept revolves around the old cliché that a chain is only as strong as its weakest link. In other words, it takes all members of the team working at an equal pace to get the log to cover the distance in a timely fashion. If the strongest pull too hard or run too fast, or the slowest or weakest can't keep up, the team will be weakened. This was also true of the Tarahumara kickball races because a team that had any significant amount of players drop out was at a distinct disadvantage in a long-distance race.

The essential nature of the log run could be duplicated in the modern physical education class or within an athletic team that needs to build some group spirit. Instead of using an extremely heavy or cumbersome object, choose something that is relatively long but lightweight. The protective cases for a pole vault might work well. Have teams of eight, with four members on each side of the "log" staggered at intervals, and contest the race around a typical running track. Assign one person to be the pacesetter at the front of the pole, whose job is to adjust the speed depending on the needs of the rest of the team. Set some rules or time penalties (perhaps a five-second deduction if any part of the pole touches the ground) to ensure that all eight team members reach the finish line still holding onto the pole.

Sources

Blanchard, Kendall. 1996. "Traditional Sports, North and South America." In *Encyclopedia of World Sport*, edited by David Levinson and Karen Christensen. Santa Barbara, Calif: ABC-CLIO, pp. 1075–1083.

"Bororo File." 1996. *The eHRAF Collection of Ethnography*. New Haven, Conn.: Human Relations Area Files.

Cook, William Azel. 1909. *Through the Wilderness of Brazil by Horse, Canoe and Float*. New York: American Tract Society.

Kramer-Mandeau, Wolf. 1992. "Games and Festivals in Latin America, 1500–1900." *The International Journal of the History of Sport*, April, Vol. 9, No. 1, pp. 63–82.

⊞   Other Ball Games

In Latin America the game known by the generic title of the Mesoamerican rubber ball game was certainly the most regal of the ball games. There were also stick-and-ball games played in Argentina and Bolivia that were markedly similar in style and objective to *shinny* or modern field hockey. These two types of ball games are treated at length in separate sections of Latin American sports.

This section provides a sampling of the many other varieties of games that were played with some type of ball—be it made of rubber, wood, plant fiber, or an animal bladder—in Central and South America. There is some speculation that all of these are descendants of the great Mesoamerican game originally played by the Olmec civilization some 3,000 years ago. Blanchard puts forth this theory: "In many ways the various types of ball games that ultimately emerge in both South and North America can be viewed as descendants of the Mesoamerican ball game. The balls are different . . . playing fields are of different design . . . equipment varies. But underneath the diversity of its outward manifestations, the American ball game is still the American ball game" (Blanchard 1996, 1080).

To say that all ball games in the Americas were ultimately the progeny of one great game would mean that in some way the flow of information went both north and south from the Olmec source in the humid lowlands of Mexico's Gulf Coast. As Blanchard notes in the preceding quotation, balls, playing fields, and equipment had striking dissimilarities. The great rubber ball game that was played at a heightened level by the Maya and later the Aztecs certainly had offshoots. There are also several instances where a ball game had institutionalized and ritualized significance, with its play often representing the dual motions of the sun and moon. Throughout Central and North America when a game was to be played seems to be associated with some type of fertility ritual, usually for a good harvest. Other ball games from South America (and North America, for that matter) were separate creations of the native and curious interest in seeing how a round object would respond if it were struck, passed, caught, or kicked. In short, if cultures from all round the globe could devise their own independent ball games, then so could the Native Americans.

Many of the ball games played in South America were simple forms of play, engaged in by either children or adults. One of the interesting aspects is the variety of material that was shaped into a ball. The Yahgan and Ona tribes of Tierra del Fuego were both especially fond of wrestling but also enjoyed an occasional game of catch, with the men standing in a circle and passing the ball back and forth by means of batting it with an open palm. Among the Ona, children, both boys and girls, did not play this game by themselves but were at times invited to join the adults. The ball was made out of a soft piece of leather (these were hunting/fishing communities) and stuffed with feathers or lichen before being sewn together into a ball roughly 3.5 to 4.5 inches in diameter. Coastal dwellers would occasionally use the webbed feet of a seabird instead of leather to make the pouch. The Bororo, a tribe that now numbers less than 1,000 people, used maize husks to make a common children's ball and then decorated it with feathers.

One of the more truly unique balls was the monkey bladder ball used by the Yanoama tribes in northwest Brazil. They form a circle and keep hitting the ball upward. This is one tribe that does ascribe to this form of play with magical and spiritual qualities; therefore, it is played only by the men. To the Yanoama this game represents the repetitive appearance and disappearance of the sun and moon, a common theme to *tlachtli*, the Aztec version of the great rubber ball game.

It has also been compared to the game played by the Paressi, who played their circle game with a hollow rubber ball that had to be kept in play only by use of the head. This calls to mind a circle of modern soccer players practicing their headers. This is a scoring game where the low score wins, with points being given to the person who allows the ball to touch the ground. The Arawak also had a head-ball game, with a ball made from the elastic extract of the gum tree. They added boundaries to define a midcourt and sidelines, meaning that their game most closely resembles the Mesoamerican games surveyed in this section. The Arawak could not use their hands or feet, which logically means that they could have used their elbows, knees, and heads. It is not known if they utilized the hips, à la the Maya and Aztecs, or specialized equipment.

Use of a ball for a game that does not utilize a stick or specialized equipment has also been reported among tribes once living along the unusually clear 1,087-mile-long Guapore River, which forms the border between Bolivia and Brazil; the Mojo in Bolivia and the Chane on the eastern slopes of the Bolivian Andes.

Sources

Becher, Hans. 1960. *The Surara and Pakidi, Two Yanoama Tribes in Northwest Brazil.* Hamburg, Germany: Kommissionsverlag Cram, De Gruyter.

Blanchard, Kendall. 1996. "Traditional Sports, North and South America." In *Encyclopedia of World Sport*, edited by, David Levinson and Karen Christensen. Santa Barbara, Calif: ABC-CLIO.

Cooper, John M. 1917. "Analytical and Critical Bibliography of the Tribes of the Tierra del Fuego." *Bureau of American Ethnology 63.* Washington, DC: Government Printing Office.

Gusinade, Martin. 1995. *The Fireland Indians.* Vol. 1: *The Selk'nam, on the Life and Thought of a Hunting People of the Great Island of Tierra del Fuego.* 1931. New Haven, Conn.: HRAF (translated from German).

"Olmec." 1994–2001. *Encyclopedia Britannica Online.*

⊞ Tejo

Tejo is one of the few games of Latin America with a high degree of standardized rules that can claim to be both indigenous and still played with some regularity today. Tejo is a Colombian sport popularly played among the lower and middle classes and has a marked similarity to the ancient European pitching game of quoits, which is the ancestor of the popular American game known as horseshoes.

The game of tejo was derived from the Chibcha Indians, who played it in pre-Columbian times. Tejo courts can be found both outside and inside, but generally they are somewhere near a source of beer since the drinking of beer—and, most importantly, which team pays for the beer—is part of the traditional custom. Basically, the team that loses the most buys the most beer. The game of tejo is considered to be the only indigenous sport or game still played with any regularity in soccer-mad Colombia, though the equipment, court dimensions, and scoring have now been standardized.

Not much is known about the exact method of play of tejo by the Chibcha, who had an estimated population of 500,000 at the time of the Spanish conquest. The Chibcha occupied the high valleys that surround the modern Colombian cities of Bogotá and Tunja and had a centralized political structure second only to the Incas among South American Indians. The loose alliance of city-states was crushed in the sixteenth century, and by the eighteenth century the Chibcha had become assimilated with the rest of the population, and their language was lost. It is known that the Chibcha excelled in the manufacture of gold, copper, pottery, and metalworks, and through trade their goods were fairly widespread.

Because of their skilled craftsmanship it is quite possible that the *tejos*, the name for the pitching piece as well as the game, were made of metal, as were the ancient quoits in Europe. The tejo today is a circular disk. One side is flat, while the other is extended slightly by pyramidal steps.

The standard court in modern play is 19.5 meters long and 2.5 meters wide. Targets are placed at both ends of the court, a half meter in, meaning that they are 18.5 meters apart. These targets are called *bocin* and are a metal cylinder that is just a bit larger than the tejo itself. Usually, the target has a four-inch hole, while the tejo, which weighs 2–3.5 pounds, is roughly 3.5 inches wide. The bocin is driven flush to the pitched landing area in a perpendicular fashion. Two features of the playing court distinguish tejo from either quoits or horseshoes. The landing area, which is of thick mud (à la quoits), is angled toward the throwing line with a definite grade of about 27–30 degrees. Also a backboard is erected to keep the tejo from skidding out of play. The backboard is in play, meaning that rebounds do count.

Surrounding the bocin are three small, triangular pouches filled with gunpowder called the *mechas*. When hit with the tejo, the mechas blow up, adding a little pop to the game. The mechas are now made from wax paper. It can be assumed that this is a relatively recent adaptation. The object of the game is similar to that of horseshoes or quoits. To get the tejo in the target, in this case the just slightly larger bocin, is the desired result of each throw. If that is done, and in the process a mecha is blown up, the throw is worth nine points, and the game is over. Interestingly, if the tejo lands in the bocin but does not blow up a mecha, it is worth only six points, although this would seem to be a more difficult throw. Exploding a mecha is worth three points. Having the closest tejo to the bocin is worth one point, but if all three (or four) team members have left their tejos closer to the target than have any of the opposing team's throws, then that is considered a *chipolo* and is an immediate victory in a game. Each player on each team gets one throw per hand, unless a mecha is exploded, in which case the hand or round is over, and the teams switch ends. It is an advantage to be the first team to play, since a hand can be won as quickly as the first throw. The team that won the previous hand always gets to throw first. This is similar to holding serve in volleyball and other court games.

Each game is played to nine points. If a team wins by a score of 9–0, then that is considered worth a bonus win, or an extra game. It is through the number of games won or lost that the end result—who buys the beer—is determined.

Suggestions for Modern Play

Part of the fun of this game, in a scholastic setting, would be building the equipment. One point not yet mentioned is that a throwing line is drawn or marked in some fashion at each end. It should be 15 meters from the front of the landing area. Tejos can be pitched from anywhere within what becomes a 2.5-by-2.5 meter box directly in front of each landing pit.

Do some experiments to determine what type of metal will produce a tejo that fits the size and weight requirements. Then figure out what can be used for the bocin. It has to be sturdy enough to withstand some pounding but also the right dimensions. According to Jernigan and Vendien, the Colombians often use the casing of an automobile generator.

Instead of alcoholic beverages as the sanctioned wager, the class should come up with some other enjoyable treat that the losing team will owe the winning team: candy, sodas, carrying books, responsibility for classroom chores, and so on. Instead of gunpowder in the mechas, stuff them with the limestone chalk that is used for lining athletic fields. Several sets of mechas should be stuffed beforehand to avoid slowing the game down.

Sources

"Colombia: Sports and Recreation." 1994–2001. *Encyclopedia Britannica Online*.
Jernigan, Sara Staff, and C. Lynn Vendien. 1972. *Playtime: A World Recreation Handbook*. New York: McGraw-Hill.

GAMES

▦　Patolli and Other Games of Chance

Games of chance in Central and South America were predominantly limited only to the more advanced societies—namely, the Maya and then the Aztecs in Central America and the Incas who came to power in roughly the twelfth century along the Andean spine of South America. In other areas of the vast and often jungle-covered continent of South America, it appears that gambling was nonexistent or at least has gone undetected in terms of traditional play.

While written records in the form of an alphabetic language are not known for the highly evolved ancient civilizations of Latin America, they did employ pictographic and hieroglyphics to record their histories. Only a very few survive. One that is not in its original form but was translated in the early years of Spanish conquest is known as the *popol vuh*. It was translated into its native Quiche language (and Spanish) using the Latin alphabet between 1554 and 1558. Quiche is the language spoken by the Mayan people who populate the highlands of Guatemala and had a highly advanced civilization that featured strong political and social organization along with numerous city-states (similar to those of the ancient Greeks), each with a town center that served as a hub of commerce and social/religious activity. The Quiche Maya were also strong advocates and experts of the Mesoamerican ball game.

While the popol vuh is predominantly a historical description of how the Mayan world was created, using both mythology and historical facts, the ball game is often cited. This is not surprising considering the strong religious and social relevance that has been attributed to the ball game throughout Mesoamerica. The popol vuh also indicates, according to Salter, that the Quiche Maya did enjoy using dice as a means of social relaxation and not just as tools for divination. While no specific games were related, the early literary work adds to architectural evidence that the Maya enjoyed playing games that fall into a category that Bell has identified as "cross and circle" race games.

At Palenque, a game board was carved into sandstone around A.D. 800. It forms a square that is then quartered by two bisecting paths (north-south and east-west directionally). Both the outer paths and the inner intersecting paths have smaller squares, seeming to indicate places where a marker would move about the board. Each of the outer edge and the intersecting lines has 11 squares (if the outer edge is counted for the intersecting lines). A description for play does not survive. Chichen Itza in the Yucatán is perhaps the most famous of all the Mayan ruins and also includes what appears to be an ancient game board, in this case cut into the top of a bench that would have allowed two players to easily sit opposite one another. This board's outer rim of playing positions is in the shape of an ellipse but again features the intersecting "cross" that is common to other race games like the Pueblo's *pa-tol* stick, the Navajo's 40 stones (see North America: Dice Games) and *nyout* from Korea.

The pre-Columbian (meaning the time before European exploration) Aztecs are known to have played a similar race game called *patolli*, which had developed to the point where the circle had been eliminated and instead the cross was expanded to include 16 compartments in each arm (see Figure 4.1). Patolli was played with such frequency that the game "board" was actually a woven mat with the cross pattern painted on, allowing the board to be quickly rolled up and tucked under an arm for easy transport.

Figure 4.1: The basic configuration of the South American game known as patolli. It has a marked resemblance to the game of pachisi, which originated in India. (Illustration by Gary Harrison)

In terms of the physical shape of the playing board, patolli bears a marked resemblance to pachisi, the national game of India that used cowry shells as its form of dice. (Pachisi has spawned many modern games, including ludo in England and parcheesi in America.) The high degree of similarity has, in fact, been the cause of considerable debate as to whether patolli was a truly indigenous invention of the Native American game players or whether patolli is instead another example of the general theory that most of American indigenous cultures and races are descendants of older Asian groups. Another theory holds that somehow there was contact between India (or at least Asia) prior to Columbus, and these unknown sailors could have brought the patolli game with them. More likely is the simpler thought that two analogous games developed independently, and it is interesting to note their similarities.

Patolli players used large black beans as their dice, with each having a hole drilled in one side that acted as a white marker. The patolli (beans) were thrown, and, depending on how many landed with the white mark up, a score was determined. The player would then move one of his or her six pieces (one player had red markers; the other typically had blue markers) onto the mat. The game has similarities to backgammon in that all of the pieces must enter the mat, cover the entire designated route, and then exit before a victory can be claimed.

The other game of chance that merits particular mention is called, among other names, *syuke*. It comes from the Gran Chaco region of the Andean mountain range. It was traditionally played in the month of March by the Choroti, Toba, Ashluslay, and Mataco tribes who now live in Bolivia and Argentina and were once part of the Incan Empire. Also, the playing terms have their origin in the Quechua (or Quichua) language, which is the native Indian language of Ecuador. (Quechua or Quichua should not be confused or connected to the Quiche Mayans.) The combination of these tribes being all within the Incan realm at one time, its widespread use and its standardized terminology suggest that syuke or at least some type of gambling game could have been part of the Incan culture. On the other hand, the Incas themselves were resistant to the concept of idle time, as their labor tax and the resulting massive roadworks would suggest.

The game is a counting game, with the board typically drawn into the ground and consisting of 23 holes in a semicircle, with the middle hole (number 12) about twice the size of the rest of the holes. The first and 23rd holes are the starting places, and the players stick arrows in those holes. In all of the rest of the holes except the 12th, small sticks or cobs of maize are placed, and they are referred to as sheep. The 12th hole is left empty and is called the river. The players start from opposite sides.

The dice are two-sided wooden sticks, with one side convex and the other flat. Four are used. The dice are thrown into the air and allowed to fall, and the number of convex sides up determines the roll.

The object is to cross the river and then land on an opponent's hole. This allows the player to "throw out" one of the sheep. The game continues until all of the sheep and finally even the opponent's marker are thrown out. Each person's turn continues until he or she throws a zero. (See later for a more detailed description of the rules of this game.)

Among the Choroti, on whom Karsten based his report, syuke was played with the express purpose of helping to guarantee a prosperous fruit crop and was played only at the beginning of winter, when the edible fruits grew scarce. The Choroti believed that the game had the effect of making the fruit crop increase, thus making them rich. This philosophy helps to explain why gambling for stakes was such an integral part of the game. The Choroti believed that in this way every game produced a winner who would gain some reward. Through the winner's luck, the whole tribe would benefit.

The aspect of associating gambling games with a purpose of increasing a tribe's overall material wealth, particularly as it related to agriculture, is a theme often repeated among native North American tribes as well.

Suggestions for Modern Play

R.C. Bell outlines an elaborate suggestion for patolli in his book.

In contrast, the Choroti game of syuke is not as well known but also much simpler to play. As stated, it begins with 23 holes or grooves. It can be played with two players or multiples of two, with an even number starting from opposite sides.

Here are some things that beginning players would need to know:

- The scoring for the dice (with accompanying Quechua term) is as follows: four convex sides up equals 4 (*tauva*); three convex sides up equals 0 (*lahipa*); two convex sides up equals 1 (*shuke*); one convex side up equals 0 (lahipa); no convex sides up equals 2 (*kima*).
- Players traditionally took two dice in each hand and tossed them up and together.
- Players could continue a turn until they tossed a zero score.
- Once they crossed the river (hole number 12), they could begin capturing sheep. If a player lands in the hole where the opponent's marker is housed, then the latter marker is killed and must start again from the beginning.
- The object is to throw out all the sheep and then the opponent's marker.
- If a player's marker lands in the river, he is drowned. He can get out on the following throw with a cast of the dice resulting in any score other than zero. If the cast is a zero, then the marker must go back to the hole closest to the beginning that still has one of his or her own sheep.

Sources

Bell, R. C. 1979. *Board and Table Games from Many Civilizations*, Vol. 1. Rev. ed. New York: Dover.

Erasmus, Charles John. 1971. "Patolli, Pachisi and the Limitation of Possibilities." In *The Study of Games*, edited by Elliott M. Avedon and Brian Sutton-Smith. New York: John Wiley and Sons.

Gillespie, Susan B. 1991. "Ballgames and Boundaries." In *The Mesoamerican Ballgame*, edited by Vernon L. Scarborough and David R. Wilcox. Tucson: University of Arizona Press.

Karsten, Rafael. 1932. *Indian Tribes of the Argentine and Bolivian Chaco: Ethnological Studies*. Helsingfors: Academische Buchhandlung.

Masters, James. 1997–2001. "Pachisi." *The Online Guide to Traditional Games*. Web site: eb.ukonline.co.uk/james.masters/traditionalgames.

McIntyre, Loren. 1975. *The Incredible Incas and Their Timeless Land*. Washington, D.C.: National Geographic Society/Special Publications Division.

Salter, Michael A. 1989. "Leisure Time Pursuits of the Quiche Maya." *Aethlon*, Spring, Vol. 6, No. 2, pp. 239–247.

⊞ MIDDLE EAST

INTRODUCTION

The Middle East, perhaps more than any other region of the world, requires a clear geographical definition. The term has many meanings to many people and different meanings for someone in the United States compared to someone in the Czech Republic. History has also changed what is called the Middle East. Middle East has a different meaning today than it had 2,000 years ago, and certainly different from any perception of "Middle East," some 5,500 years ago when cities first started to form in this oldest region of the so-called civilized world.

Rather than trying to debate eminent scholars, historians, and politicians, we give the boundaries of the Middle East used in this book, where "Middle East" is more restrictive than in many perceptions, particularly those of the modern politician. For this book, Middle East has a northern border that includes the modern countries of Turkey, Iraq, Iran, and Afghanistan, which is, in general, consistent with most perceptions of Middle East. It includes the countries of the southeast corner of the Mediterranean: modern Israel, Lebanon, Syria, and Jordan, the whole of the Arabian Peninsula (Saudi Arabia, Yemen, Oman, Bahrain, Qatar, and the United Arab Emirates), as well as Kuwait, the small buffer state between Iraq and Saudi Arabia.

Countries *not included* in this book's definition of "Middle East" are also significant. To the west, Egypt has been included with Africa, as a matter of simplifying the geographical assertion of seven "regions" of the world. This is admittedly in conflict with most of Egyptian history since the Egyptians are, from a sociological and anthropological view, more closely aligned with their Arab neighbors than with their continental brothers below the Sahara Desert. So, too, the North African countries of Tunisia, Libya, Algeria, and Morocco are sometimes included in modern descriptions of the Middle East (due in large part to the preponderance of the Islamic faith), but, like Egypt, they have been included in Africa for the purposes of this book. To the east, Pakistan and India are grouped with the Asian group, again due primarily to geography.

Therefore, the Middle East is by far the smallest of the regions into which we have divided our modern world for the study of ancient sports and games. The counterbalance is that it is home to some of the most ancient civilizations. Often called the cradle of civilization, it is the nascent home to Christianity but is now predominantly Muslim in religious orientation. Adding further to what is a very diverse tapestry of historical perspectives is that the dominant rule of the region fluctuated and changed many times during ancient history, including several segments of time when the ruling culture was from "outside" the native area. Particularly along the Mediterranean border, changes in control were frequent. The ancient city of Tyre, located in Lebanon, serves as a vivid example. Considered Phoenician in heritage, it was, in order, an island colony of Sidon, under Egyptian rule (fourteenth Century B.C.), self-ruled, under Assyrian control (eighth and seventh centuries B.C.), caught for 12 years in Babylonian king Nebuchadnezzar II's unsuccessful siege, ruled by the kings of Persia (535–332 B.C.), crushed by Alexander the Great in 332 B.C. (who turned the island city to rubble to make a causeway through the sea that literally turned the area into a peninsula), controlled by Ptolemaic Egyptians, controlled by a Hellenistic kingdom around 200 B.C., under Roman rule in 64 B.C., a predominantly Christian area by the second century A.D. In the last of its "ancient" days, Muslim rule began in A.D. 638 and continued for five uninterrupted centuries. Granted, all of this change took place over a significant amount of time, but the fact of 10 distinctly different ruling groups in Tyre over a 2,000-year period—9 of which were non-Phoenician—demonstrates that this region of the world has been in a repetitive cycle of upheaval for more than 4,000 years.

As Christianity and Judaism were planting their religious roots into the soil of the Levant (modern Lebanon, Israel, and Jordan), the region was under Greek and then Roman control. This meant that the Hellenistic themes of striving for victory and bodily perfection, along with the daily practices of training in gymnasiums and in the nude, were often in conflict with the teachings of the new religions. From a more secular perspective, early Christians and Jews had to choose between following strict policies (particularly the Christians) that inhibited shows of physical strength and the use of the gymnasium as a means of assimilating into the overall Greek culture, which could help their stations in life.

The Middle East—even in our relatively narrow definition—is an area with a long history of political and spiritual turmoil. Finding consistent threads in terms of activities that could fall under the categories of sport, play, or games *and are indigenous in origin* is a challenging task. Still, a couple of important trends make this region of the world unique.

First are the importance of the horse and the evolution of its use in the Middle East. Throughout the rest of this book the horse has been relatively de-emphasized. In the Americas this was a simple matter of fact: the horse was brought to the continents by European explorers. Even though it would become a significant part of the North American Indian's way of life, it was not native.

In the Middle East the Arabian horse, perhaps the oldest and purest of all breeds, was carefully raised. The horse as a tool of war was instrumental in shaping the region because the "chariot team was an essential element for political control from about 2000 BC until . . . about 500 AD" (Mandell 1984, 10). Further, the care and studied breeding of horses began in this region, as evidenced by the "Kikkulis text," a Hittite cuneiform dating to approximately 1360 B.C., which over four volumes outlined a specific, 184-day training program for horses. Therefore, the "horse sports" of polo and *buzkashi* are included in the section on ancient sports of the Middle East.

A second trend in the Middle East is the preponderance of what can be termed "tabletop games," or board games involving varying degrees of chance and strategy that were played in this region of the world during ancient times. This is where the book's narrowing of the term "Middle East" becomes a problem. While the ancient lands of Mesopotamia and the Persian Empire were certainly bastions for board games, often funneling them both east and west to Asia and Europe, very few of the ancient games have been verified as originating in this small area. With one glorious exception known as the royal game of ur, the ancient games of the Middle East seem to have gotten their start in either Egypt or India.

Another general statement that can be made about the region is that there is a relative lack of emphasis on competing in sports and on playing games strictly for the pleasure of the moment. Sport, when it was practiced, was a tool used to promote a warrior spirit among the military and/or to buttress the superiority of elite princes.

This philosophy seems to spring from Mesopotamia itself, the swath of deltas between and along the Tigris and Euphrates Rivers that are often referred to as the cradle of civilization. Located in what is now Iraq, this is where it is presumed that widespread agriculture and construction of cities first took place around 3500 B.C. While the Sumerians, the first major ruling group of this area, did have festivals that included pugilistic sports and running races, it was not an area that was ripe with playful recreation.

So, too, the Arabian Peninsula has a limited sport history, in part due to the harshness of its desert environment, making survival a significant task and thus limiting any sense of organized play. Even when the Prophet Mohammed was setting forth the earliest edicts of the Islamic faith around A.D. 700, the emphasis was on a militarist trinity of physical preparedness. "You shall teach your children how to ride, shoot and swim" was a statement from one of the first of Mohammed's spiritual successors.

Finally, it is important to address how, if at all, the ancient sports history impacts the Middle East's role in modern sports, particularly as it relates to the relative lack of female participation at all levels and the lack of success that these countries have experienced (by men or women) at the international level.

Women of the Middle East are noticeably absent from competitive sports. This is usually attributed to the region's high density of Muslims and the Islamic religion's generally restrictive social policies toward women. According to Sfeir's exhaustive research, from 1956 to 1984 a total of 51 women from the 29 countries that she described as "predominantly Islamic" participated at the Olympics. Of them, 16 came from Indonesia, a distinctly Asian country with a large Muslim population, and 13 from the relatively Westernized country of Turkey. Egypt—which began sending men to the Olympics as far back as 1912—did not send its first six female representatives until 1984 (Sfeir 1985, 286).

Sfeir makes observations that have pertinence to the role of ancient women in sports. First, that the practices of seclusion and veiling, so often associated with the limited social role of women in Islamic countries, were borrowed from cultures that adopted the Muslim religion, including seclusion from the Persian scholars who were among the first to translate the Koran. This would indicate that the severe limits on female social rights had a historical foundation in pre-Islamic times. Second, the Prophet Mohammed in his own writings actually encouraged equal participation in physical health and readiness for women, while stressing the overall need for children (of both sexes) to oblige their fathers to "teach them writing, swimming and archery." It would appear that it was not Mohammed's intent to keep women away from a physical education. Instead, the region's historical predilection toward strict limits on female sport participation (which by no means was unusual compared to Greek, Roman, or Asian practice) put the focus on other aspects of the Koran's teaching that were restrictors of woman's rights. Exclusion of women from sports and games in the Middle East is an ancient practice, made more rigid in recent times by Islam, and is only in the past two decades being slowly reversed.

Seclusion of the whole region from international competition is also slowly being rescinded. While Turkey and Iran have a 50-year history of success in international weight lifting and wrestling, modernization and, in some cases, some very significant wealth among the ruling elite are bringing other countries into the international sports mainstream. Soccer has taken hold strongly in several countries, significantly, Saudi Arabia, which qualified for the 1994 World Cup. Still, in terms of overall competitiveness, this often-fractious region of the world—where nationalistic pride and religious differences have created many ongoing and global concerns—significantly trails the rest of the world.

There is no small irony that probably the most public breakthrough by modern Middle Eastern sportsmen has been in thoroughbred horse racing. Oil billionaires have become increasingly conspicuous and successful in this extremely costly sports environment as owners, breeders, and racetrack impresarios. Once the horse—attached to the swift and deadly chariot—allowed Arab kings the means of securing power and great riches. Now the Arab sheik uses his power and great wealth to secure the best horses.

Sources

Conti, Mary. 1996. "Breeds." In *Encyclopedia of World Sport*, Vol. 2, edited by David Levinson and Karen Christensen. Santa Barbara, Calif.: ABC-CLIO, p. 446.

Decker, Wolfgang. 1996. "Chariot Racing." In *Encyclopedia of World Sport*, Vol. 1, edited by David Levinson and Karen Christensen. Santa Barbara, Calif.: ABC-CLIO, p. 177–183.

Lamont, Deane Anderson. 1995. "Running Phenomena in Ancient Sumer." *Journal of Sport History*, Fall, Vol. 22, No. 3. pp. 207–215.

Mandell, Richard D. 1984. *Sport: A Cultural History*. New York: Columbia University Press.

Poliakoff, Michael. 1984. "Jacob, Job and Other Wrestlers: Reception of Greek Athletics by Jews and Greeks in Antiquity." *Journal of Sport History*, Summer Vol. 11, No. 2, pp. 48–65.

Rosandich, T. J. 1991. "Sports in Society: The Persian Gulf Countries." *Journal of the International Council for Health, Physical Education and Recreation*, Spring, Vol. 27, No. 3, pp. 26–30.

Sfeir, Leila. 1985. "The Status of Muslim Women in Sport: Conflict between Cultural Tradition and Modernization." *International Review for the Sociology of Sport*, Vol. 20, No. 4, pp. 283–304.

SPORTS

▦ Archery

One problem in studying the history of archery in the Middle East relates to a group of archers who significantly impacted the history of the region and beyond but are still relatively unknown and not well understood. They are the Hyksos, and they have been described as an "enigma," a force that swooped into the scene, dominated, then left as abruptly as they had come.

Who were the Hyksos? The reason the question is so relevant is that even though the particulars about the Hyksos—like where they came from and what happened to them—are difficult to know, their effect on the spread of both archery and the use of the chariot is well known. The Hyksos, one of many Semitic intruders, swept across the Sinai and invaded Egypt. Little is known of them, but two things are certain. They put the Egyptian people under complete rule for the span of two dynasties (fifteenth and sixteenth), and they introduced the horse to the Nile Valley. The bow that they brought to Egypt was a composite make. They also brought the chariot, which became a critical element of Egyptian battle and the sport of the pharaohs in future dynasties. It is probably not a coincidence that the pharaohs' supreme power began to be proven by their ability with the bow not longer after Egyptian sovereignty was reclaimed.

The Hyksos, also known as the Shepherd Kings, seem to be the original forerunner of the nomadic horsemen who would follow every 700–1,000 years in history: the Scythians (700–300 B.C.), Attila's Huns (ca. A.D. 430–453), and Genghis Khan and the Mongols (thirteenth century). These horsemen from different eras shared the ability to strike terror into more sedentary people. In each historical case, the invaders used their bows to dominate in battle to the point where they could take ruling control, but eventually their grip weakened, and they would retreat or go elsewhere. Presumably, the Hyksos were not much different from their successors. They needed pastureland for their horses (the Nile Valley would have provided this), and they used speed, intimidation, and missile fire to overwhelm slower, less mobile forces.

The Hyksos were not the first Middle Eastern peoples to effectively utilize the bow. That honor falls to Sargon of Akkad in northern Babylonia. In 2,340 B.C, using an infantry of mostly archers, Sargon conquered the Sumerians of southern Babylonia.

Following the Hyksos, the next great archers of the Middle East were the Assyrians, one of the many groups to rule over the rich valley between the Tigris and the Euphrates known in ancient history as Mesopotamia and now part of the country of Iraq.

The importance of the bow is seen repeatedly in the narrative stonework art in the palace of King Ashurnasirpal II in Nimrud. It shows Ashurnasirpal shooting lions with his simple bend bow (as opposed to the recurved then in use in Central Asia) from a two-wheeled chariot. The shape of the bow, if it accurately displays the bows used by Assyrians, would mean that it was not a particularly powerful instrument and that extremely long arrows were used, in part, because the pull of the bow extended to the release shoulder. The work also shows that the Assyrians shot from atop a horse and wore what could be considered a prelude to the armor of the Middle Ages.

A study of the gestures of Assyrian archers and, in particular, non-Assyrian archers in the stonework around Ashurnasirpal's palace is also informative. The king is often shown with his bow raised and ready. In contrast, non-Assyrians are shown with their bow either drooping or actually dropped onto the ground. This sends the message(s) that the non-Assyrians are defeated, near death, and basically inferior to the Assyrian conquerors. The bow as symbol is not unique to Assyria. In the literature of many western Asian cultures, the bow appears "as a metaphor for potency—political, military even sexual" (Cifarelli 1996).

To that end, the Hittites, who also had their time of influence in Mesopotamia, used the bow in their primitive attempts at increasing sexual strength. Apparently, it worked equally well for men and women and may have been a means to combat homosexuality. The essence was that a man was handed a spindle (sign of woman), and then the spindle was replaced with a strung war bow (the symbol of masculinity) by the local shaman. Following a magical incantation, all manners of a woman had been cast away, and the manners of a man had been taken up.

To the north of Mesopotamia and stretching west toward Greece was the land once called Persia. Its heart was in what is now Iran but at times stretched across the southern rim of the Black Sea, what is now Turkey. The Persians were expert archers and horsemen and are generally credited with inventing and popularizing polo. It is said that from the ages of 5 to 25 Persian boys were instructed in three areas only: riding, archery, and truth telling. Knowing the importance of quality, a good Turkish bow might take 5 to 10 years to make. This was particularly important for the princes and sons of noblemen. The process was emphasized from the time of Cyrus the Great (539 B.C.) and for the next 1,000 years until the end of the Sassanid dynasty (A.D. 651). The importance that Persians placed on the training in physical arts as a means of increasing the likelihood of heroism in battle was attested to in Persian literature as well as by Greek author/historians like Herodotus.

While Cyrus was able to bring together the varied tribes of this large region into one nation that looked to the king for leadership and protection, there were variables in bow design. According to the legendary Athenian warrior Xenophon in his tale of mercenary warfare, he encountered many different types of archers as he tried to escape from Persia. The most formidable test came from a mountain people of the area that Xenophon called Carduchi, likely what came to be known as the mountainous region of Kurdistan where Turkey, Iran, and Iraq meet. They used long arrows that were almost the width of a javelin and that could easily pierce a shield. Burke suggests that such a bow would have had an immense draw of 200 pounds: "The Carduchian bows seem as strong as any we find mentioned in antiquity, except for those of legendary kings and princes." (Burke 1957, 57).

The Persian influence, which extended into a stage of controlling Egypt, extended until the empire was destroyed by Alexander the Great in 331 B.C. While the Greeks generally did not extol the virtues of the bow in their own training, regarding the heavily armored, tightly packed group of spear holders called the phalanx as their favored approach, Alexander himself was fond of the archer. It just usually wasn't Greeks pulling the bows, but rather hired mercenaries, often from the island of Crete. In the closest calls of his undefeated career, Alexander was twice pulled out of dangerous situations by his adept maneuvering and use of his archery regiments—once in Persia.

The bow both fits symbolically into the formation of Persia as well as helps to decide one area where it would not tread. Legend has it that Persia's northern boundary (with the Scythians) was decided when a hero soldier climbed a mountain and shot an arrow with an agreement in place that where the arrow landed would serve as the boundary. Supposedly it flew for most of the day, landing 600 miles away (remember, this is a legend), and the Scythians honored the agreement.

In the days of Persian expansion, they were stopped short by a particular warning from Ethiopian royalty, which sent back a huge bow with emissaries. The message was, if you can use this Ethiopian bow, then attack. If not, be thankful the Ethiopian kings have no intention of furthering their boundaries. Persia stopped its progress in Egypt.

Sources

Burke, Edmund. 1957. *The History of Archery*. New York: William Morrow.

Cifarelli, Megan. 1996. "Gesture and Alterity in the Art of Ashurnasirpal II of Assyria." *Art Bulletin*, June, Vol. 80, Issue 2, p. 210.

Decker, Wolfgang. 1992. *Sports and Games of Ancient Egypt*. Translated by Allen Guttmann. New Haven, Conn: Yale University Press.

Knauth, W. 1976. "Sport Qualifications of the Ancient Persian Princes." *Stadion: Journal of the History of Sport and Physical Education*, Vol. 2, Issue 1, pp. 1–89.

Levinson, David, and Karen Christensen, ed. 1999. *Encyclopedia of World Sport*. (paperback) Oxford: Oxford University Press.

Ziegler, Earle F., ed. 1973. *A History of Sport and Physical Education to 1900*. Champaign, Ill.: Stipes.

▦ Buzkashi

The ancient contest known as buzkashi still is considered the national sport of Afghanistan. Buzkashi is a contest between two teams of horsemen over the possession of a dead calf or goat carcass, with the object being for one talented and fearless rider to gain control of the slippery carcass and then separate from the pack of horseman vying for the same prize. Buzkashi means goat, but a calf carcass is often used because it reportedly stays intact longer. The animal is beheaded, bled, and behooved before being used. It can be either gutted or not.

The sport was spread by the Mongol hordes that swept out of China and across the vast steppes of central Asia. Currently, buzkashi is played mostly by Turkic people, including the Uzbek, Turkomen, Kazakh, and Kirghiz.

In the midst of the frenzy, a horseman is likely to be whipped by the other horsemen—from either team—and slammed into by other horses. If the carcass is secured (which would not be easy in an empty field due to its weight; it is often doused in water, and the rider must bend low enough in his saddle to virtually touch the ground), then horse and rider race away to a predetermined area with the carcass. That feat wins a prize for the horseman (money, a handkerchief), a point for his team, and the right to briefly celebrate his effort.

The value of the prize helps determine how many players participate and thus how intense the competition is. A team can consist of as few as 5 horsemen and as many as 1,000. The number of competitors typically increases as the buzkashi continues, or if one cycle of play lasts a particularly long time, as the value of the prize can increase as the game goes on.

Then the carcass is returned to the center of the field and the melee of man and horse begins again until another player gains possession and races again outside either the predetermined area or, as he did in ancient times, to a point where he is "free-and-clear" from pursuers, at which point the calf is dropped and the prize claimed.

The process is repeated until an agreed-upon point total is reached or until one team withdraws. The latter often happens due to a dispute, and the defection of a team detracts from the overall quality of the buzkashi. The final cycle of the daylong buzkashi is extra special, and the winning horseman rides off with the tattered, but honorary, bit of carcass draped over his saddle.

Certainly, buzkashi is a wild spectacle. Its origins can be found in a harsh environment of nomadic, warring populations of the Central Asian steppes. These were the people once known as Mongols and Huns, who were fearsome invaders. Swooping into battle upon their stout, swift horses, usually with a recurved bow made of composite materials, they were an awesome fighting force. Buzkashi demanded the horsemanship and fearlessness that a man would need to be successful in battle and to take away enough of the spoils in its aftermath to make the effort worthwhile.

Buzkashi "provided excellent training for the mobile shock cavalry which developed in Central Asia and which even Alexander the Great could not defeat." (Dupree 1966). It has also been suggested that the Mongol nomads used prisoners of war instead of goats or calves (Blanchard and Cheska 1985, 130). If that was the case, then the game served not only as practice for warfare but also as a vivid warning of the consequences awaiting anyone captured by the fearless horsemen.

A more recent author, G. Whitney Azoy, disputes the human carcass claim. Azoy contends that there is no evidence to support this "lurid notion, advanced to horrify tourists in the 1960s and 1970s" (Azoy 1999, 69). Regardless, it was not, and is still not, a game for the fainthearted. The Afghans' obsession with buzkashi has been pointed to as an example of why the Afghanistan rebels were able to torment and eventually stymie the military of a superpower like the old Soviet Union in the Afghan–Soviet War of 1979–1989. To play buzkashi is to not give up, no matter what the odds or the danger. An old buzkashi legend says that once a father and son ended up on different teams because the son was trying to win the favor of a young girl whose father was affiliated with a rival team. During the buzkashi, father and son contested the carcass so fiercely that they rode their horses over a cliff. So intense was the need to win or, at the very least, to not give up that father and son were desperately clawing for control of the carcass even as they fell to their certain death.

As in the past, buzkashi teams are still sponsored by wealthy khans, or community leaders. While centuries ago the objective was to train an effective cavalry, now the khan's motive has more to do with winning influence. His political fortunes can rise and fall depending on the outcome of a sponsored event, called a *tooi*, where buzkashi is played. It is up to the sponsoring khan to supply housing and prizes as well as to be able to settle the disputes that inevitably arise. If he can do all of these things well, then his name will rise in prominence. If not, he will fall from public favor.

A fine buzkashi horse is still considered one of the most prized possessions of the Afghan warlord, and he will usually choose specially trained riders, called *chapandazan*, for his best mounts. The rough-hewn glamour, sort of an Eastern version of the American rodeo, has become a subject for the big screen on more than one occasion. Sylvester Stallone has a bonding experience with Afghan rebels during a buzkashi match in *Rambo III*. In 1971, director John Frankenheimer used buzkashi as the focus of his film called *The Horseman*.

The Navajo of North America play a similar game called the chicken pull, with a live rooster buried in the ground replacing a four-legged carcass.

Suggestions for Modern Play

Buzkashi can be simulated, perhaps using bikes instead of horses and a 50-pound bag of grain instead of the goat or calf. Instead skip the transportation and use a football in a basic playground game. Divide into two teams simply for point-scoring purposes. Put the ball in the center. On a signal, everyone runs for the ball. Once it is secured by one person, he or she is now free to be tackled and to have the ball tugged, pulled, or otherwise dislodged from the person's grip. Someone who can make it all the way to a predetermined boundary (the swing set to the left, the softball fence to the rear, etc.) wins that round and a point for his or her team. Play to 10.

Sources

Azoy, G. Whitney. 1999. "Buzkashi." In *Encyclopedia of World Sport*, edited by David Levinson and Karen Christensen. New York: Oxford University Press, pp. 68–70.

Blanchard, Kendall and Alyce Taylor Cheska. 1985. *The Anthropology of Sport*. South Hadley, Mass.: Bergin and Garvey.

Burke, Edmund. 1957. *The History of Archery*. New York: William Morrow.

McGirk, Tim. 1996. "The National Game." *World Press Review*, August, Vol. 43, Issue 8, p. 33.

▦ Polo

A glorious game of horseman and mount, polo has been enjoyed by the powerful and the rich for centuries and in many different locations around the world, but it is to the ancient kingdom of Persia that the birthplace of polo most likely belongs.

One of the earliest descriptions of polo comes from the Persian poet Firdausi, who describes a match between the Persians and the Turkomans that took place about 600 B.C. For the herdsmen of Central Asia, polo was both a knightly pursuit and a royal pastime in an age when the Persian Empire challenged any of its strongest neighbors.

By the time of Firdausi's writings, the emphasis on the horse in the ancient Middle East had been a serious endeavor for centuries. A well-known, four-volume, 184-page book detailing specific practices for successful care and breeding of horses has been dated to the fourteenth century B.C. and was written by a Hittite known to us only as Kikkulis. In the seventeenth century B.C. the Hyksos had come streaming across the Arabian Peninsula with horse-drawn chariots to overwhelm the Egyptian pharaoh's reign and would control the lands of ancient Egypt for the next century.

The mysterious "Hyksos, Hittites (central Turkey), Assyrians of Mesopotamia (modern Iraq) and many other peoples of the ancient Near East devoted enormous amounts of time and energy to care and breeding" of horses (Guttmann 1992).

At Isfahan, in central Iran, the remains of an ancient polo grounds 300 yards long have been unearthed with the original stone goalposts set eight yards apart—still the standard width of a polo goal.

Polo remained the national sport of the old Persian Empires of the Achaemenids, Parthians, and Sussanids. It was the principal manly pastime at court, which was not surprising, since the cavalry was always the decisive arm of the Persian armies. It was primarily because of its army's ability atop horses, as archers and swift attackers, that the Persian Empire came close to overwhelming the Greek civilization around 490 B.C., had succeeded in conquering Egypt, and were still a formidable threat until the empire was destroyed by Alexander the Great in 331 B.C.

At times, polo was also known as *chuvigan* and *Tshougan*. By the end of the ancient times, polo had spread from the steppes to Mesopotamia, Syria, and Byzantium to the west and across Asia to China and Japan. In China, it was supported by all 16 emperors of the Tang dynasty (A.D. 618–907), several of whom were reported to be excellent players. The Tang emperors viewed polo, or *jiju* as it was called, as an excellent form of military training, as the horse had increasingly been introduced into military life. In this way, polo replaced Chinese football (*t'su chu*), which reached its height in the Han dynasty (206 B.C.–220 A.D.) as the preferred "game" for military training.

Polo in the time of the Persian Empire probably did not look much like the highly refined, four-horse-per-side game that is played today at some of the most exclusive locations around the world. It was not, however, the wild free-for-all that is *buzkashi*. As with the charioteers of Egypt and Greece, there had to be a significant level of wealth achieved before polo could be pursued with any amount of vigor. Good polo "ponies" were highly valued and well cared for. Therefore, it was the domain of the ruling class and at times a conversation point between rulers from different regions of the world.

Umminger details a tremendous bit of verbal sparring between Darius, the Persian king of kings and the not-yet-great Alexander. Darius reportedly brought Alexander a mallet and a ball as would be used for polo and tells him to "play with these and leave the serious matter of war alone." To which Alexander replied, "I will—with the earth as my ball and myself as the stick." As it turned out, Darius had significantly underestimated Alexander.

Interestingly, polo had disappeared from its origins and existed only in a few relatively remote areas of the northern Indian subcontinent when British soldiers rediscovered the game in the nineteenth century and heartily adopted it. This spawned its spread again around the still-huge British Empire and other areas of the world, including the increasingly wealthy enclaves in the United States. World War II was another tough blow for the game, limiting its play in most countries. By the 1970s, Argentina, benefiting perhaps from its *gaucho* heritage, had established itself as the foremost country for polo in the world.

Suggestions for Modern Play

Could polo be played by American schoolchildren? It's not likely to be done on horseback, due to the high cost and large playing field required. The fact that only a fraction of children are capable equestrians would also discourage true polo as a pastime. Still, the thrill of trying to control a speeding vehicle while striking a moving ball can be replicated to a degree with bicycles. In fact, bicycle polo has been played for over 100 years and has developed strongly enough to have associations and clubs in Europe and the Far East, where it has even been included at times in the Asian Games. Bicycle polo is usually played on a grass field roughly the size of an American football field. Goalposts could be used as the goals. Teams can consist of both boys and girls (or men and women) with up to six per side, though four is the preferred number. As with polo, the game is divided into "chukkers" (usually six 15-minute intervals), and a wooden ball is advanced by means of striking it with a mallet.

Sources

Arlott, John, ed. 1975. *The Oxford Companion to World Sports and Games*, London: Oxford University Press.

Guttmann, Allen. 1992. "Old Sports." *Natural History*, July, Vol. 101, Issue 7, pp. 50–57.

Riordan, James, and Robin James. 1999. *Sport and Physical Education in China*. London: New York, E and FN Spon.

Umminger, Walter. 1963. *Supermen, Heroes and Gods*. English ed. London: Thames and Hudson.

Ziegler, Earle F., ed. 1973. *A History of Sport and Physical Education to 1900*. Champaign, Ill.: Stipes.

⊞ Running

Among the earliest bits of evidence of a physical activity being turned into a sporting contest where victory appears to have mattered, at least to some degree, are references to footraces as part of an annual celebration in the Sumerian city of Umma over 4,000 years ago.

Ancient Sumer was a collection of city-states that was a significant force in the area from about 3,000 B.C. until 1,800 B.C. Through art and cuneiform carved into clay tablets it is known that the Sumerians put a significant amount of interest in the physical body and in fine-tuning it.

Further, as with many other ancient civilizations, the ruling class employed a corps of running messengers to communicate with their subjects and with other rulers.

Because of the written records of a relatively simple governmental nature it can be ascertained that footraces were sanctioned and supported by Umma in the reign of King Shu-Suen, who held power from 2,038 B.C. to 2,030 B.C. These are basically order forms for necessities for festival offerings to the king to be placed at gates in honor of significant gods and goddesses. These were to be delivered "on the occasion of the city race-making," which was identified as the eighth month, which is roughly the period between October 15 and November 15 in the Sumerian calendar. While specifics about the races are not known (how many runners, what the distance was, exactly what the purpose was) the mention of "race-making" indicates a celebration run of some type.

About 1,800 B.C. another tablet, this one from southern Sumer, indicates that a certain payment is to be made in the "footrace month." Again, the tablet was not written as a sports record, but rather as an accounting record. The specifics regarding the footrace month are missing, but it is another clue that footracing was established well enough that the debtor would understand when payment was expected.

When it comes to ancient history, myths and legends also help to illuminate what was considered important to the people associated with the legends. Many of these legends, particularly when they pertained to kings and royalty, were undoubtedly embellished to enhance the grandeur of the ruler (see Africa: Running; Africa: Archery as they relate to Egyptian pharaohs). That is probably the case for the next example of running in Sumer, one that does offer specific—albeit hard to believe—details.

The father of the previously mentioned Shu-Suen was King Shulgi of Ur, who ruled the southern cities of Sumer from 2,094 B.C. to 2,047 B.C. In a hymn written to commemorate his greatness, Shulgi is reported to have made a round-trip run between the cities of Nippur and Ur in one day during the year 2,088 B.C. The distance between the two cities was roughly 100 miles. The supposed purpose of such an arduous task was to allow Shulgi to take part in annual celebratory feasts in both cities on the same day, thus gaining fame and universal respect for himself. While at first glance it seems totally out of the realm of possibility, it might have been able to be done, particularly if the king ran to Nippur the day before the festival and then ran the 100 miles back to Ur. Since a day was considered sunset to sunset, the king would have had 24 hours to complete the 100 miles. It would not have been easy, but a pace of a little over five miles an hour—essentially a marching pace—would have completed the trip.

Whether Shulgi was among the first of the great endurance runners or simply a king with a very inflated ego, the hymn would have served a purpose only if the audience could conceptualize the difficulty of such a task. To do that effectively, it would seem to follow that the audience would have needed some knowledge of running and what was a standard of excellence in the messenger service.

Beyond the realm of kings and legends, it can be stated with a high degree of certainty that several of the major cities along the Mediterranean were introduced to Hellenistic-style games in the final centuries before the birth of Christ by means of having stadiums erected. One such case is in Amrit, site of a onetime Phoenician city that is virtually uninhabited now. The stadium, in ruins, is a virtual replica of the dimensions at Olympia, with a length of 220 meters and a width of 30 meters. The *stadia* race of the Olympics is known to have been one length of the track and has been consistently agreed to have been roughly 200 meters.

Thus, this stadium fits the nature of a Greek stadium designed to house running events as well as the typical jumping, throwing, and wrestling that also would have taken place in a Panhellenic festival. Boutros, the author of the source of this information, invariably tries to make a case in several published articles that the Phoenicians had Festival Games that predate the Greek Olympics. The implication is that the Greeks "borrowed" the concepts from the Phoenicians as opposed to the more accepted notion that the Greeks spread their emphasis on physical competitions to the many places where their cultural ideals took root. Boutros has had little support of his Phoenician-first theories. Regardless, it can be accurately assumed that the people of Amrit were participating in sanctioned sporting events, including footraces, in ancient times at their own stadium.

This can also be said of several other cities in the Near East. Antioch in Turkey, Ephesus and Ismir in western Asia Minor near the Aegean coast, Damascus in Syria, Tyre in Lebanon, and Alexandria in Egypt are among the locations considered to have hosted athletic contests during either Hellenic (332 B.C.–64 B.C.) or Roman (64 B.C.–A.D. 395) rule.

Sources

Boutros, Lahib. 1977. "The Phoenician Stadium of Amrit." *Olympic Review*, No. 112, pp. 114–120.

Lamont, Deanne Anderson. 1995. "Running Phenomena in Ancient Sumer." *Journal of Sport History*, Fall, Vol. 22, No. 3. pp. 207–215.

⊞ Wrestling

There has been a repeated emphasis in this book that wrestling is a universal sport that can reasonably be surmised to have evolved from man's natural need to subdue opposing forces—both animal and human.

Therefore, it is only natural that wrestling was known as an activity worthy of practice and depiction in the area of the world often called the cradle of civilization, the modern Middle East.

The Sumerians and their immediate successors as sovereigns in Mesopotamia, the Hittites, both engaged in wrestling and boxing as a means of physical exercise that was worthy of visual representation. The Sumerians also used wrestling as an attribute that was associated with their mythological heroes as well as epic poetry of the great King Gilgamesh (ca. 2,600 B.C.). Gilgamesh's exploits predate the suspected time frame for Homer's famous Greek sportsmen/warriors by nearly 1,500 years.

The Sumerians offer some of the oldest archaeological evidence of sportlike activities, stemming from the early dynastic period, which ranged from 3,000 B.C. to 1,500 B.C. Several types of combat sports, including boxing and wrestling (as well as bull jumping), are depicted in statues, seals, and *stelae*. They are also noted in administrative documents. In the early stage of this period gaming boards, now known as the royal game of ur, have also been dated (see Middle East: Royal Game of Ur). This would seem to indicate that the Sumerian elite, at the least, participated in sports and games.

Artifacts from the Hittite era (second millennium B.C.) indicate they had begun to have formal exhibits of gladiatorial combat sports. Some 600 years later in northern Italy, the Etruscans would also engage in contests that foreshadowed the bloodthirsty circuses of Rome. It has also been suggested that the Hittites may have used funerals and festivals as an occasion for hosting competitions, which included wrestling, to honor the deceased or the gods. (The Hittites are also famous for being among the earliest and most detailed practitioners of breeding horses; see Middle East: Introduction.)

In the areas to the west, in what is now modern Israel and Lebanon, it is almost certain that the early Christians and early Jews took part in wrestling while the region was under Greek and then Roman rule. As Poliakoff wrote, there are numerous literary references to the religious heroes Job (Christianity) and Jacob (Judaism) taking part in wrestling matches, often in the context of fighting some form of evil spirit force. In the case of Job, the opponent is often Satan, and the wrestling context can certainly be interpreted as merely a literary metaphor for Job's continued need to struggle to overcome his hardships and not succumb. Poliakoff contends, however, that even if the references are not evidence that Job was a wrestler, the specificity of some of the passages about techniques and intricacies of wrestling indicates that the authors felt that their audience had a significant understanding of wrestling.

The primary reason that the early Jews in outposts like Jerusalem (where both a gymnasium and an *ephebion*, or school for the physical and intellectual training of youths age 16 to 21, were erected about 175

B.C.) and Alexandria, Egypt, would have taken an active role in the physical models of Greeks and Romans had to do with the ability to attain certain rights. The first step toward obtaining rights of being a citizen within the city-states were often taken by attending the gymnasiums through active participation. This does not mean that the Jews gave up all of their beliefs, only that they worked within the system to assimilate into the Greek, then Roman political structures as a way of obtaining more direct control of their own lives. Taking part in the physical aspects of the gymnasium, particularly wrestling, was at that time a vital part of earning the status of citizen.

To the north, in the regions more closely associated with the Persian Empires, there is little doubt that wrestling has a vital place in traditional Turkish and Iranian cultures. *Yagli* is still a national sport in Turkey and attracts large crowds to its national tournaments. While Turkey has become a significant force in both freestyle and Greco-Roman wrestling in Olympic competition, the traditional form of wrestling known as yagli is still practiced extensively.

Yagli is marked by the leather breechcloths worn by the competitors and the fact that they grease themselves with oil, making any firm grip difficult to secure and maintain. A contest ends when one shoulder and one thigh are touching the ground. The yagli wrestling takes place outdoors, and the annual Kirkpinar contests can draw a field of over 300 wrestlers from across the country. Multiple matches are the order of the three-day tournament. In ancient times, the sultans were extremely generous in bestowing gifts upon champions. With the high stakes, competition was fierce.

(The practice of anointing the skin with oil prior to athletic events is an extremely ancient practice. It has been well documented that the Greek athletes not only used oil when competing but also were often awarded olive oil as a prize and regarded it as very valuable. There is also evidence that the Sumerian royal messengers used oil for anointing often enough that the supply of the oil was part of a ration supplied by the city of Ur to the runners.)

In neighboring Iran, wrestling has a long history, going back to the Persian Empire. Not only were the wrestlers expected to be strong and good enough to be champions, or *qahraman* in Persian, but they also aspired to reach the rarefied state of sportsmanship that was expressed by the Persian notion of *pahlavan*. This means that the athlete is not only a formidable opponent but also fair and just, does not take pleasure in promoting his own superiority, and can still be kind to the weak. Pahlavan as a concept is not restricted to wrestling, but it is worth noting that in Iranian legends and history three of the greatest examples of a pahlavan man—the pre-Islamic legend Rostam, the early Islamic leader

Imam Ali (a son-in-law of the Prophet Mohammed), and fourteenth-century champion Mahmud Kharazmi—were all wrestlers.

Throughout Iran there are many regional forms of wrestling, and as the country crossed into Islamic control, they were often practiced in a special venue called a *zurkhaneh*, or "house of strength," which included seating areas encircling a center pit for the wrestlers, thus allowing for spectators. Of the many styles of Iranian wrestling, a form called *kushti* is similar to the Turkish yagli in that it takes place on grassland. The wrestlers wear tight-fitting leather trousers, and the object is to win as many matches as possible by the means of throwing a wrestler to his back and onto the ground.

Wrestling tournaments have also been recorded in the ancient and extinct Middle East civilizations of Babylonia and Assyria.

Suggestions for Modern Play

High school wrestling teams could use a demonstration of Turkish yagli wrestling as a fund-raising event that would probably draw some interest from the community. The wrestlers should make sure that they oil their bodies to emulate the ancient practice. Equipment should consist only of tight-fitting bicycle shorts (for modesty) and a sturdy breechcloth (for getting a grip on something other than an oily body). Hold the event at one end of a football field where seating is available for spectators, with the "grassland" consisting of approximately 30 yards by the width of the football field. Make sure that several matches are going on at once. Money could be raised by means of having each wrestler solicit pledges from family and community members for each successful fall recorded. In this way, the wrestlers will be motivated to continue to wrestle new opponents for an extended period of time.

Sources

Arlott, John, ed. 1975. *The Oxford Companion to World Sports and Games*. London: Oxford University Press.

Chehabi, H. E. 1995. "Sport and Politics in Iran: The Legend of Gholamreza Takhti." *The International Journal of the History of Sport*, December, Vol. 12, No. 3. pp. 48–60.

Lamont, Deane Anderson. 1995. "Running Phenomena in Ancient Sumer." *Journal of Sport History*, Fall, Vol. 22, No. 3. pp. 207–215.

Palmer, D., and M. Howell. 1973. "Sports and Games in Early Civilizations." In *A History of Sport and Physical Education to 1900*, edited by Earle F. Ziegler. Champaign, Ill.: Stipes.

Poliakoff, Michael. 1984. "Jacob, Job and Other Wrestlers: Reception of Greek Athletics by Jews and Greeks in Antiquity." *Journal of Sport History*, Summer, Vol. 11, No. 2, pp. 48–65.

Soreq, Yehiam. 1985. "Diasporal Jewish Participation in Gymnastic Life." In *Sport*

History, Olympic Scientific Congress 1984 Official Report, edited by Norbert Muller and Joacim K. Ruhl. Schors-Verlag: Niedernhausen, pp. 432–441.

PLAY

▦ Magura

Magura, also known as pecan hole, is a traditional children's game of Iraq that emphasizes accuracy while pitching an object and also the need to be able to keep score mentally to determine when an off-target throw is the best throw to make.

In terms of equipment it is a simple game, consisting of a small hole dug in the ground about four inches in diameter and three inches deep, with a small wooden backstop set up about a foot behind the hole. Also needed are enough pecans so each player (there can be any number) has 10.

The game involves two types of players—the "throwers," who stand about seven feet from the hole and try to pitch their pecans into the target, and the "protector." As the latter name implies, the protector is the person who stands near the hole, but he does not actively try to keep the pecans out of the hole. Instead, the protector is there to secure what could be considered rent for using the hole. Each thrower throws all 10 pecans toward the hole. Some will be returned, but others—unless all 10 go in the hole—will be kept by the protector. The key component in determining who gets which pecans is whether an even or an odd number of pecans go in the hole.

If an even number of pecans goes in the hole, then the ones in the hole are returned to the thrower, and the rest are given to the protector. If an odd number goes in the hole, then the protector keeps the pecans in the hole, and the misses are returned.

Therefore, the game rewards the thrower who can throw many and an even number of pecans in the hole but exacts a penalty for many and an odd number in the hole.

For example, if the thrower deposits 8 of his 10 pecans in the hole, then he gets back those 8, and the protector has only 2 pecans. But if the thrower has, for example, made his first 8 shots and then tries to get greedy but misses one of his last two attempts, thus putting 9 in the hole, the protector keeps 9 pecans and gives only 1 pecan back.

Throwers continue their turn until they are out of pecans. The protector has the option of "selling" the hole to a buyer. This gives the former protector a chance to pitch a few pecans himself.

The game is obviously played for fun, as opposed to high stakes, since the protector has the distinct advantage of always being able to keep at least some of the thrower's pecans unless the thrower can pitch them perfectly. Even when a perfect round is accomplished, the protector does not lose any previous pecans that have been gained. This means that a protector's pecan stash continues to increase, or, at worst, stays the same, while the thrower's pecan total inevitably decreases.

Suggestions for Modern Play

Any type of nut or small stone or even marbles would work in the place of pecans, since pecan trees may not be common to your neighborhood. One modification to the game is the manner in which a thrower becomes a protector. This could be done on a rotational basis. When a single thrower is out of nuts, it must follow that the protector now has 10. At this point the former protector goes to the end of the throwers' line, and the previous thrower becomes the protector. This would be a good game for preschool, kindergarten, and early primary students to play in small groups of three to five children. It would give practice in counting and recognizing even- and odd-number sets while providing a simple eye-hand coordination task and a rudimentary lesson in strategy. Keeping the number of players to a minimum should help decrease the boredom level for a thrower who is waiting his or her turn.

Source

Jernigan, Sara Staff, and C. Lynn Vendien. 1972. *Playtime: A World Recreation Handbook.* New York: McGraw-Hill.

GAMES

⚏   Royal Game of Ur

The Royal Game of Ur is actually a modern name ascribed to board games that have been uncovered in the royal tombs of Ur in ancient Sumeria. One example currently on display at the British Museum has been dated to 2600 B.C., making it one of the oldest game boards in existence.

The board certainly has the look of royalty. Made of wood, it is inlaid with lapis lazuli and shell fragments. The board features finely crafted rosettes and a unique shape, somewhat akin to a square hourglass. Typically, the boards were constructed in this way: a straight pathway, marked by 2 squares, connects two larger areas of playing surfaces; one is a 2-square by 3-square section, the other 3-squares by 4-squares, equaling 20 squares in all.

While the recovered boards do vary in their decorations, one consistency is that each has squares that are decorated with an ornate rosette

The elegant game board unearthed by Sir Leonard Woolley during his famous excavations of the royal tombs of Ur, an ancient Sumerian city. The wooden part of the board had deteriorated when Woolley found it, but the beautifully inlaid playing area, consisting of shell plaques inlaid with lapis lazuli and red limestone and separated by lapis lazuli strips, was intact enough to allow for a beautiful reconstruction. Now known as the Royal Game of Ur, its exact method of play remains unknown but has generated many possible theories. (© The British Museum)

symbol. The other squares are either left blank or also contain significant symbols. Most often there have been five rosettes, though a board uncovered some distance from Ur itself had three rosettes.

Like the game's name, the actual rules of the game, as it was played in the Ur palaces, are lost. However, the same style of boards was in use less than 200 years before the birth of Christ, and rules have been found on a cuneiform tablet of Babylonian origin dated 177–176 B.C.

While the actual rules can only be guessed at, it would appear that this game board is set up for a race game in backgammon style. There are similarities in shape and configuration to the Egyptian boards for *senet* (which had 30 squares) and 20-square boards, which are also considered to be backgammon ancestors. One reason for this theory is that the boards of Ur have been recovered with five to seven "pawns" or playing pieces for each person and some type of dice to determine the number of squares that could be moved.

The most famous (and elegant) board is on display at the British Museum. Uncovered in the excavations done jointly by the British Museum and the University of Pennsylvania and headed by Sir Leonard Woolley from 1924 to 1934, the find also included unique, pyramid-shaped dice. In all, the Woolley-led expedition found five gaming boards in various states of repair and also with various decorative touches.

Because of the similarity of the senet and 20-square boards, it is assumed that the game was played beyond Ur and even outside the realm of Sumeria. Games with 20 squares have been found from Egypt to India and dating from around 3000 B.C. to modern times. Of particular interest is a board discovered in Cyprus and dated at about 1580 B.C. At that time, Cyprus was under the control of Egypt. This board retained the five rosettes and also had a 3-square-by-4-square pattern at one end. The major difference is that from the 3×4 block there extended an eight-square path down the middle with no other squares, as if some game-maker had decided that the game was better served to change the 2-square "bridge" and the 2×3 configuration into one long path. What is interesting is that there are no depictions of anyone actually playing the game (as there are with senet), and for several years after Woolley unearthed the game boards no one had even a good guess as to how the game was played.

The cuneiform tablet from Babylonia, however, shed some significant light on the subject, most significantly that the rosette squares were considered good luck and, in fact, that failure to land on them could require paying a penalty (this would imply that the game was usually played for stakes). This description indicated that five pawns were used for play and that each required a specific throw of the dice to gain entrance onto the board. One important point is that by the time of the Babylonian cuneiform the standard dice were knucklebones, as opposed to the odd, pyramid-shaped dice uncovered by Woolley. This tablet also indicates that the game board was used for fortune-telling.

The Royal Game of Ur has generated significant amounts of conjecture in terms of exactly how it is to be played. There are a number of variables: the number of pawns, the starting and exiting locations, exactly what type of "good luck" is gained from landing on a rosette, and what number (or numbers) was needed to place a pawn onto the board. The matter of the pyramid dice and how the rolls would have been counted is also a quandary.

On the latter subject, some explanation about the dice is needed. First, they are three-sided pyramids, not four-sided, meaning that there are four vertices. Two of the four vertices were dotted with an inlay. Here we refer to Bell's description of what the rolls would be worth, with which Soubeyrand agrees

Three jeweled corners up equals five and another throw
Three plain corners up equals four and another throw

Two plain corners up equals zero and the turn is finished

One plain corner up equals one and another throw

The British Museum, which has an instructive and interactive game that is reached by either its general Web site or by going directly to the Web address: www.mesopotamia.co.uk/tombs/challenge/cha_set.html, changes the dice pattern for simpler play. They still use simulated pyramid shapes but use four of them and just put one dot on each, thus the possible rolls are 4, 3, 2, 1, and 0. If you roll zero, you miss a turn. This simulation shares the opinion with other theories that the rosettes are "safe" squares, meaning a pawn can not be taken while resting on one. Also, landing on a rosette is good for another turn. Two pawns of the same color cannot occupy one position, even a rosette square. The Oriental Institute (which sells a modern reproduction of the game) suggests that any number of pawns can rest at a rosette. If a pawn lands on a (nonsafe) space already occupied by an opponent's pawn, the opponent's pawn is sent off the board.

Both Bell and the British Museum simulation contend that players enter the board on their own side, with the entrance point being the non-rosette corner of the 3-by-4 portion that is nearest the bridge. The exit squares are the two rosettes on the 2-by-3 section. This means that one player moves his or her pawns in a counterclockwise direction, while the other player moves in a clockwise fashion (Figure 5.1). The object as in backgammon, is to get all of the pawns through the board and off the exit.

Suggestions for Modern Play

The first suggestion is to try the interactive game at the British Museum site. It will quickly become apparent that this game is not easily completed because of the frequency with which pawns are sent back to start over.

The second suggestion is to make the game yourself and then play it with a friend. The basic pattern is simple enough to draw onto a piece of cardboard, and regular chess pawns or checkers can be used as playing pieces. Players should experiment with different types of dice and maximum scoring throws to see the different patterns of play that develop. One thing to remember: there is no "absolute" when it comes to the rules. Even though experts in the field of game play and ancient games have suggested the methods of play that have been presented, it is quite possible that none are exactly how the ancient Sumerians played the game.

Sources

Bell, R. C. 1979. *Board and Table Games from Many Civilizations*, (revised double edition). New York: Dover.

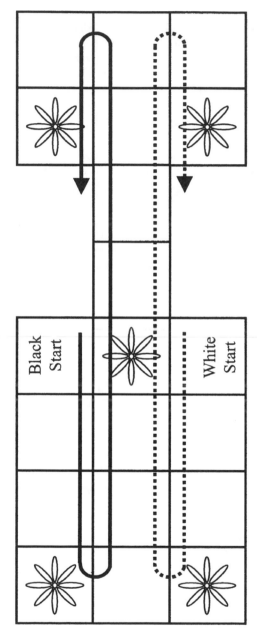

Figure 5.1: The Royal Game of Ur is considered to be a backgammon-style game. Though there is no positive proof on how to play the over 4,500-year-old Sumerian game, the starting point, pattern of play, and exit points presented here emphasize the rosettes as signifying special squares. (Illustration by Gary Harrison)

"The Challenge." 2001. Interactive Web site game from the British Museum (www.mesopotamia.co.uk/tombs/challenge/cha_set.html), played June.

Soubeyrand, Catherine. 2000. "The Royal Game of Ur." *The Game Cabinet* (Web site: gamecabinet.com/history/), September.

Westerfield, Jennifer T. 2001. "The Royal Game of Ur." The Suq, *Oriental Institute, University of Chicago*, April, (Web site).

▦ Shatranj: An Early Version of Chess

Shatranj is generally considered by historians of games to be one of the earliest and truest ancestors to modern chess and was developed in the latter stages of the Persian Empire, around A.D. 600, and then codified and popularized in the Middle East within the next three centuries.

To understand shatranj, however, it is first necessary to look a little farther east to India, where Sanskrit records detail the games of *chaturanga* (also called *shaturanga*) and *ashtapada*. Both games are considered to have ancestral ties to the more refined Persian version.

A Sanskrit name for a battle formation, chaturanga has two important rules that are still used in chess but were not common to games to that point. These were the concepts that playing pieces could be assigned different values and properties of movement (i.e., in modern chess, the queen can move in any direction, the rook goes at straight lines, the bishop diagonally, etc.) and that victory would be determined by the fate of one particular piece. This piece was known as the rajah in chaturanga and can be accurately compared to the king in modern chess. The other pieces in chaturanga were the elephant, cavalry, ship, and pawns, with the first three possessing special moves.

Bell contends that chaturanga was likely an early sixth-century creation that had its origin in the form of a 64-square board used for an ancient Indian race game called ashtapada. Others feel that the two games developed more or less simultaneously, since both are mentioned in very early Sanskrit records from as far back as 800 B.C. Regardless of whether chaturanga followed ashtapada or developed in a parallel fashion, they both played a significant role in the Middle Eastern development known as shatranj, which is considered a true chess ancestor and was written about in detail in Arabic about A.D. 920 in a book called *Kitah Ash-Shatranj* (Book of Chess).

Chaturanga showed some early signs of modern chess but two primary factors had to evolve to make it more chesslike. When this evolution took place, the game became shatranj. Neither development is difficult to explain, but both obviously changed the game considerably. The first is that chaturanga was a four-person game, with two players being, in Bell's terms, "loosely allied" against the other two players. The other major difference is that dice were used, marked with the numeric choices of 2, 3, 4, or 5. This second consideration limited exactly what a game player could do, since the dice determined which pieces could be moved.

According to Bell, a 2 meant that the boatmen moved; a 3 allowed a cavalry piece to move; 4 meant that the elephant moved; and 5 allowed the rajah or the infantry (also known as a pawn) to move.

Based upon a translation of the early Sanskrit writing known as *Bhavishya Purana*, the details of how the chaturanga pieces moved are known. This was an epic story that, in part, told of a prince who had lost his fortune at dice and asked a friend to teach him the mysteries of chaturanga so he could earn back his losses, which included his wife. From this tale of a gambler gone awry, more similarities to modern chess are revealed. The rajah's movements are exactly like those of the modern king: one space in any direction. The elephant, too, had a direct connection. Its movement was the same as the modern castle or rook, being able to move any number of squares directly forward, backward, to the left, or to the right, though not able to jump an opponent. The cavalry had the same mode of transfer as the modern knight, often referred to in beginner's slang as "the horse." The chaturanga cavalry could move one square orthogonally (meaning directly forward, backward, left, or right) and then one space diagonally. The ship was similar to the modern bishop in that its moves were diagonal, but they were always limited to two spaces, with a jump allowed.

The ships and pawns could capture only other ships and pawns. Each player had four pawns, with one playing piece of each of the other varieties—at least when the game started. It was possible for a player to basically usurp his ally's playing pieces and his turn by "seizing the throne," which was done by occupying the throne of a player, which is the starting spot of the rajah on the board.

The basic principle of the game was to try to combine forces in such a way as to increase power and ultimately win the game by capturing all of an opponent's pieces. This was done by seizing the throne and also by establishing something known as a "concourse of shipping," which meant that all four ships were in a four-square block arrangement. The fourth ship into the area, the one completing the concourse, captured the whole fleet and then was allowed the power to move any ship when a 2 was rolled on the dice.

A significant part of the game, as evidenced by the story of the prince who wanted to learn the "mysteries" of chaturanga, was its gambling nature. Wagered stakes were established beforehand, and the capture of enemy rajahs involved the gain of a stake.

Interestingly, the power of religious leaders helped to push chaturanga toward becoming shatranj and thus to make an even closer connection to modern chess. Since gambling was outlawed at an early date by

Hindu culture, the chaturanga players dropped the use of the dice to take away the element of chance, thus increasing the element of tactical skill. Gradually, the four-person format was whittled down to two, leaving each player with eight pawns, a pair each of ships, elephants, and cavalry, and an extra rajah, which was now given title of prime minister with significantly less power. Somewhere the powers of the ships and the elephants were switched, helping to explain the term "rook." The Sanskrit name for ship is *roka*.

Through histories written several centuries later in Persia, there is evidence that after A.D. 600, the more refined version known as shatranj had become an extremely popular court game in Persia. Shatranj gradually spread across the whole of Europe either by means of territorial expansion, marriage arrangements, and gift-giving between Persia and Byzantium and from there into Europe or, at the very latest, as a result of the Crusades.

The previously mentioned book, written by Abu-Bakr Muhammad Ben Yahya as-Suli about A.D. 920, aided the diffusion of shatranj across Europe. The author was considered a chess master at the court of the caliph (religious leader) of Baghdad.

Sources

Avedon, Elliott M., and Brian Sutton Smith, eds. 1971. *The Study of Games*. New York: John Wiley and Sons.

Bell, R. C. 1979. *Board and Table Games from Many Civilizations*, (revised double edition) New York: Dover.

"Chess." 1994–2001. *Encyclopedia Britannica Online*.

⠿ NORTH AMERICA

INTRODUCTION

When asked who the indigenous, ancient North Americans were, many people who live in the United States would say, "The Indians." That answer is a number of things: correct in its most basic sense but politically incorrect as far as many are concerned who do not view the word "Indian" as appropriate, since it was first used by Christopher Columbus to describe the aboriginal population of this continent because he mistakenly thought that he had found a new trade route to the spices and riches of India. Most significantly, the answer is woefully incomplete. The people of this vast land may have shared many spiritual and lifestyle approaches, but they also had and still have many distinct differences. There are an estimated 260 Native American nations in the United States today, and it is believed that there were over 300 languages, with many more subdialects, among the indigenous people of North, Central, and South America in pre-Columbian times. Many such peoples are as different from one another as the French are from the English.

The "Indian way" in the Northeast was not the culture of the bountiful Great Northwest or the muggy, near-tropical jungles of Florida and Louisiana. So it is important to bear in mind that any generalization about Native Americans based on the observation of one group or just a few groups can never be viewed as an absolute. Further, as with any civilization, the purpose of sport must be looked at from within the constraints of the individual culture, not with imposed values from the observer's life history. Many early writers and observers of Indian sport are suspect when it comes to gauging the significance of games and play in the aboriginal societies because they looked at the leisure activities as little more than wasted energy.

Joseph B. Oxendine, author of *American Indian Sports Heritage* and a Lumbee Indian and former three-sport athlete in high school and college, contends that several important factors characterize traditional Indian sports, including:

1. Strong connection between sport and social, spiritual and economic aspects of daily life.
2. Both participants and spectators seriously prepared the mind, body and spirit for competition.
3. Standardized rules and technical precision were assumed unimportant.
4. Sportsmanship and fair play were strongly adhered to.
5. Men and women participated at high levels, though with different expectations.
6. Gambling was widespread and viewed as a vital component in all sports. (Oxendine 1988, pp. 3, 4)

Sport and games were a central part of Native American cultures. While not all shared the same sports, or the same approach to a similar sport, the notion of play was pivotal to a child's early years as a preparation for adulthood. Further, particularly for men, participating in aggressive and physically challenging sports continued to be an important part of their lives until old age. That is not to say that women were not athletes. In fact, if there is any culture in the world that can proudly look back on its ancient heritage as a source of equal opportunity for women athletes, it would be that of the Native North Americans. It was not only accepted that women would be athletes and could exhibit strength, quickness, and agility, but was actually encouraged. Double-ball, the first entry in the "Sports" section was a women-only game.

Because of the vast number of sports that have been documented by early writers, nineteenth- and early twentieth-century researchers, and modern scholars, some activities have been excluded. One conscious omission was the sport of wrestling. Certainly practiced by Native Americans, wrestling, in general, did not have quite the same degree of prominence as it does in other ancient histories, nor was it given as much emphasis as other physically demanding sports. The various Eskimo tribes had a number of wrestling/submission-type games to test endurance and a person's pain threshold. Some of those are included in the section entitled "Eskimo Endurance Contests."

In deciding which sports and games would be included, the most important consideration was to choose subjects that are most likely to have been traditional pursuits. Though archaeological evidence does help to a certain degree, the Native Americans' record of their own sports and games comes to us in the form of oral history, as opposed to written documents. This makes specific time frames much harder to pin down. Therefore, it is quite likely that some of the subjects covered here are not as old as those from the lands of Egypt, Greece, or China covered in other sections of this book. They are, however, games that are considered to be creations of the Native American populations and predating European influence. For that reason, there is no mention of games or activities that involve the horse, which was introduced to the North and South American continents by the Spanish explorers in the early sixteenth century.

In the following discussions, the terms "Native Americans," "Indians," "American Indians", and indigenous people are used synonymously.

Sources

Altherr, Thomas L. 1997. *Sports in North America: A Documentary History* Vol. I: Part I: *Sports in the Colonial Era 1618–1783*. Gulf Breeze, Fla.: Academic International Press.

Eisen, George, and David K. Wiggins, ed. 1994. *Ethnicity and Sport in North American History and Culture*. Westport, Conn.: Greenwood Press.

Oxendine, Joseph B. 1988. *American Indian Sports Heritage*. Champaign, Ill.: Human Kinetics Books.

SPORTS

⊞ Double-Ball

Compared to the European settlers who often displaced them from their own lands, the Native North Americans were advanced in several areas, namely, agriculture, hunting, woodsmanship, and general holistic health practices like sweat-bathing, which were once viewed as hedonistic but have since been proven beneficial. They also were far ahead of the Europeans in the notion of a woman's right to participate in sporting activity. At a time when playing the role of spectator was still the most important task of a sporting woman in Europe (though horseback riding, falconry, and archery afforded some recreational opportunities), the settlers must have been a bit surprised the first time they witnessed double-ball.

Double-ball was a sport for women that was both physically demanding and team-oriented and, for the most part, was something that they could call their own. (Double-ball also has been called the women's ball game, maiden's ball, twin ball and other local variations and was played by men in only a few northern Californian tribes.) Culin (1907) reported that double-ball was played by women in more than two dozen tribes primarily west of the Mississippi (in Gilmore 1926).

The ball was, as the name suggests, unique. It was actually more like a pair of pouches, usually made of buckskin and holding sand. They were held together either by a strong string or by leather thong. Sometimes a larger piece of buckskin, in a dumbbell shape, was used, with the ends then folded and sewn in such a way as to hold the sand, creating a tapered, slender centerpiece. What resulted was a device with two weighted ends about 6 to 12 inches apart. The Chippewa would use billets of wood instead of a ball, tied together by string or a thong. Regardless, the "double-ball" would hang from a stick about three to four feet long (some reportedly up to six feet) with a curved or notched end, while the women ran across vast expanses of a field. As with virtually all Indian ball games, the ball could not be touched or advanced with the hand. At either end of the field were goals in the shape of an inverted "capital U," a couple of unconnected posts, or simply mounds of earth. The objective is to hang the double-ball from the crossbar, if there is one, or to drive the ball through the goal area. In Fletcher's instructions of how to play the game, she indicates that points or "counts" should be taken away from a team's score if the double-ball hits the ground and that counts would be gained if a team can move the whole distance of the field and score a goal without the double-ball's touching the ground.

Whether points were actually discounted for having the double-ball hit the ground is unclear. It is apparent from folktales, though, that the preferred trajectory for the double-ball is in the air. In several tales, including the Wichita's "Seven Brothers and the Woman," a woman uses the double ball as a means of escape when being chased by men or animals. In the Wichita tale she tossed the double-ball into the air and then followed it. Returning the double-ball skyward must also have been fitting since some groups believed that the moon gave the game to the women (Fletcher, 1994 [1915]).

Like most tools used for sport, the double-balls and the sticks would be brightly decorated, sometimes including etchings and carvings. Since the game could get rough and since dropping one's stick was highly possible, it was also important for the players to mark their sticks with some sort of identifying sign.

In descriptions, double-ball is a close cousin of lacrosse. It is a game that ultimately rewards possession and uses a stick to propel the projectile. Also the fields for both sports were huge by modern comparison, though double-ball didn't go to quite the extreme of spanning the distance between villages as lacrosse did on occasion. Most double-ball playing areas were described as 300 to 400 yards long. Some, particularly those of the Cree, were a mile or more in length.

Any number of women might play, and, while not restricted to un-married women, it was most popular with them. The women of the Missisauga in Ontario would remove all unnecessary clothing and paint their bodies, working feathers into their braided hair. The double-ball game was an attraction and, at least for some women, was a way of gaining notice from the men. There is evidence that once a woman reached adulthood and marriage, the emphasis on sport in general was severely reduced, which was not the case with men.

Overall, the game was taken as serious sport. When women competed, they did so vigorously. As such, betting on the outcome was routine, as it was with virtually any organized Indian activity, though to a some-what lesser degree. As Oxendine states, (1988, 58) "Accounts of double ball play make it clear that women, like men, took sports participation seriously. They played with a high level of enthusiasm and physical abandon."

Suggestions for Modern Play

The most obvious component is that this is a game for girls and women, and the men come to watch and cheer (or jeer) the action. To simulate double-ball, the first stage is to have the women make their own equipment. Traditionally a rough piece of animal hide was turned into buckskin by chewing on the hide to soften it. Instead, purchase a tough material. Cut out several elongated figure-eight shapes, with about a six-inch strip between the two bulbous ends. Fill the ends with sand and stitch them up. Since sticks varied in length, it is possible that it was done with a purpose, as is the case in modern lacrosse, where the longer sticks are used by defensemen to increase their reach, but shorter sticks are used by attacking players because they are easier to handle and hold onto the ball. This can be the players' decision, to choose a stick from three to six feet in length. The game time should be set in advance, and much proclamation of the event be made in the community to ensure a large crowd. After ceremonial painting of the equipment and the ath-letes' bodies (adorning long hair with feathered braids would be appro-priate), the players take to a very large field. Ideally, it would be larger than a football field. Three soccer fields situated side by side and then played across their widths would be good. A football field does offer the advantage of preexisting goals. If a football goalpost (or some equivalent) is used, score the game in this manner: three points for hanging the double-ball on a crossbar, one point for driving the double-ball under the crossbar and through the posts, zero points for flinging it over the crossbar. Play the game for an extended period of time with free substi-tutions made on the fly.

Sources

Fletcher, Alice C., 1994 (1915). *Indian Games and Dances with Native Songs*. Lincoln: University of Nebraska Press.

Gilmore, Melvin R. 1976 (1926). "The Game of Double-ball or Twin-ball." In, *The Games of the Americas*, Part 2, edited by Brian Sutton-Smith. New York: Arno Press.

Oxendine, Joseph B. 1988. *American Indian Sports Heritage*. Champaign, Ill.: Human Kinetics Books.

▦ Hoop-and-Pole

Whether it was the Choctaw in Mississippi or the Eskimos in Canada, rolling a hoop and throwing a spearlike pole toward it was a popular pastime that was also steeped in cultural and often deeply religious meanings. It was probably a very naturally occurring game among the indigenous people of large parts of North America. It has also been reported in similar forms across Africa and, to a lesser degree, in South America.

The game probably had its origins in the southwestern United States and northern Mexico but is recognized as being played throughout the entire continent north of Mexico. It was originally a game of great religious ceremony. The game involves rolling a hoop and then throwing spears or long poles at it. The object was usually not to throw the spear/pole through the hoop but rather to throw it to a spot where it would stop rolling. Ideally, the pole would end up underneath the hoop.

One reason that the hoops were not pierced by the poles is that they were not designed in such a manner. Many had a spider's web of buckskin sewn and stitched across the diameter of a young sapling of wood that had been bent into a circle. *Chungke* (also known as *chunke* or *chunkey*) was a form of hoop-and-pole that utilized a smaller stone hoop and was confined primarily to the southeastern U.S. tribes.

It seems almost certain that the hoop-and-pole and chungke games had significant meaning to the tribe. It has been suggested that they were used as healing tools, as well as games that symbolized sexual intercourse, with the hoop and the pole representing the female and male genitalia, respectively. This may be taking things too far, but certainly games were often played to promote fertility. It was also usually the case that women were not allowed to play the hoop-and-pole game. In one report on the Apache tribe from 1868, which admittedly seems fraught with exaggerations of the tension between men and women, it is stated that women were not even allowed on the hoop-and-pole site. Compared to women in most traditional cultures, the Native American woman had a high degree of athletic choice and high levels of achievement in everyday life. Still, there were aspects of life where she was subordinate, particularly in terms of control over food, property, political power, and sexual access.

It is not reasonable to speculate about the meaning of the hoop-and-pole types of games because they were already in decline in terms of play by the late nineteenth century. Further, many elders appear to have been resistant to detailing what the origins and meanings of the game were to outsiders and even to play the game in front of the white settlers. This reticence hints at the importance attached to the game, while hiding the details of its meaning.

That hoop-and-pole was an important game as opposed to a mere diversion is evidenced by the great care given to the playing surface. Impediments were cleared away, and every effort was made to be sure that the hoop would roll straight and true. Sometimes even a layer of sand was put down. The Mandan (North Dakota) went so far as to construct timber floors 150 feet long. The Creeks from the Southeast had enclosed seating areas for their chungke games.

Because the hoop-and-pole playing surfaces were often quite large, this could be a strenuous game (though not as fatiguing as lacrosse), especially if played for long periods of time, as it reportedly was. When the hoop was rolled out, usually by an impartial third party, two players would run after it, one on each side, and track its path from a prescribed distance behind the hoop (usually at least six feet to the rear) before throwing their pole at the spot that they felt would be the end of the hoop's momentum. As the first throw was made, the opponent could—at least in some tribes—choose to try to deflect the pole to earn points with his own throw.

Two writers from colonial times were alternatively aghast at what they saw as "stupid drudgery" (Adair 1775 in Altherr 1997, 459) and the expansive betting that accompanied the game and amazed at the skill with which players "hurl the stone and pole with wonderful dexterity and violence" (Romans 1775 in Altherr 1997, 460). To his credit, while noting that the game would seem foolish to any European, Adair did recognize that chungke stones were rubbed smooth from repeated use and had deep social significance. "They are kept with the strictest of religious care, from one generation to another, and are exempted from being buried with the dead. They belong to the town where they are used and are carefully preserved" (Altherr 1997, 460).

The hoop-and-stick game popular among the Canadian Eskimos had the distinction of using two hoops, one at least a foot in diameter and the other only about four inches. Men, boys, and unmarried women could play the game. Usually, it was a team game, with one group rolling the hoops past the other party, with the big hoop going first. The goal was to spear the hoops as they rolled past. Despite the one target being more difficult due to its smaller size, no extra points were awarded for spearing the small hoop or for spearing both. Each team had a pile of evenly distributed counters. Once their run was completed, they would take a counter for each successfully speared hoop. The team that cleaned out its pile of counters first was declared the winner. Then another game started. The game reportedly was never played in the summer.

That Eskimo hoop-and-pole play included women was highly unusual. As previously mentioned, in most cases this was a game solely for the men.

Suggestions for Modern Play

Hoop-and-pole would be relatively easy to simulate. Most hoops were in the 12- to 16-inch range, while chungke stones tended to be smaller, only about three inches in diameter. The poles' length varied widely. Six to eight feet would be appropriate, with tapered ends. Some poles were marked at the center and then at regular intervals to the end, and these marks were used as a scoring mechanism, that is, more points the closer the stone fell toward the exact center of the pole. This game would probably be best played in an empty parking lot or an outdoor basketball court. The surface should be smooth and relatively hard. Award two points for each time the hoop falls on your pole, one point to the person whose pole is closest to the hoop. That means each player could get two points on a turn if both poles are under the hoop, and the extra bonus point would go to the player who was most accurate. Decide beforehand whether the ideal is to have the center of the pole covered by the hoop, or one particular end. If neither pole is covered by the hoop, then one point is awarded to the player whose pole is closest to it. Play to 15. Tournaments could be created.

Sources

Altherr, Thomas L. 1997. *Sport in North America: A Documentary History*, Vol. 1: *Sports in the Colonial Era 1618–1783*, Gulf Breeze, Fla.: Academic International Press.

Blanchard, Kendall. 1996. "Traditional Sports, North and South America." In *Encyclopedia of World Sport*, edited by David Levinson and Karen Christensen. Santa Barbara Cal.: ABC-CLIO.

Glassford, Robert Gerald. 1976. *Application of a Theory of Games to the Transitional Eskimo Culture*. New York: Arno Press.

Oxendine, Joseph B. 1988. *American Indian Sports Heritage*. Champaign, Ill.: Human Kinetics Books.

⊞ Lacrosse

The North American game most described and discussed in the literature of the European settlers is lacrosse. It was a game that was played with great intensity, seriousness, and ceremonial purpose across large expanses of the North American continent.

Lacrosse is actually the name ascribed to the frenzied, community-oriented game that Europeans witnessed the Native Americans playing. It has been theorized that the stick, with its webbed end, resembled a bishop's crosier, at least to a French missionary, thus, the name *la crossier*, shortened to lacrosse. The American Indian gave it a name that in its simplicity implied its place of prominence. It was known most often as simply the *game of ball*. It was also known as *baggataway*. Especially in the southern part of the United States it was often referred to in early writings as *rackets*, with lacrosse usually a term reserved for northern reaches.

Usually a game only for men, native folklore supports the idea that lacrosse was of great prominence for tribes in the South, Northeast, Midwest, Plains and across Canada.

While the game was virtually universal among North American tribes—despite the fact that few tribes shared a common language—it is uncertain where the game developed. Some feel that the Algonquin tribe in the southeastern United States created the game approximately 1,000 years ago. The Iroquois contend that their forefathers first played the game in the areas of upstate New York and eastern Canada.

In relation to a strict time frame used in many cases as a guideline for this series, it can be contended that lacrosse is not an ancient game. However, it was most certainly a traditional game, created and popularized without interference from European settlers. It was given great importance to the overall health and welfare of tribes. Also, as Oxendine (1988) points out, it is one of the very few truly American-invented team sports actively played by large numbers today.

The games were often part of a religious festival and would at times be prescribed as a healing remedy by either the village medicine man or the sick individuals themselves. As Paul Le Jeune, the French Jesuit reported from his travels in the Huron area in 1636–37: "No matter how little may be his credit, you will see then in a beautiful field, Village contending against Village, as to who will play crosse better, and betting against one another Beaver robes and Porcelain collars, so as to excite greater interest" (Altherr 1997, 437–38).

The lacrosse season depended on the tribe and the climate, but it was usually connected to significant seasonal activities, like the first thaw until the harvest. Games were scheduled with social, ritual, and religious purposes in mind. Games were played to help secure fertility, end drought, cure illness, prolong life, secure a victory, and, in general, please the gods.

Early observers were quick to understand that the game was also a valuable tool for training the warriors. As a commandant of French outposts in the Upper Mississippi Valley and Great Lakes region, Nicolas Perrot wrote about "the games and amusements of the savages" in 1718. "If one were not told beforehand that they were playing one would certainly believe they were fighting together in the open field," Perrot reported (Altherr 1997, 440). But, as Perrot and others state, the mishaps of the game that were sure to happen were always attributed to the luck of the game, not malice from another player.

Often referred to as the "little brother of war," at least once lacrosse was used specifically as a battlefield tactic. At Fort Michilimackinac (the northern tip of Michigan's lower peninsula) in June 1763 a game of baggataway was used to distract the British soldiers inside the fort. When the game ball "accidentally" flew into the fort, the gates were opened. The baggataway players rushed the doors. Three British survived.

Still, lacrosse was much more than simple warrior training. As with most American Indian sports, there was considerable preparation prior to games for both the players and the communities. Since lacrosse was the unchallenged king of contests, the preparation and participation were especially impressive. Players would often put themselves on strict dietary guidelines for weeks leading up to a particularly important game. The Cherokee of what is now North Carolina would abstain from eating rabbit because they did not want to ingest any of the negative traits of what they perceived to be a timid and witless animal. They would also abstain from sexual activity. Individual and community prayer, dance, and ceremony were common. Often elders of the group would give long, dramatic orations detailing past highlights of a tribe's lacrosse history. The combination of music, dance, speech-making, and calling upon the memories of past victories to inspire another great triumph gave the whole pregame aura a feel not unlike the modern high school pep rally (Oxendine 1988).

There was no uniformity of rules and regulations across tribes. The number of players for small, informal games was usually one or two dozen per side with an average field size being 200 to 300 yards long. As the contest gained in importance, the number of players and the size of the field grew. A mile-long field and teams with 200–300 players were not uncommon. Teams were of equal size, however. George Catlin (1976/1841) reported that the Choctaw of Mississippi had games with as many as 1,000 total players and as many as 6,000 to 8,000 spectators. These games routinely took a half to a full day to complete.

In most northern areas of the country players carried one stick, about five feet long, with some type of a webbed end for catching and carrying the ball. In southern areas it was common for players to use two smaller sticks, often with a smaller, circle-shaped web. Points were scored for throwing or running the ball through the large, gate-like goals at either

Early Native American ethnographer George Catlin illustrated this scene of ball play near Fort Gibson, Oklahoma, around 1840. While the game is similar to lacrosse, the fact that both men and boys are playing at the same time would have been considered unusual among most tribes. In general, the game of lacrosse was taken quite seriously and was a game for the warriors. (Library of Congress, Prints and Photographs Division [LC-USZC4–4810])

end of the field. Occasionally, the target would be something thicker, like a tree, and it had to be struck with the ball. The ball itself could be made out of many things. The two most common were a hard piece of wood, usually carved from a knot, or an animal skin sewn around some type of stuffing (feathers, hair, cornhusks).

Despite the huge numbers of players, there would be only about four officials. These were elder, esteemed members from both competing tribes. Neither their calls nor their integrity were ever questioned. Fair play was a staple of the competition. Injuries, which were relatively frequent and at times severe, were attributed to luck and were not a cause for retaliation, for the most part. (There are a few scattered references to fistfights breaking out during the course of the games. These were discouraged, however, by several factors, including that at times the officials carried whips or clubs to beat miscreants until they stopped unacceptable behavior; two players grappling on the ground stood a good chance of being trampled if the ball came into their area; and, most importantly, there was a pervasive attitude that sportsmanship was important and that the results were determined by a higher power anyway.) Despite the rough, vigorous nature of the game, tempers were kept in check.

As with virtually all American Indian activities, gambling was an important part of the ball play, with significant wagers being made. For many early European settlers, the fact that the Indians put such emphasis on "games," combined with the pervasive element of gambling, was a source of admonition and criticism.

The Protestants, including Roger Williams, the founder of Providence, Rhode Island, were harsher critics of Indians' games primarily because they saw them as a waste of time. They were also offensive to the Protestant work ethic. Gambling was most offensive. What the Protestants did not understand was the social significance to the games, how lacrosse and other games were played with the direct purpose of pleasing their own gods as well as themselves. The Protestant ministers, according to Eisen, saw only "Christian" sins. That the natives were "happy and content in their present state apparently could not filter through the thick curtain of moral bigotry" (Eisen and Wiggins 1994, 7).

Suggestions for Modern Play

For those who want to experience the basic energy and enthusiasm of this fast-paced sport, which involves strength, stamina, skill, and an ability to hand out and sustain some physical punishment, there is probably a lacrosse club nearby. Not too long ago lacrosse was played at the high school-age level almost exclusively at prep schools. Now it is becoming increasingly popular as a public school sport.

To truly get a glimpse of the social and ritual importance of lacrosse, or ball play, to Native Americans, it would be best to expand the level of participation. Organize a game between two high schools with as many players as possible, making sure each team has an equal number of players. Play the game at a large park, with the goals at least 300 yards apart. Make it a game to 21, so it will last a significant amount of time. Encourage full school participation in the preparation stage. Put an emphasis on learning more about the nuances and subtleties of the interconnectedness between Native American sport and Native American society at large.

At game time, wear shorts and sneakers, but males can forgo the tops and protective equipment. Remember that fair play is paramount and that the game itself must be pure for it to be pleasing to the gods.

Sources

Altherr, Thomas L. 1997. *Sports in North America: A Documentary History*, Vol. 1: *Sports in the Colonial Era 1618–1783*. Gulf Breeze, Fla.: Academic International Press.

Catlin, George. 1976 (1841). "A Choctaw Ball Game." In *The Games of the Americas, Part II*, edited by Brian Sutton-Smith. New York: Arno Press.

Eisen, George, and David K. Wiggins, ed. 1994. *Ethnicity and Sport in North American History and Culture*. Westport, Conn.: Greenwood Press.

Oxendine, Joseph B. 1988. *American Indian Sports Heritage.* Champaign, Ill.: Human Kinetics Books.

Spears, Betty, and Richard A. Swanson, 1978. *History of Sport and Physical Activity in the United States*, edited by Elaine T. Smith. Dubuque, Iowa: Wm. C. Brown.

⊞ Running

The trait of being a long-distance runner was a value seen as praiseworthy among the Native North Americans. Certainly running, which did involve community-wide competitions in pre-Columbian (prior to 1492) eras, was more than solely sport. It was also essential for commerce. Virtually all evidence suggests that the horse did not exist in the Americas prior to the Spaniards' arrival. That meant that intertribal trade, as well as the return of all hunted or gathered food, had to be done by foot and that there would be instances when time was of the essence.

In the Southwest of the United States the Zuni, Hopi, and other Pueblo Indians were known as excellent long-distance runners, and the Zuni youth began training at an early age. Also, the Crow nation from the region of North Dakota was said to value the reputation of being a fast and long-distance runner as second only to being a good warrior and hunter.

Depictions of what most people would consider superior running feats were routinely reported by white settlers and then again by early researchers around 1900. The primary reason for the Indians' superiority when it came to long-distance running is similar to the theory on why East Africa has become the preeminent source of marathon and top-flight distance runners. In both areas running is the primary and best means of transportation and is often done in hilly conditions. Therefore, the training for running begins at an early age and never really stops until well after adulthood is reached.

Running is intricately and fully interwoven into many Native American myths and folktales, helping to describe the natural order of animals and humans and even the arrangement of the constellations. Numerous variations of the "Tortoise and the Hare" story are told, emphasizing the importance of sticking with a task and making sure that one is not distracted.

That type of steadfastness would have been essential for Native American runners, particularly those who used their skills for the purposes of hunting and communication. Particularly impressive are the various communication systems across North and South America that relied on the speed and stamina of runners, as well as their ability to accurately transfer a message.

One reason that the Iroquois Nation was such a powerful force in the early colonial period of the United States was the effectiveness of its 240-mile Iroquois trail, which, with the help of running messengers, bound the various tribal groups together. The text of a late eighteenth-century Quaker settler marvels at how one of the best Iroquois runners reportedly could cover 90 rolling miles from Canandaigua, New York, to Niagara between sunrise and sunset. While the Quaker author may have found the feat unfathomable, some simple math indicates that the athlete, known as "Sharp Shins," might not have been particularly impressed with his own effort. Presuming that it was a summer day, there could be as much as 16 hours of daylight. That means that Sharp Shins would have needed to average 5.625 miles an hour. Certainly, Sharp Shins' endurance would have been tested, but his pace of 10 minutes, 40 seconds per mile is equivalent to a slow jog.

The Seneca messengers often took along small quantities of scorched cornmeal to nibble on while making their long journeys. Long-distance solo treks were not the norm, however. Usually, the Native Americans emphasized teamwork by establishing a relay of runners, each passing on the message. Accuracy was paramount, since often times the relay runners were used to send messages about war and invaders. Even more benign messages about trade with other tribes needed to be correct to create trusting relations with neighbors. The running messengers were sometimes the beneficiaries of well-maintained road systems. In New Mexico's Chaco Canyon some 200 miles of curbed roadways, at times including staircases to clear bluffs, have been unearthed by archaeological research. Similar (and more extensive) road systems have been uncovered in Central and South America (see "Latin America: Running" for a discussion on the famous Incan messengers).

Formal races were not only held but also prepared for by means of special diet and exercise regimes. Reports indicate that both the Ojibwa and the Cherokee would routinely tie sacks or pouches filled with sand or shot around their ankles for the weeks leading up to a big race. This would help strengthen the leg muscles. Then just before the start the pouches would be removed, creating a feeling of being especially light-footed. There are also strong indications that at least some North American tribes (the Mandan and Crow along the Missouri River among them) had regular racetracks that were cleared of debris and kept in order for running purposes. The Crow reportedly used a 300-yard track, and such was the emphasis on winning that most races featured several false starts. The Mandan track was significantly longer, up to three miles, and shaped like a giant horseshoe. In this way, spectators could be at the starting line and then leisurely stroll to the finish area about 100 yards away. The Mandan races attracted large numbers of competitors and spectators.

In the early nineteenth century an Osage chief named Black Dog promoted intertribal races in what is now the Kansas/Oklahoma border. The racetrack was 2.5 miles long, and the races were seen as valuable training for the Osage couriers. The notion of intertribal races has also been reported for the far-flung Iroquois in upstate New York and the Mississauga in Ontario.

The importance of running is also testified to by its place in ceremonies where a sense of competition was only part of a greater festive and/or spiritual ceremony.

In an elaborate and revered Pawnee ceremony known as "Bringing in the Tree," in which a cedar tree was cut from a timber growth so it could stand in the tribal lodge, an integral part of the ceremony consisted of a women's run. When the men could be seen from a distance of about three miles, dragging the tree back behind their ponies, the word went out and women gathered with gifts that would be placed upon "Mother Cedar." The women then raced toward the men to have the honor of tying their gifts to the tree. The first four women who reached the tree got to tie their gifts on; which would remain on the tree even when it was returned several months later to the timber where it was cut. The remaining women threw their gifts onto the tree, but their gifts did not have the permanence of the gifts the winners. While there was much merriment involved (and the middle-aged women recognized that they would not win the race), the younger women got caught up in the competitive spirit, and "when they near where the men are coming, the women run harder, for it means something to them" (Murie 1989, 341)

The Tarahumara of northern Mexico are an example of an entire culture revolving around running in general, highlighted by long-distance endurance games called kickball races. The Tarahumara's emphasis on long-distance running is given extended discussion in the next section. They were not the only people to have kickball races, however. The Hopi of Arizona participated in kickball races similar to those of the Tarahumara, but much of the Hopi's physical activity had significant spiritual meaning, including a ritualized custom of running and pursuit. On the last day of the Snake ceremonies and for four days following, male youths would gather up food and run about the village. The boys ran knowing that they would be pursued by women and maids who would attempt to catch them and take the goods. "This custom of running and pursuit is believed to have beneficial effects on crops and rain, the fields belonging to the household of the girl strong and fleet enough to secure many articles, being particularly favored with good crops" (Beaglehole 1937, 48).

For the Hopi, running was an essential part of their history, in terms of both individual achievements and their myth-legends. Among the

Hopi, "fleetness of foot and endurance are regarded as supreme psycho-physical accomplishments" (Courlander 1982, xxix).

In the early part of the twentieth century, the traditional talents of Indian distance runners began to translate to international success. Three athletes are of particular noteworthiness. Lewis Tewanima of the Hopi nation, a classmate of Jim Thorpe's at the Carlisle School, was a member of the 1908 and 1912 U.S. Olympic teams, winning the silver medal in the 10,000-meter race in 1912. Ellis "Tarzan" Brown of the Narragansett tribe was the winner of the 1936 and the 1939 Boston Marathons. The last great Native American distance runner at the international level was Billy Mills, who is of Sioux descent. Mills shocked observers when he won the gold medal in the 10,000 meters at the 1964 Summer Olympics. Mills ran 46 seconds faster than his previous best to beat the then world-record holder Ron Clarke of Australia.

Suggestions for Modern Play

Necessity was a great motivator for preparing superior long-distance runners. Each tribe needed at least some long-distance stars in order to have good channels of communication and in many cases a farther reach in their territory for hunting. The fortunes of United States world-class distance running, which took a decided downturn in the last quarter of the twentieth century, have often been cited as an example of how a soft, transportation-laden society is at a disadvantage when it comes to pro-ducing great long-distance runners. External motivation for running is a great aid. Track and field teams could use the communication relay model. Station groups of runners assigned to different teams along a course. Teams race to the finish but also must be sure to transfer the message accurately.

Sources

Beaglehole, Ernest. 1937. *Notes on Hopi Economic Life*. Oxford: Oxford University Press.

Blanchard, Kendall, and Alyce Taylor Cheska. 1985. *The Anthropology of Sport*. South Hadley, Mass.: Bergin and Garvey.

Courlander, Harold. 1982. *Hopi Voices: Recollections, Traditions and Narratives of the Hopi Indians*. Albuquerque: University of New Mexico Press.

Murie, James R. 1989. *Ceremonies of the Pawnee*. Edited by Douglas R. Parks. Lincoln: University of Nebraska Press for the American Indian Studies Research Institute

Oxendine, Joseph B. 1988. *American Indian Sports Heritage*. Champaign, Ill.: Human Kinetics Books.

▦ The Tarahumara Kickball Races

While foot racing is virtually universal in some form among the native peoples of North and South America, one mountainous group surely runs in front of all others in terms of endurance, both on their feet and in life.

The Tarahumara of the high country of the Chihuahua state in northern Mexico, located approximately 300 miles south of El Paso, Texas, are an extraordinary example of an entire community of runners. To this rough, hardscrabble location these shy and private people fled following their first encounters with the Spanish colonists in the 1500s. They call themselves the *raramuri*, meaning "foot runners." They have been known to run modern marathons and then ask in wonder why the race ended so soon.

The motto of the people says a lot: "Why walk when you can run?" Considering that foot travel is the only means of transportation, there is plenty of opportunity to run. It appears to be something that the culture of the Tarahumara accepts and actually reinforces through its daily rituals.

Traditional tales indicate that the Tarahumara would chase a single deer until the deer would drop from exhaustion. Further, "many daily activities were structured to tax the limits of one's endurance" (Blanchard and Cheska, 1985). Explorer Carl Lumholtz lived with indigenous groups in Mexico for five years in the 1890s and visited several Tarahumara groups.

No doubt the Tarahumares are the greatest runners in the world, not in regard to speed, but endurance. A Tarahumare will easily run 170 miles without stopping. When an Indian is sent out as a messenger, he goes along at a slow trot, running steadily and constantly. A man has been known to carry a letter in five days from Guazapares to Chihuahua and back, a distance of nearly 600 miles by the road. Even considering shortcuts, which he, no doubt, knew, it was quite a feat of endurance; for he must have lived, as the Indians always do while travelling, on pinole and water only. (Lumholtz 1902, 282)

The Tarahumara were not unique among Native Americans (whether North America or South America) to be very adept at the long-distance run as it related to communications, hunting, or livestock herding. The Tarahumara were unusual in their extreme emphasis of running when it came to their sport as well as how pervasive the notion of running was throughout the whole culture, including the women.

The Tarahumara are famous for their kickball game called *rarajipari* (also known as *dalahipu* or *dalahipami*), which involved kicking a small, wooden ball up and over the tough mountainous terrain, whether it was full of cacti and loose gravel or not. The kickball game was communal and involved many runners on different teams. Estimates range from as few as 2 runners to as many as 20 per team. Those not able to compete took part by marking the path, often with torches since the game would routinely last overnight. If it was agreed upon, spectators could also help their favorite team by finding the ball when it went into the reeds, high grass, or a crevice and on rarer occasions were even allowed to place the ball for their favored team, much in the manner of a golfer setting up his ball on a tee to allow for a longer strike. These endurance tests were normally around 35 miles, but some were 48-hour, 200-mile tests of will.

The shorter races were and still are held quite frequently, sometimes as the result of two men boasting about their prowess during a *tesguinada*, which is essentially a lengthy drinking binge that takes its name from the corn-and-grass beer called *tesguino* that is consumed. (Champion notes that the Tarahumara's legendary stamina for running is equaled by their stamina at the tesguinadas. Failing to drink in moderation could have something to do with the brew itself. The alcoholic drink will turn lethal within a few days, thus requiring it to be consumed rapidly.)

In these smaller races, the course is decided on immediately before the race, but in the serious, larger races, which pit one communal group against another, the courses are clearly marked beforehand. The courses range from 2 to 12 miles in length, and then a number of "laps" are decided upon. At the start of the race a row of stones is laid out, one for each lap. As a lap is completed, a stone is removed. This provides both competitors and spectators with a visual scoreboard of how much of the race has been completed.

Each team has its own ball, made of wood and about three inches in diameter. A stick is often carried by each runner to allow him to extricate a ball from a difficult location. Occasionally, it is agreed upon that hands can be used to set the ball into position, but it can never be advanced with the hands. This is done only by the feet. For this reason, the traditional Tarahumara ran barefoot. Practiced ball-racers would have thick, hardened toenails. They would stop while addressing the ball, scoop their foot underneath it, and then kick it high into the air. While the one runner stopped to address the ball, his teammates would keep moving, thus getting in position to receive the pass. Runners were allowed to drop out of the race to eat, drink, or receive medical treatment in the way of herbal rubdowns or other "cures" by the group's shaman. Once they reentered the race, however, they were not allowed to kick the ball again unless they had completed the same number of laps as the leaders of his group. "Obviously, the team that can keep the greater number of runners in the race can keep the ball moving faster, and thus win the race easier" (Bennett and Zingg 1935, 336).

Training usually took the form of men and women kicking a ball while moving down a trail during their daily routines of work, visits, and livestock herding. It could be said that they were in constant training since all members of the community ran from early childhood.

Prior to the larger races runners and their supporters undertook serious mental and physical preparations, according to Bennett and Zingg, who did their study of the Tarahumara in 1930–31. Runners would "cure" their legs for three nights before a race with boiled cedar branches and goat grease or olive oil. On the third night the team members would gather together in one house, and on this night the curing of the legs would be administered by a special man while the runner would hold his stick and the ball. Then the stick and ball would be passed to a teammate, and the process would be repeated.

During the formal races, several things would be carried or worn by the runners, including plant extracts, bits of food, dried animal blood mixed with tobacco, and dried parts of eagles or crows. Each had a purpose, either as ointments for tired muscles and joints, sustenance, or to ward off evil spirits. The latter was necessary because it was accepted practice that the opposing group's shaman would attempt to create spirit obstacles that must be encountered and overcome.

Betting was a vital part of the race, both for spectators and for the runners themselves. In fact, it was viewed as bad karma if the runners were not involved in some serious wagering. When that happened, the spectators usually curbed their own wagering.

The Tarahumara women also had their own race, called the *dowerami*. The major difference is that they used a hoop that was flung forward with a stick three to four feet in length as opposed to kicking a hard wooden ball. While their races were usually shorter, they were still serious endurance tests that typically went through the night and were accompanied by significant wagering. The women's legs were also cured the night before by old men. Both married and single women participated.

The Tarahumara's historical running feats have brought them a measure of fame. *Runner's World* magazine proclaimed these short, relatively stocky people (the average height of the men and women were 5 foot 3 and 4 foot 10, respectively, in a study done in the 1920s) the "World's Toughest Runners" in 1979. Serious medical journals have marveled at their ability to run endurance races like the Leadville, Colorado, 100-miler while wearing tire-soled sandals and being very competitive despite subsisting on a diet of about 1,500 calories a day.

Unfortunately, that fame has not translated to fortune. In the late 1990s the Sierra Tarahumara was hit with a multiyear drought, and several hundred Tarahumara children died from starvation. In fact, the runners in endurance races like Leadville were at near starvation stages themselves and competed to help bring awareness of the plight of their people.

Suggestions for Modern Play

A high school cross-country or track team would be especially well suited for the following small-scale simulation of the Tarahumara's kickball races. Since the races quite often included multiple laps, a high school track could be used. Divide into teams of eight, with the object being to move the ball around the track four times—roughly the distance of one mile. Make it mandatory for each team member to advance the ball at least once in each lap. That means that the whole team has to keep up its pace, as do the Tarahumara. A good equivalent of the Tarahumara ball would be a wooden croquet ball. Remember, the motion for propelling the ball is not so much a kick as a careful placement of the foot underneath the ball and then a forward fling.

This could be an effective exercise for building team spirit and camaraderie while breaking the monotony of the daily distance runs often used as a warm-up to the more serious and event-specific practice.

Sources

Bennett, Wendell C., and Robert M. Zingg. 1935. *The Tarahumara: An Indian Tribe of Northern Mexico.* Chicago: University of Chicago Press.

Blanchard, Kendall, and Alyce Taylor Cheska. 1985. *The Anthropology of Sport.* South Hadley, Mass.: Bergin and Garvey.

Champion, Jean Rene. 1970 (1963). *A Study in Culture Persistence: The Tarahumaras of Northwestern Mexico.* Ann Arbor, Mich.: University Microfilms.

Lumholtz, Carl. 1902. *Unknown Mexico: A Record of Five Years Exploration of the Western Sierra Madre; in the Tierra Caliente of Tepic and Jalisco; and among the Tarascos of Mcihoacan.* Vol. 1. New York: Charles Scribner's Sons.

Oxendine, Joseph B. 1988. *American Indian Sports Heritage.* Champaign, Ill.: Human Kinetics Books.

⊞ Shinny

Today the name *shinny*, especially in Canada, refers to the practice of playing a game of keepaway while on ice skates with a hockey puck and hockey sticks. Centuries ago, shinny was a relative of the noble and widespread Native American game that we call lacrosse and something of a precursor to modern field hockey.

Prior to the late nineteenth century, shinny may have been the most frequently played of all ball games in terms of the number of tribes and geographical range. Shinny was "practically universal among tribes throughout the United States" (Culin 1907, in Oxendine 1988, 50).

In most tribes shinny was the domain of women and small children and served a similar role for those people as lacrosse did for the adult male. There were areas of exception where men played, sometimes separately from women and sometimes even together.

The object of the game was to drive a ball past opponents and through their goal. The ball—ranging in size from as small as a modern golf ball to slightly larger than a baseball—was usually carved from a tough knot of wood or stuffed buckskin. Infrequently it was bone, which was the case with the Makah Indians of the Pacific Northwest, who used a whale-bone as a ball and played shinny in celebration of the capture of a whale. The stick was very much like a modern field hockey stick in that it was made of wood and had a curved end that was relatively small. One example from the Wyoming Wind River Reservation has a head that more closely resembles that found on the 1-wood in a golfer's bag, being quite thick and heavy. While sticks ranged in length from two to four feet, the norm among preserved sticks is 30 to 36 inches in length. Of course, since strict regulations were virtually nonexistent in any Native American sport, a stick was going to match the size and style of play of the person using it.

Shinny does not seem to have carried nearly the same degree of preparation or ceremony as did lacrosse. It was not marked as a means for healing the sick or changing the fates of nature, as was lacrosse. It was possible, however, to have magic enter into the equation. In "Sioux Games," written by J. R. Walker (1905–6) it was known among the Sioux that anyone could make a club (stick) but that certain people possessed the ability to make a magic club. The people possessing such a club were highly sought after for team membership, and extra-heavy wagering was placed on their team's being able to win. The Sioux men regarded shinny as "their roughest and most athletic game" (Walker 1905–6).

Shinny did share some significant characteristics with lacrosse, most of which reflected Native Americans' general emphasis on participating in vigorous play. As with lacrosse, the shinny field was usually at least 200 yards long and rectangular and at times could literally extend between two villages. There was a goal at each end, and the object was to strike the ball through the goal. Teams could be made up of very large, though always even, numbers, and touching the ball during play with the hands was illegal.

One difference is that shinny seems to have had more organization in terms of position than most of the early reports on lacrosse would indicate was the case with that game. The game was started with what we would call a face-off as two players would try to dig the ball out of a shallow hole and then pass it to a teammate. Some players defended the goal; others stayed near the middle of the field and initiated an offensive thrust toward an opponent's goal.

The game did not have the long duration of important lacrosse matches. The best of three goals and the first team to score four goals were two common ways to determine a winner.

While the references to positioning and passing sound much like modern field hockey, the Native game was played with significantly more airborne hits. A report from 1891, cited by Culin (1907) and Oxendine (1988) says that in a game in California the small ball, when hit with the hardwood, would stay airborne for "two or three hundred yards." Considering that 300 yards is considerably longer than most people can strike a golf ball (even with its roll), the distance is dubious. It does, however, suggest that the shinny players could smack it a considerable distance and that the game was often characterized by a fast-breaking style of a long hit that was then chased down by a teammate. At least in areas where long smacks were part of the game, it may have looked more like Irish hurling (see Europe: Hurling) than field hockey.

While similar games were played in Europe, particularly in the British Isles (where they were known as *bandy* in England and *shinty* in Scotland), shinny was a native and traditional sport for the indigenous people of North America.

Suggestions for Modern Play

For suggestions on how to adapt traditional shinny to a modern format, see the sections on double-ball and lacrosse. Shinny could be played by either females or males but, in respect to tradition, should probably not consist of coeducational teams.

Sources

Levinson, David, and Karen Christensen, 1999. *Encyclopedia of World Sport*, (paperback). Oxford: Oxford University Press.

Oxendine, Joseph B. 1988. *American Indian Sports Heritage*. Champaign, Ill.: Human Kinetics Books.

Spears, Betty, and Richard A. Swanson. 1978. *History of Sport and Physical Activity in the United States*. Edited by Elaine T. Smith. Dubuque, Iowa: Wm. C. Brown.

Walker, J. R. 1976 (1905–90) "Sioux Games, Parts I and II." In *The Games of the Americas*, edited by Brian Sutton-Smith. New York: Arno Press.

PLAY

▦ Archery

As was the case with so many aspects of Native American culture, the role of the bow and arrow and the skill with which it was deployed have been vastly misrepresented in the history of popular American culture. Particularly guilty of making sweeping and often erroneous generalizations about the American Indian were the moviemakers of Hollywood and that staple genre of film, the American Western.

For many Americans, their first reference to Native American culture is through the medium of television and movies. Few of these references offer anything more than gross caricatures of indigenous populations. Such was the case with archery, only this time, instead of a demeaning characterization, television and film have actually exaggerated the skill of the Indian archer.

Simply put, the American Indian archer did not typically have the technological advancements in his bow to allow for accurate, long-distance shooting. Compared to the high sophistication of archery that took place in the Middle East, Asia, medieval Europe, and even ancient Egypt, what the first European explorers encountered when they met the Indian archer—particularly in the Northeast—was rudimentary. The bows were generally made from a single piece of wood, meaning that they lacked the strength and flexibility of composite bows that were the norm in Egypt, the Middle East and Asia before Christ. Few were re-curved, which means that the end of the bow where the drawstring is attached is bent back toward the front of the bow. This allows for a shorter bow with more power.

Burke contends that "there is little if any evidence to show that the average American Indian was more than a fair shot with his bow" (Burke 1957, 170). Burke bases his opinion primarily on the quality of the in-digenous archer's equipment, namely, that the bows were not particu-larly strong, arrow shafts were often less than perfectly straight, and the fletchings (what a nonarcher would possibly call the feathers) were more ornamental than beneficial.

Burke wholeheartedly contends that the cradle of the bow is in what is often called Asia Minor, and, as he repeatedly points out, the nomadic warring tribes that swept repeatedly across the Eastern European and Western Asian steppes were superior archers. He seems to take a dis-missive approach to American archery. To state that there is "little evi-dence" to support that the indigenous archers were nothing more than ordinary is an injustice. The bows might have limited what and where they could shoot, but within that bow's range, their accuracy was very good.

Early colonial reports from New England marvel at the marksmanship and especially the speed with which Native Americans could shoot. Also, since the Indian hunter tended to be an expert stalker and was usually in a heavily wooded area, he neither needed nor could have particularly used a bow that shot extremely long distances (150 yards seems to be the outer limits for a killing strike).

Despite the technical limitations, archery was an important part of everyday life as well as a ritual custom of the American Indian and was practiced nearly universally. Young people and adults both practiced archery in a competitive format to hone their skills because it was an important tool for securing food and in warfare. By the age of five it was common for young boys to be given their first bows. At first the arrows would be blunted to avoid dangerous aspects, but as their aim became truer, they were given real arrows. Numerous are the references to chil-

This is a reproduction of a drawing of a Florida warrior with his bow and arrow. The original was by John White between 1585 and 1593. The picture demonstrates the relatively limited technological advancement of the native bow. (United States National Museum)

dren, some as young as seven, being able to hit the intended target of a bird in flight with an arrow. This is a strong refute to Burke's contention. Native Americans were indeed more than a "fair shot" with a bow.

What seems to set the Native American archer apart from traditional archers in other parts of the world are these key points: (1) he never achieved a high degree of technical advancement with his bows or arrows, (2) he did not emphasize long-distance shooting, (3) he practiced

A popular archery game among some tribes of North America was known as the "game of arrows" and involved shooting one arrow as high as possible into the sky and then trying to reload and shoot as many arrows as possible before the first hit the ground. The photograph was taken in 1906. The photographer, Edward S. Curtis, commonly staged photos for dramatic effect. (Library of Congress, Prints and Photographs Division [LC-USZ62–96723])

at moving targets more often, (4) he could find his arrows and reuse them with great frequency, and (5) a wager was usually involved when it came to competitions, with the arrows themselves often serving as the gambling stakes.

Among the popular shooting games was one often referred to as "game of arrows." The object was to shoot an arrow as high as possible into the sky, then reload, and shoot as many arrows as possible before the first arrow landed. The Mandan of the Dakota area and the Apache were both reportedly expert at this, with the Apache able to fire as many as 10 arrows into the air at once.

There were many other games created and played to test and improve an archer's marksmanship. When it came to stationary targets, the target was often an arrow itself, shot at some distance. The object would then be to strike the arrow or perhaps to have an arrow land that would cover the first arrow. Other times the target would be moving. Usually in sporting competitions this would be accomplished by having a runner who dragged something like a tarp of animal skin behind him or carried a target aloft while moving about.

Another game had a similarity to the popular hoop-and-pole (*chungke*) game, with the primary difference being that arrows were substituted for the javelin-shaped pole. Played in the Great Lakes region by young boys, the object was to stop the rolling hoop by hitting it with an arrow.

The Pima in Arizona were particularly fond of shooting at moving targets, whether it was human (as in the tarp game) or a tossed bundle of grass (à la modern-day skeet shooting). They also played one of the most challenging games in terms of skill and quick judgment. It would start with one person's shooting a target arrow. Before the target arrow landed, several others would unleash their arrows, trying to hit the spot where the lead arrow would indeed land.

In a generalized sense, the farther West one travels, the better the archery equipment of the American Indian, with the greatest degree of advancement being found in the Northwest, the Plains, and the Rocky Mountain regions. While not immediately associated with archery, Eskimo tribes were one of the few to use composite bows (perhaps out of necessity due to the relative lack of good timber) and also developed waterproof quivers and bow cases made from sealskin. It has also been theorized that the Americas were populated by migration through Asia and across the Bering Strait. In part due to their similar physical features, it has been postulated that the Eskimos were the last of the Asiatic migrators and may have already had knowledge of composite bow construction. The Inuit of North Alaska took their archery indoors during the coldest months, setting up small bird targets hung from the roof of a communal center and using miniature bows.

By the mid- to late nineteenth century, archery was becoming more popular among non-Indians as a sporting endeavor in America. This is another instance of a traditional sport (lacrosse being the best example) that had enough crossover appeal to be adopted by the settlers.

Suggestions for Modern Play

To adapt traditional archery to a modern game, the bow, shafts, and arrowheads must be made by hand. Witch hazel, beech, and ash were common woods for bows and shafts, and usually a sharpened piece of bone was the everyday arrowhead. The classic flint arrowheads that are highly prized by collectors were viewed as valuable by the Native shooters as well and thus were used only when needed (for war and for bigger game). Turkey feathers were common fletchings. Play the "game of arrows" with your homemade bows. Chances are it will be difficult to even fire a second arrow before the first lands. One tip: the arrows were held in the bow hand in this game, not in the quiver.

Sources

Altherr, Thomas L. 1997. *Sports in North America: A Documentary History*, Vol. 1: *Sports in the Colonial Era 1618–1783*, Gulf Breeze, Fla.: Academic International Press.

Burke, Edmund. 1957. *The History of Archery*. New York: William Morrow.

Levinson, David, and Karen Christensen, ed. 1999. *Encyclopedia of World Sport*, (paperback). Oxford: Oxford University Press.

Oxendine, Joseph B. 1988. *American Indian Sports Heritage*. Champaign, Ill.: Human Kinetics Books.

▦ Eskimo Endurance Contests

Testing the limits of endurance is a fairly common human endeavor. It is done today by masses in the New York City and Boston marathons, any number of triathlons, which combine swimming, bicycling, and running, and a myriad of other sporting events designed primarily to test an athlete's physical and mental stamina.

In ancient civilizations, races and sports were often routinely used as a means to test both stamina and strength. Native American sports often included a grueling component. Lacrosse, *shinny*, and double-ball games were played on huge fields and often for the entire day. The Tarahumara Indians of northern Mexico have been famous for centuries for their community-wide practice of participating in ultradistance running—both as sport and as the primary means of transportation.

Far to the north, in the cold, often desolate lands near and above the Arctic Circle, the various tribes of the Eskimo seemed particularly fond of games of endurance in their traditional cultures. They often involved some type of unique contortion of the human body, creating the opportunity for rather humorous results.

Several were what could be termed "race" games, though the race was not to be the fastest but usually to be the longest-lasting. Others seem to have been more a test of a person's pain threshold. Together they constitute a group of games that are not only illustrative of the Eskimos' approach to sport and play but also indicative of some of the generalizations that can be made with a relatively fair degree of accuracy about any number of Indian contests. Among these points are:

1. Stamina was an important characteristic of the Indian athlete.
2. Physical, even rough games not only were accepted practices but were often undertaken by both men and women.
3. It was important to be able to laugh at yourself and to accept others laughing at you with a degree of grace and humility.

The various Eskimo tribes had a number of games that tested strength and endurance, but many were done with a certain amount of lighthearted fun being at the center of the activity. One of the favorite communal games was the blanket toss (or in this case a walrus-skin toss), with the person in the air being encouraged to strike different poses while airborne. (Library of Congress, Prints and Photographs Division [LC-C2688–583])

This last point seems to be particularly important when one considers a couple of the staple Eskimo contests, outlined by Glassford. For instance, the *ikuskikmiag* is well described as the elbow-ear walk. The player supports himself by his toes and his elbows. The hands, meanwhile, are kept out of the action because it is required that they grasp the ears. Give this one a quick try. The objective was to travel the greatest possible distance before giving out or toppling over.

The elbow-ear walk had some cousins when it came to *tulugauyak*. In this competition, both the legs and the arms were placed in the sleeves of a parka and in this position, resembling a calf with its legs bound in pairs, the contestants raced to a predetermined mark. The Eskimos, not being herdsmen, did not consider the unique body position to have a connection to cattle. Instead, they saw it as a representation of a squatting raven. Glassford contends that this was an ancient game. It is possible that the race developed from ritualized imitation of the raven. Other games included the knuckle hop and the hand hop. Both involved having the weight supported by the toes and then some part of the hand (only the knuckles in knuckle hop). The idea was to move forward in a hopping motion by using only the spring generated by the toes and hands, with a rigid body. No opportunities for rest were given, and the person traveling the greatest distance was the winner.

There were also team forms of race games. One is best described as a spread-eagled carry and involved teams of five people. The person to be carried would lie face down with arms and legs apart. Each of the four limbs would then be grasped by teammates, who would carry the fifth player as far as possible before the person being carried collapsed due to the strain on the stretched limbs.

While some of these race games probably became painful as they went on, others were painful from the start. These included the *igiruktuk*, or mouth-pull, where two players would stand face-to-face, wrap their right arm around their opponent's head, and then insert their fingers in his mouth and pull, with the person turning his head toward the pull being declared the loser; and an ear-pull game that operated on the same principles, with the two contestants linked by a leather thong wrapped around their ears and the object being to back up and "pull" the opponent with you or to get him to twist his head to release the thong.

The Eskimo also had a very rough, at times deadly game called *ungatanguarneg*. This contest involved two opponents standing face-to-face and then taking turns slugging the other in the temple, shoulder, or chest, until one either succumbed or relented. The Eskimo did not engage in boxing as we know it, but it is easy to see how ungatanguarncg, because it did not allow for a defensive posture, could be lethal, especially when it was used to settle a personal dispute, leading to both more angry blows and a greater reticence to give in.

Suggestions for Modern Play

The Eskimos have both some wonderful and easy-to-adapt tests of endurance particularly the elbow-ear walk and the raven hop. These seem like good contests to promote friendly competition and a light nature where players should not take themselves too seriously, much like the old reunion picnic favorites like the sack and wheelbarrow races.

Sources

Blanchard, Kendall, and Alyce Taylor Cheska. 1985. *The Anthropology of Sport*. South Hadley, Mass: Bergin and Garvey.
Glassford, Robert Gerald. 1976. *Application of a Theory of Games to the Traditional Eskimo Culture*. New York: Arno Press.

▦ Ring and Pin

Forms of this game are frequently found throughout the Americas. The form used for this discussion was a particular traditional favorite of the Eskimo.

An easy way to think of the ring-and-pin game is to remember the cup-and-ball game that you probably played as a child. The ball is attached to a string, which is, in turn, attached to a stick that has a cup at one end. The ball will fit in the cup but not easily.

The Eskimos called the traditional game *ajagak, ayagak* (which was also the name of a string game akin to a highly developed form of cat's cradle) and *ajaguktuk*. Ajagak may have referred to the team version of the ring-and-pin game.

The pin was usually some type of sharpened stick, whether it was made from wood or more likely a sharpened bone or ivory. The word "ring" is something of a misnomer since it usually wasn't a ring shape at all. Instead, it was usually some type of a cap or object that had an opening (or many openings) that could be impaled on the "pin." Rings were often unadorned skulls of a rabbit, while others were highly stylized pieces of ivory artwork. Depending on the shape of the ring, the game might have some changes in the goal. For instance, when a bear-shaped ring was used, the game usually represented a polar bear hunt and was coupled (as it often was) with a chant. The best catch of all was to put the pin into the bear's nose hole, at which point the player would shout "*piyalga*," which means roughly, "I got him" (Glassford 1976).

The ring was attached to the pin by means of a thong of leather. A successful catch usually started with the ring being swung in as wide a half circle as possible, making for a longer vertical descent. Then players used the pin to catch or spear the ring.

The ring-and-pin games were popular across the continent. Interestingly, they were favored more by adults. The Gros Ventres tribe in Montana called it the matrimonial game as it was a favorite pastime of young men and young women. In the Northeast, some tribes used it as a means of determining marital ties. If two suitors were in line for one woman's hand, they would play the ring-and-pin game. "The winner of the game was also the winner of the maiden" (Oxendine 1988).

The means of play among the Eskimo could be quite varied but were agreed upon beforehand. Sometimes a player simply kept his or her turn until missing. Another version used a childlike counting chant that is reminiscent of some of the verbal accompaniment found in jacks games. "Thumb, first finger, second finger, third finger, little finger," and then so on for the next hand. If all 10 fingers were accounted for—meaning 10 successful and consecutive catches—then the player would give the ring a bigger swing and catch it after one and a half revolutions, signifying completion.

Making a tougher move to end a game is similar to what many people do when playing the basketball game H-O-R-S-E when they have to "prove it" by making the "E" shot a second time. Also, the 8-ball in billiards often has to be pocketed with at least a single bank shot when competitors reach a certain level of skill. Even from such a simple game as the ring-and-pin there is something to be gained from having to make a clutch move at the end to actually secure a victory, even when the player has done everything well up to that stage. Certainly, a hunting society like the traditional Eskimo community can appreciate such an exercise. A hunter may be expert at tracking and stealthily approaching a seal across a frozen patch of ice, but he must be able to steel his anxiety at the most critical moment to be able to make the deciding kill.

Sources

Glassford, Robert Gerald. 1976. *Application of a Theory of Games to the Traditional Eskimo Culture*. New York: Arno Press.
Oxendine, Joseph B. 1988 *American Indian Sports Heritage*. Champaign, Ill.: Human Kinetics Books.

▦ Snowshoeing

While probably developed in Central Asia some 6,000 years ago, the snowshoe figures most prominently in the earliest settlement of North America. This combination of wooden frame and leather straps and harnesses helped the migratory spread of the people who made the journey into North America and became an indispensable mode of winter transportation for the aboriginal peoples from Labrador to the Great Plains. During the westward expansion, traders, hunters, explorers, and surveyors all depended on snowshoes.

In Canada, particularly in the province of Quebec, the Native peoples designed a shoe made out of hardwood and leather thongs that was called a "Beaver tail" design by white settlers due to its rounded shape. This design was used to enhance travel over mountainous or rough terrain where the "traditional" tennis-racquet shape that most people are familiar with could cause problems. Historically, the Athabascan, Algonquin, and Iroquois tribes were known to have hundreds of snowshoe designs to fit varying snow and topographical conditions.

It seems reasonable to assume that indigenous people would have held races or contests on snowshoes. Certainly, they showed a propensity for athletic competition in other endeavors that simulated or enhanced hunting and warfare (*baggataway*, hoop-and-pole) as well as games that were played in winter, most prominently snow snake. There is evidence of dances and celebrations staged by snowshoe-wearing warriors to honor the snowfall, which would slow down animals like bison and deer. With their snowshoes and their abilities they would now be faster and more agile than the beasts that they hunted.

The western artist George Catlin painted a scene in the mid-1800s of 10 shirtless Ojibwa men dancing in newly fallen snow around a pole that suspended two snowshoes because they were thanking the gods for snow because now "they can run on their snowshoes in their valued hunts and easily take the game for their food" (Wolkomir 2000, 91).

Still, the first recorded "race" on snowshoes took place in 1840 and was staged by the fledgling Montreal Snow Shoe Club. In that inaugural contest, Indians were invited to participate, and the race was won by a clever native who, noticing that the course was icy, added nails to the underside of his shoes for added traction.

Snowshoeing as a recreational sport took off in Quebec in the latter part of the 1800s and was a critical element in the organization of sports and a sporting culture in Canada. Only lacrosse exceeded the total number of urban snowshoe clubs at the time. It would take ice hockey several years to surpass snowshoe in terms of popularity and level of participation.

Suggestions for Modern Play

For someone wanting to try snowshoeing, lightweight metal composites have allowed the size of the shoe to shrink, making it exceedingly easier for the novice to begin to move around. Interestingly, most new "techno" snowshoes have also dropped the tail and gone to a more rounded or oblong shape, much as the indigenous people of Quebec incorporated different design principles to fit certain utilitarian needs.

There are often snowshoe trails at ski resorts and in city parks. All it really takes is some open and, at first, relatively flat terrain to give it a try. It quickly becomes evident that it can be an exceptional cardiovascular workout, similar to cross-country skiing. Snowshoes, once mastered to a degree, can also open up previously inaccessible areas of narrow trails or hikes with steep inclines that are difficult to cover with skis.

To experience what it must have been like for the earliest Americans or the French Canadian trappers who followed, you'll need to add some extra gear, like a heavy backpack.

Sources

Morrow, Don. 1988. "The Knights of the Snowshoe." *Journal of Sport History*, Vol. 15, No. 1, pp. 5–40.
Wolkomir, Richard. 2000. "Shod for Snow." *Smithsonian*, December, Vol. 31, Issue 7, p. 90.

⊞ Snow Snake

Snow snake is about as simple a game as can be found: throw a stick across frozen ice and determine who can throw it the farthest. Sticks were of hardwood, usually about six feet long, and usually carved at both ends to imitate the head and tail of a snake. The "snake" was grabbed by its tail and thrown across a long patch of ice and snow. The objective was to get the snake to slide on the slippery surface for maximum distance. The head was usually carved to be a bit wider than the rest of the stick and to be tapered or curved upward, much like a modern ski tip. This helped the snake to slither up and over any bumps or ruts that it might encounter.

Snow snake was not what could be termed a universal Indian game. It was popular only in areas where lakes and rivers consistently froze in winter, typically the northern United States and across Canada. Called *kow-a-sa* by the Iroquois, perhaps its most passionate players, snow snake was considered a sport for its own sake. Usually the reserve of men and boys, it was played by women and girls at times. Only occasionally did it become a spectator event. It was played to determine a winner, however, and gambling on the outcome was common. According to Oxendine (1988), the bet was quite often the snakes themselves. Each player usually had several. They were typically works of folk art, with eyes and decorations included, and the wood had been buffed and sometimes even oiled to reduce the amount of friction when sliding across a cold surface. Since a well-made snow snake took considerable effort, the bets had significance.

Compared to other Indian activities, snow snake was not a particularly religious or socially significant activity. Still, the supernatural was enough of a factor to make some New England tribes throw away the snakes in the spring to make sure that they didn't turn into real snakes.

Snow snake trails had to be long, straight, and essentially flat. It was also best if they were hardened. For that purpose, boys would occasionally prepare a snow snake trail by grabbing a friend by the feet and dragging him on his back, thus flattening down a long strip of snow. If it was played on a frozen pond, lake, or river of any width, then banks of snow would be piled up to create the preferred narrow runway.

The throwing motion was usually underhanded. The most common grip was to place the forefinger or middle finger at the very end of the pole in such a manner that a flick of the finger would create more momentum. The thumb and other fingers would be wrapped around the "tail," and the nonthrowing hand would be used to balance and stabilize the long "snake" in a manner that brings to mind the very beginning stages of the run-up in the modern pole vault.

As with almost all Indian sports, the exact distance (or time) was unimportant. All that mattered was to be the farthest on that day against those competitors. In this way the Native Americans were very much like the ancient Greeks, who cared little for record keeping despite having the means to do it. Reports from the nineteenth century indicate that distances of 300 yards were common. Others have suggested that the snow snakes can travel a mile or two, though it is significant to mention that by the late nineteenth century the Iroquois, at least, had taken to the practice of adding lead to the head of the snake, thus giving a greater inertial mass. A long-distance throw could be explained by a downhill course. A well-thrown snake on smooth ice would certainly travel farther than on hard-packed snow.

This was not in the truest sense a team sport. Individuals were competing to try to achieve their longest throws. Usually, though, individuals were banded into groups of two or six, much like a bowling or billiard team, and cumulative totals of comparative wins and losses were kept for the team as well as the individual. The game was finished when the predetermined winning score had been reached.

Snow snake is a uniquely American Indian game but is not one (like lacrosse) that has had any degree of crossover appeal for non-Indian populations or in mainstream school athletic contests. Therefore, it is rarely played today, and the Iroquois are the only tribe that ascribes much prominence to the activity.

There are some "cousins" of snow snake in the world of traditional sports and games. In the southwestern areas of the United States a similar game was played with a bone or horn used as the thrown object. In the islands of Polynesia several different groups of people play a markedly similar game that they refer to as dart throwing.

Sources

Beauchamp, W. M. 1976 (1896). "Iroquois Games." In *Games of the Americas*, Part 2, edited by Brian Sutton-Smith. New York: Arno Press.

Blanchard, Kendall, and Alyce Taylor Cheska. 1985. *The Anthropology of Sport.* South Hadley, Mass.: Bergin and Garvey.

Milne, A. A. 1928. *The House at Pooh Corner.* New York: E. P. Dutton.

Oxendine, Joseph B. 1988. *American Indian Sports Heritage.* Champaign, Ill.: Human Kinetics Books.

▦ Swimming

Perhaps more than any other large region of the world, swimming was a natural and essential part of life for the Native American. The natives of North America typically grew up around water, with almost all establishments being situated on a river, lake, or bay.

Geographic location alone, however, does not explain why the American Indian was such a superior swimmer. Most European sailors couldn't swim at all, even though they literally spent months on the open water. What made the difference for the Native American population is that they consciously made the art of swimming a fundamental part of childhood lessons for both boys and girls, recognizing that to be able to swim could make life safer and more fruitful.

Hieroglyphic and early written evidence indicates that the ancient Egyptians and probably the later Greeks knew of the "crawl" stroke. Both of these societies emphasized swimming lessons, at least for the upper class. For that reason, it cannot be said that the crawl was invented in North America. It can, however, be confidently stated that the Native Americans popularized the stroke that today is known as the freestyle, the fastest of the strokes used in competitive sprint events. The crawl is the first stroke that most swimmers learn today (at least after the dog paddle). Its essential element is that while one arm reaches forward with a slightly cupped hand, the other arm is under the water pulling back toward the waist.

If the crawl had been once known in Europe, it had long since disappeared from disuse by the time of European colonization of North America. The breaststroke, where both hands come together under the chin and then are spread apart, was the European standard.

George Catlin has left us a detailed description of the technique used by the Mandan in the 1830s, but earlier accounts from the Eastern shore also indicate that the crawl was in use. William Wood, an English settler, writing ca. 1634, says the indigenous peoples swam "not after our English fashion of spread arms and legs which they hold too tiresome." Wood goes on to note that they swam well in swift and rough waters, could float still like a log, enjoyed diving and then surfacing some distance away like a fishing duck, and taught their young to swim (in Altherr 1997, 22). A hundred years later a Virginia planter in Roanoke named William Byrd tells of how on one frosty morning several people went for a swim, including "one of our Indians." "They strike out not both hands together but alternately one after another, whereby they are able to swim both farther and faster than we do" (Altherr 1997, 24).

That Catlin went to such pains, in the late 1830s, to give a detailed description of the arm motion and side-to-side rocking of the upper body indicates that the standard American Indian stroke was still not a common sight among the non-Indian population, a fact that Catlin himself directly states. Benjamin Franklin, in a lengthy personal letter to a water-phobic friend written before 1769, takes pains to describe the breaststroke—not the crawl—as the preferred manner for swimming. At some point, the general populace came to the same conclusion that Wood, Byrd, and Catlin had made years before: the Indians had a better way to swim that was worth adopting.

Swimming was not confined to Native American men. In fact, all children were encouraged to learn to swim, and women would routinely go, as a group, for dips. As was the case with other sporting endeavors, women learned to swim with skill, endurance, and enthusiasm.

Sources

Altherr, Thomas L. 1997. *Sports in North America: A Documentary History*, Vol. 1: *Sports in the Colonial Era 1618–1783*. Gulf Breeze, Fla.: Academic International Press.

Oxendine, Joseph B. 1988. *American Indian Sports Heritage*. Champaign, Ill.: Human Kinetics Books.

GAMES

⊞ Gambling

Whether it was a well-planned lacrosse game pitting hundreds of players from separate villages against each other or a small group of children playing with tops, gambling was a standard accompaniment to Native American sports and games. The question is both obvious and multidimensional. Why was gambling such a pervasive part of life in the many varied tribes of North America?

A number of answers or suggestions to this question have been raised. Especially in small-stakes, friendly games of chance, betting added to the enjoyment of the contest. Others have claimed that gambling created a circular form of economics, since the goods would, in most cases, stay within a tribe even as they were passed from loser to winner. Since the notion of sharing wealth with the whole tribe was prevalent among many indigenous people, there have been suggestions that gambling practices were reinforced not by the notion of economic gains for the winners but rather that gambling practices were "influenced very much by concern for altruism and accord" (Flannery and Cooper, 1976/1946).

Perhaps a better explanation for the preponderance of gambling in indigenous American cultures is that prior to European colonization and the subsequent loss of their native lands there was a great deal of natural wealth and leisure time. Combine inherent wealth with a philosophy of sharing and gambling loses many of the evil connotations often ascribed to it by Puritan settlers of the seventeenth century.

Gambling by all accounts was pervasive and seems to be spread across tribal groups. Colonial-age observances from New England, Virginia, Carolina, the Great Lakes, and Louisiana all mention gambling. European commentators spoke of gambling in varying degrees of criticism, some simply stating its prevalence and others condemning the practices as a sign of the heathen nature of the natives.

Gambling was also a cause of consternation for some within the tribes, at least according to French Jesuit de Brebeuf, whose narrative was liberally spiced with valuable anthropological observations (Eisen 1994, 10). He says that "gambling never leads to anything good; in fact, the Savages themselves remark that it is almost the sole cause of assaults and murder."

It is significant to note that gambling was a sport in itself. The issue was to win the bet, not to win something that was necessarily of monetary value. Eisen's research indicates that there were times when the items wagered were wildly disparate in terms of value. Others have disagreed, like Flannery and Cooper in their study of the Gros Ventre of Montana, who specifically noted that like items had to be wagered (a handkerchief against a handkerchief, a swift horse against a swift horse) and that in the rare cases where two different items were wagered, they were seen as having equal value to the two bettors.

There do seem to be some standard precautions against creating social havoc through gambling. One was that only items in a gambler's personal possession could be wagered. That way no gambling debt was incurred. As it relates to games of chance, it was also understood that in the long run winnings and losses would be relatively equal for everyone involved. The matter of being a good sport about losing was important. Much as a player injured in a lacrosse game knew not to attempt to seek personal revenge against the person who delivered the blow, the losing gambler understood that it was important to pay up and accept the outcome. This was not always the case, as de Brebeuf's narrative suggests. Also, success in gambling did not translate into significant social status within a tribe, especially compared to successes in athletics or battle. Conversely, a person who gambled in a foolhardy fashion or was known to repeatedly engage in high-stakes affairs was looked down upon and would not be considered for important tribal positions. Even gamblers considered touched by magic "power" were not given any great amount of prestige within the tribe. If anything, they were given fewer opportunities to gamble because it was assumed that they would win.

Gambling was a part of virtually all sports and games. As such, children often wagered what goods they had (often arrows or the gaming pieces themselves). Women were also allowed to gamble. Many games of chance, which could be grouped into the category of dice games as well as guessing games like the moccasin game and the hand game, were prominent parts of American Indian leisure activities. The Navajo created literally hundreds of songs to accompany gambling pursuits.

Sources

Eisen, George, and David K. Wiggins, 1994. *Ethnicity and Sport in North American History and Culture.* Westport, Conn.: Greenwood Press.
Flannery, Regina, and John M. Cooper. 1976 (1946). "Social Mechanisms in Gros

Ventre Gambling," *Southwestern Journal of Anthropology*, Vol. 2, No. 4. Reprinted in *The Games of the Americas*, Parts 1 and 2, edited by Brian Sutton-Smith. New York: Arno Press.

Oxendine, Joseph B. 1988. *American Indian Sports Heritage*. Champaign, Ill.: Human Kinetics Books.

⊞   Pa-Tol Stick and Plum Stone: Two Examples of North American Games of Chance

In 1907 Stewart Culin's huge work, *Games of the North American Indians*, detailed the games and sports of approximately 250 tribes in North America. Of those, 95 percent were determined to engage in one or more activities that Culin termed "games of chance" (Oxendine 1988, 142).

These differed from the other primary category that Culin outlined, games of dexterity. A simple way of thinking of the difference is that games of chance were essentially like our current tabletop games. Games of dexterity were closely associated to what we would commonly term sports and involved physical skills and often required strength, speed, endurance, keen hand–eye coordination, or some combination of them. This section looks at two of the more common games of chance. Both could be easily adapted for modern play by following the descriptions.

Pa-tol stick was one such game. There were elements of both luck and strategy involved in the game. It has some similarities to backgammon (one of the world's most ancient "race" games). The most important aspect of the game was the stick itself, which was flat and had two sides, with one side marked, the other side blank. Throughout the Americas, the "dice" were two-sided implements, as opposed to the six-sided cube that is our most common die. Two-sided dice were also the norm in other areas (see Africa: Abbia).

The dice could be many different things: flat stones, bone, seeds, strips of sugarcane, or flat sticks. Fletcher describes a game that she calls the pa-tol stick game, played by the Pueblos. The Navajo called the same game forty stones. The sticks were similar in shape to a modern domino, being about four and a half inches long, an inch wide, and a half inch thick. The game would be played with only three sticks. Two would be marked in the same fashion on one side only. The third would be marked the same way on one side and then would have a separate, distinctive mark on the opposite side. (In other variations, all three sticks have one blank side, and the opposite side is marked in the same manner. The manner in which the fall of the sticks was scored also varied greatly between tribes.) Play was almost exclusively by men in the Pueblo tribe. In other tribes men and women played dice, though usually separately.

The pa-tol sticks would be thrust down upon a stone, which would cause them to bounce before they landed. How they landed determined the number of points that were scored. While at first glance this would seem to be strictly a matter of luck, it was reported by Lummis and quoted in Culin's work that the experienced players were very adept at getting the score that they desired by the way that they held the sticks and how much force they exerted on the downward thrust of the sticks.

What makes it a race game is that the sticks were thrown inside a circle formed by 40 stones, divided into quarters of 10 stones each, easily distinguished because there would be an open space between each group of 10 stones. The object was to race around the circle, using a wooden stick or reed as the counter, and return to the space where one had started. Landing in an open space (a roll of 10 at the start of the game) meant a second turn. There was danger, though. If another player (this version of the game could accommodate more than two players) landed in the same space as another player, then the first player was "killed" and had to go back to his or her original starting spot. Players could move in either direction around the circle, but only expert players chose to charge around in an opposite direction because this left them vulnerable to attacks from both behind and in front. The first person to successfully make his or her way around the full circle was the winner. As was typically the case, gambling by both players and spectators was a vital part of the festivities. According to a Navajo legend, the Navajo invented the game.

Plum stone is played by tossing a certain number of plum seeds into the air and catching them with a basket. This game had any number of variations and was also routinely called the bowl game. Fletcher describes a version played by the Omaha women that used five stones. Other descriptions indicate seven stones were tossed with the bowl.

In each, specific point totals related to certain configurations of how many marked or unmarked sides were up. Generally, the ideal throw was to have all like sides land facing up. Several combinations of throws would not be worth any points, and at that point the other player would have the chance to throw the dice and then catch them in the wide bowl, which required a flat bottom. The contest would be played to a predetermined score, be it 50 or 100, with the same number of beans used as capital. A player who scored points would take that same number of beans from the pile. The game continued until one player had captured all of the beans.

The importance of these games is difficult to gauge. In ancient times it has been suggested that such games were often played as a means to cure the sick. Later they were played primarily for diversion. Evidence recovered from burial grounds suggests that dice games have been played in the southwestern United States for more than 2,000 years. While the popularity of such games waned in the late nineteenth century (in part, due to the introduction of playing cards), Culin's exhaustive

Gambling was a central part of Native North American culture. Women were also ready gamblers. These late nineteenth-century women from the Central Plains of Oklahoma play a form of plum stone, where marked seeds are tossed into the air and caught in a basket. (Library of Congress, Prints and Photographs Division [LC-USZ62–112332])

survey indicates that such games of chance were played by virtually all tribes across the breadth and depth of North America.

Suggestions for Modern Play

When adapting either pa-tol stick or the plum seed game to modern play, the key element for the players is to determine how to score the sticks or seeds once they have landed. To do this, make a diagram of the possible scenarios and affix the higher point total to the most difficult throws. In pa-tol stick, written descriptions indicate that the top score was 10 if all three sticks had a blank side, 15 if one stick was marked on both sides. For specific ways to mark the plum seeds when the game is played with five seeds, Fletcher's book is instructive.

Sources

Eubank, Lisbeth. 1976 (1945). "Legends of Three Navaho Games." *El Palacio*, Vol. 52, No. 7, July. Reprinted in *The Games of the Americas*, Parts 1 and 2, edited by Brian Sutton-Smith. New York: Arno Press.
Fletcher, Alice C. 1994 (1915). *Indian Games and Dances with Native Songs*. Lincoln: University of Nebraska Press.
Oxendine, Joseph B. 1988. *American Indian Sports Heritage*. Champaign, Ill.: Human Kinetics Books.

⊞ The Moccasin Game

This was a guessing game where the object was to find an object after it had been hidden under four pieces of cloth. The moccasin game's name comes from the traditional practice of using moccasins to hide the ball. It was also at times known as the bullet game because the round lead bullets used in older-style guns were often used as the gaming pieces. It is the ancient forerunner to the favorite of scam artists commonly known as the shell game.

The moccasin game was similar to other Native American guessing games in several ways: it did not involve any type of complex calculations like checkers or chess; it generated considerable gambling interest, from both the players and the spectators; it involved trickery and sleight-of-hand deception; and participants often felt that they could be more successful by calling upon spiritual input to aid their perceptive ability. Because it was a game that moved quickly and was played for stakes, part of the equipment of the game consisted of sets of sticks to keep track of the scoring. Usually, a set of 20 sticks was used for counting, with larger sticks used to mark when a set of 20 had been reached.

One interesting characteristic of the moccasin game was that it was played with musical accompaniment. Traditionally, it involved both a double-sided drum and chanting songs. By the 1960s, as the game's popularity had faded and it was being played by relatively few tribes, the Chippewa or Ojibway of Minnesota among them, the songs had disappeared from the game's lexicon because even the elders could not remember them (Flaskerd, 1976 [1961]).

The drums and songs were not designed to soothe, however. They were used in an effort to distract the person who was guessing from watching the person who was hiding the ball or bullet under the moccasins. According to some reports, the moccasin game most resembled the modern shell game in this manner because the person dealing the bullet would often add his or her own incessant chatter to the musical accompaniment while mixing in facial and body hitches and feints, all in an effort to throw off the person trying to choose the correct moccasin. The process of selecting a moccasin was done by slapping it or turning it with a long slender pole, usually made of some type of hardwood. Flaskerd reports that in his own personal collection he has two of varying lengths, with handles made of different styles. "This may be due to the user having the idea that the nature of the handle might affect his luck" (Flaskerd, 1976 [1961]).

The moccasin game's origin is not exactly known, but it is regarded as one of the oldest of all Native American games and appears to have been played by most groups long before European settlement. The Navajo have a wonderful old folklore that explains both how the game began and also why our day is split into darkness and light. As the story goes, before there were humans, sometimes the gods would tire of being simply gods and at times would change themselves into animals and birds. During one such time they began to argue about the proper degrees of lightness and darkness in the world. To solve the problem they formed two teams and played the moccasin game. They used a stone of turquoise hidden under a pair of moccasins. They played a long time but eventually ended in a tie and decided that the tie meant that the day should be split evenly between light and dark. (A tie in such a game makes sense. If only two moccasins are used, the chance of being right would be 50 percent. The longer the game is played, the greater the likelihood that such an outcome will occur.)

There were some variations to the game. Flaskerd suggests that the Ojibway used four balls, with one marked distinctively. This seems to be more the exception, and it would certainly have required a high degree of dexterity to manipulate the balls in such a way that each was hidden but still moved about. At other times the objective was not to pick the moccasin hiding the ball on the first try, but to get it on the second try or to avoid it for as long as possible.

Many tribes along the northern Pacific Coast played a game referred to by Fletcher as "hiding the disks," which had the similar characteristics of hiding a designated piece under cover and then trying to deceive a group of guessers. In this game, nine disks were used with one marked in a special way and referred to as the chief. The player doing the hiding, with much dramatic flair, pools the disks into two groups, both covered with some type of bark, leaf, or other material. A member of the guessing group chooses the pile, the disks from that pile are rolled out, and if the chief is in the pile, then a counting stick is given to the guessing group. Another game, which had an "either one or the other" component, was the hand game and involved guessing which hand a small stick was in. This was a very common guessing game. The moccasin game was quickly adopted by white settlers, who also used it as a means for gambling. It became popular enough with colonists that laws were written prohibiting the play of "bullets" and making it a finable offense.

Suggestions for Modern Play

As was the practice among most Native groups, play the game while seated around a large blanket. Instead of gambling valued possessions like lacrosse sticks, food, clothing, and housing, as was often the case, choose another item that was sometimes used as the wager, especially in an informal setting—the loser cooks dinner for the winner. Play the game at first in a quiet manner, with no audio distractions. Then add the drum and make up a song that keeps time with the deceptive motion of hiding the bullet. Finally, let the person doing the hiding add his or her own array of words, movements, and facial expressions and then determine how the ratio of correct to incorrect guesses is impacted by adding distractions.

Sources

Flaskerd, George A. 1976 (1961). "The Chippewa or Ojibway Moccasin Game." *The Minnesota Archaeologist*. Reprinted in *Games of the Americas*, Part 2, edited by Brian Sutton-Smith. New York: Arno Press.

Fletcher, Alice C. 1994 (1915). *Indian Games and Dances with Narrative Songs*. Reprinted, Lincoln: University of Nebraska Press.

Oxendine, Joseph B. 1988. *American Indian Sports Heritage*. Champaign, Ill.: Human Kinetics Books.

⊞ OCEANIA

INTRODUCTION

Oceania is a vast area defined primarily by its geographic presence in the Pacific Ocean as opposed to specific shared racial or national heritage. Perhaps that is why the region is marked more by its differences—to other regions of the world and from one culture to another within its own region—than by broad similarities. In the study of its ancient and traditional sports and games, Oceania is especially noteworthy because of these differences, some large and others more subtle.

For our purposes, Oceania includes Australia, Melanesia, Micronesia, and Polynesia. The latter includes both New Zealand and the Hawaiian Islands and most of the thousands of islands—many still uninhabited—that lie between the two far-flung locations. The broadest similarity among all of these people that was significant to how sports could be shaped is that they were a Stone Age population until modern immigration from Europe or Asia. That means that their tools, thus their sports equipment, were confined primarily to rock and plant life. Another important similarity across the region that impacts the modern scholar of traditional and ancient sports is the lack of written language. This is not unique to Oceania. The same situation exists in sub-Saharan Africa and throughout most of the Americas.

WHAT CAN BE CONSIDERED "ANCIENT" IN OCEANIA

Once again it becomes necessary to be willing to make a leap of some faith when we apply the word "ancient" to any of the games of the indigenous Oceanic population. While the ancient civilizations of Greece, Egypt, China, the Middle East, Persia, and India left copious documentation in both language and visual depictions, many Oceanic cultures are devoid of such permanent history. Part of this can be attributed to the climate combined with the construction skills: plant-based implements won't survive thousands of years in a tropical jungle. Theirs is instead a history of oral record and repetitive practice and refinement of traditional patterns of behavior. It can simply not be stated with any high degree of certainty what these people were doing for amusement or physical challenge (other than subsisting) 2,000 years ago. Even in the cases of the rare archaeological finds that can be dated (stone tools and totems, a boomerang), taking the next step of describing what exactly the inhabitants were doing with these things is by its very nature a supposition.

This is why most of the research used to formulate the section on sports and games of Oceania is ethnographic in its approach. The early studies of ethnic groups at a time when they had encountered little previous contact with settlers, industry, or modernization offer clear and sometimes detailed descriptions of traditional games and sports. Activities considered traditional forms of play by the people of Oceania when records first began to be kept must stand as their "ancient" history.

THE PEOPLE

The diversity of the people and cultures in Oceania is huge. In Australia alone it has been estimated that between 500 and 900 tribes existed at the time of European colonization. Some geographic descriptions should help familiarize the reader with the primary regions that make up the relatively arbitrary heading known as Oceania.

Australia is the largest island in the world and is considered a continent. Much of the interior of this huge mass is considered essentially inhospitable and most of the traditional populations (numbering a rather scant 300,000 people at the time of European colonization) were located around the island's lengthy perimeter. *Melanesia* is a group of islands in the South Pacific that form a crescent shape to the northeast of Australia and lie between the equator and the Tropic of Capricorn, including New Guinea, the third largest island in the world (after Australia and Greenland). *Micronesia* is a Greek derivation meaning small (*mikros*) island (*nesos*). The smallest group in Oceania, it is actually a series of islands located in the Western Pacific and north of the equator and includes the Federated States of Micronesia, the Northern Mariana Islands, and the Marshall Islands. *Polynesia* is the general term for the many island countries that are commonly thought of when someone uses the term "South

Seas." Together they form a rough triangle with the axis points being New Zealand in the southwest, the Hawaiian Islands in the north, and the isolated Easter Island in the extreme east of the Pacific Ocean. Other major islands of Polynesia include Tahiti, Fiji, and Samoa.

At times, Oceania is defined as including the island groups of Indonesia, Taiwan, and the Philippines. This book has agreed with most recent definitions that these islands are more closely associated with Asia in their history and their present-day culture. Because part of New Guinea is under Indonesian rule (known as Irian Jaya) there are a few brief instances where the tribal groups mentioned may actually live in Indonesia but are considered of Melanesian descent.

Even without including Indonesia, Taiwan, and the Philippines, there are still more than 10,000 islands in the vastness of the Pacific Ocean that are considered to be part of Oceania. While some are rather small, in total, excluding Australia, they still account for approximately 317,000 square miles. In 1990 there were an estimated 26.5 million people living in Oceania, with more than 17 million of those living in Australia.

Much of the history of these people is through tales and songs, some of which have been described by dedicated researchers in the past century. They can be called a Stone Age people, since they did not have metals or a written language. They are not, however, uncivilized as was often the implied or directly stated assertion of nineteenth-century observers who were either colonists or missionaries. It is now known that there was a fairly extensive amount of trade, travel, and interaction between various groups. Often this was in the shape of war. The concept of war—the banding together of like-minded people under the direction of a military leader to do battle against an opposing force—is itself a sign of an advanced civilization, no matter how savagely or brutally the combatants wage their battles.

As has already been suggested, the people of Oceania form a very heterogeneous population. Even the ocean itself was not as omnipresent a factor as one might first conclude, since many separate tribes or cultures who lived in the substantial inland areas of Australia, New Guinea, and New Zealand never encountered the ocean. Still, the element from which the region's name springs is a binding force for a majority of the Oceanic people. This relation to the sea from infancy helped to tone young bodies into strong, agile athletes. The process of natural play creating island upon island of athletes has been suggested as the one great binding similarity of the diverse and far-flung Polynesian peoples: there was "an unbroken rhythm of life handed down the generations, an athletic and musical ritual governing their mental and bodily activities" (Umminger 1963, 42). Throughout Oceania, dance and music often were intertwined with contests of an athletic nature, either through direct rhythmic accompaniment or with post-match festivities.

A DIFFERENT NOTION OF SPORT

Still, the differences seen in this region of the world do much to define Oceania in terms of its play, games, and sports among traditional societies. There are two specific sporting activities prevalent in all other areas of the world that large numbers of the Oceanic people had little interest in: archery and gambling games.

The overall lack of competitive archery and a corresponding lack of development in the craftsmanship of the bows and arrows that do exist are a regionwide phenomenon, with the Australian Aborigine the prime example. Australia is the only continent where native archery was not developed. Whether due to isolation keeping the spread of trade and ideas from reaching its shores, a lack of raw material, or the fact that an alternative weapon (the boomerang) was developed is a matter of conjecture. Regardless, the bow and arrow were significantly less important throughout Oceania than in Asia, Europe, Africa, North America, and the Middle East. Primarily for comparative purposes with other world regions, a short section on archery in Oceania is included.

The more sweeping concept of gambling is known to have existed, but there is a significant lack of the specific types of games that might be grouped into a classification of "board games" or "tabletop games." Ancient history is rife with games that emphasized numeric skill along with chance and were often used as vehicles for gambling. There are *senet* from ancient Egypt and the similar backgammon-style counting game from the royal Sumerian tombs of Ur in what is now Iraq; *mancala* and all of its derivatives throughout Africa; games with knucklebones throughout Europe and the Middle East; *weiqi* (go) in China; *pachisi* in India; and a wide array of gambling-inspired dice games in North America. In Bell's classic, two-volume set *Board and Table Games from Many Civilizations*, only one game hails from Oceania, and it, the Maori game of *mu torere*, was a late addendum to the second volume, which was published nine years after the first volume.

The theory that differences define the region is also applicable when it comes to comparing the various groups within Oceania. A matter of great variation in Oceania is the relative degree of competitiveness ascribed to games and matches. Among the Australian Aborigines very few games of physical skill and chance were played with the primary purpose of determining a winner or the "best man," according to Roth in his 1902 field survey "Games, Sports and Amusements," a work still considered to be among the most comprehensive on the subject.

In contrast, the Hawaiians trained for specific events, placed bets on the outcome of sporting events, and held elaborate sporting festivals that have been compared to the ancient Olympics of Greece. The ancient Hawaiians held the *Makahiki* Games each year. In terms of its annual duration, it far surpassed the Greek Olympics. While the Greeks wrapped up their affairs in five days, the Makahiki lasted up to four lunar months from mid-October until mid-February. Work ceased, and war was forbidden during this time while competitors came together to test their skills against one another in surfing, spear-throwing, wrestling, bowling disks, and the *holua*, a uniquely Hawaiian sport that could be described as dry-land bobsledding.

The reader will find that many of the topics are general in nature and try to be inclusive of the different practices or approaches to things like games that featured a ball, the use of canoes, and different approaches to physical-contact sports like wrestling and boxing.

It also is worth highlighting two of the more exotic sports that give us another hint that the people of Oceania did perhaps share one common trait—that of daredevil. One of those already mentioned is the Hawaiian holua. This competition of sledding on dry land was highly organized, extremely dangerous, and especially exciting. Courses have been estimated to be as long as two miles and were constructed with smoothed surfaces, primarily on the island of Hawaii. Sleds were narrow and long with two runners, and riders rode headfirst. Being the fastest was the objective. This competition was especially popular with Hawaiian royalty.

Several thousand miles away in New Hebrides (one of the Melanesian Islands), the natives of Maleka were enjoying the forerunner of modern bungee jumping. They constructed a tower some 80 feet in height with attached vines that dangled down toward a cleared pit. The young men of the region would take turns diving off the tower with vines of various length tied around their ankles. The person who dared to dive from the highest point was declared the winner.

Sources

Bell, R.C. 1979. *Board and Table Games From Many Civilizations* (revised double edition). New York: Dover.

Blanchard, Kendall, and Alyce Taylor Cheska. 1985. *The Anthropology of Sport*. South Hadley, Mass.: Bergin and Garvey.

Howell, Reet. 1996. "Traditional Sports, Oceania." In *Encyclopedia of World Sport*, edited by David Levinson and Karen Christensen, Santa Barbara, Calif.: ABC-CLIO, pp. 1083–1093.

"Oceania." 1994–2001. *Encyclopedia Britannica Online*.

Roth, Walter E. 1976 (1902). "Games, Sports and Amusements." *North Queensland Ethnography*, No. 4, Brisbane, Australia: George Arthur Vaughan, Government Printer. Reprinted in Studies in Play and Games series. New York: Arno Press.

Umminger, Walter. 1963. *Supermen, Heroes and Gods*. English ed. London: Thames and Hudson.

SPORTS

⊞ Canoe Racing

In the Melanesian and Polynesian societies canoe racing was one of the most important sporting activities and was deeply seated in the social and economic activities of the total community. For traditional communities, the canoe was the primary means of transportation to fishing grounds and other off-island locations and usually was vital in any type of warfare. Therefore, being skilled and strong in a canoe—whether it was a single or double hull or outfitted with a flotation device, a sail, or both—was an essential part of adulthood. The natural urge to test one's skill against another led to informal races, which led to organized, ceremonial regattas in some regions of Oceania.

In the Melanesian societies in southern New Guinea, Guadalcanal, Manus Admiralty Island, Hall Sound, Aroma, and Gaile the practice of canoe races has been reported. Often these took the shape of challenge races between older children who were still honing their skills. Thus, they were not spectator sports. Nor were they especially well organized or monitored. An exception to the rule of Melanesian canoe races being spontaneous acts of natural childhood competitiveness can be found among the Trobriands of Papua New Guinea. They held special races with miniature canoes, and these were competitive endeavors performed as a *kayasa* ritual. A kayasa was an obligatory festival with a specific purpose, organized by the headman and accompanied with great feasting. While not always centered on a source of amusement—as would be the case with the miniature canoe races and other common themes like dancing and the tug-of-war—the kayasa did create feelings of community and shared direction. In this particular case, the miniature canoe races had the purpose of enhancing community spirit.

In Polynesian societies like Hawaii the canoe races were definitely accredited significantly greater pomp and ceremony. They were fond of betting on the outcome of the races, and wagering was a strong component of the sport. In general, Hawaiians enjoyed betting on their sports and games. In this way they are similar to the indigenous North American Indians while separating themselves from many Oceanic cultures. In Rotuma, a large volcanic island that was annexed by Fiji (then a possession of Great Britain) in 1881 and is relatively isolated from the two main Fijian islands, canoe races for women were also reported.

While Howell states that canoe racing was of greater significance in Melanesian and Polynesian societies in his thorough overview of traditional sports of Oceania, one should not infer that it did not take place in Micronesian societies. (In general it is fair to say that canoe racing was not a central activity for the Aboriginal Australians. Their canoes were very rudimentary—usually little more than strips of broad bark lashed together at the ends and plugged with mud. There is no significant evidence to suggest that the Australians practiced sea travel. Oliver suggests that the Aborigines' sparse population, general abundance of resources, and the fact that there was no visual destination to sail toward would have effectively rendered the notion of sea travel a moot point. Instead, the Aboriginal canoes, rafts, and floating boards were means of getting around in rivers and coastal areas and were propelled by hand or a push pole.)

The inhabitants of the Micronesian Truk Island, known now as Chuuks, were fond of any type of race, and canoe races were especially popular. They used paddle-powered canoes. Usually, the races were of a spontaneous nature, but once a race had begun, "spectators on the shore shriek, run up and down, and express their opinion about the individual canoes" (Bollig 1927). They also were fond of racing model canoes.

The canoe was of such vital importance that significant rituals often accompanied its manufacture and continued care. For the Tikopia of the Solomon Islands, these were of a complex religious nature where the construction of the canoe, the tools used for the construction, and repair were dedicated to guardian spirits. Even with a canoe well protected by the afterlife spirits—or extra human beings, as they were sometimes referred to—it was still necessary to hold rites on occasion to get continued cooperation during the use of the canoes in fishing activities.

The canoe race stands today as one of the most significant symbols of Hawaii's significant sporting past, which was effectively denuded by missionaries in the 1800s, who repressed the native Makahiki games in the belief that they were heathen in nature. They also resented the extensive, four-month curtailment of work. Today during Aloha Week the most popular event is the Moloka'i-to-O'ahu canoe race, a competition where six-man crews propel their outrigger canoes at speeds up to eight knots over the 40-mile course.

Beyond its significance to sport, the canoe stands as a much more important tribute to the Polynesian and Melanesian sailors' daring, seamanship, and willingness to explore. It was also a testament to a group or clan's ability to work together and to provide an economic surplus to sustain the building process, which spanned several months and usually involved the effort of an entire village.

In the case of the Lauans (a group in the Fiji Islands), the prospect of building a single-hulled sea canoe, with sailing mast and an outrigger float, took much planning. Just the aspect of choosing, felling, and extricating a suitable tree trunk from the jungle took significant work, effort and resources, since the workers had to be fed and often an initial payment made to the master carpenter.

When the amount of work and effort is considered, it is easy to understand why even neighboring villages would take part in the initial launch of a new canoe, as is evidenced by the following account of a ceremonial launching among the Trobriands of Papua New Guinea in the early 1900s:

Soon after the painting and adorning of the canoe, a date is fixed for the ceremonial launching and trial run, the *tasasoria*, festivities as they are called. Word is passed to the chiefs and headmen of the neighbouring villages. Those of whom own canoes and who belong to the same . . . community have always to come with their canoes and take part in a sort of regatta . . . (O)n the *tasasoria* day a whole fleet of brand new or renovated canoes assemble on the beach, all resplendent in fresh colours and decoration of cowrie shells and bleached pandanus streamers. (Malinowski 1922, 147).

Malinowski went on to report that as many as 1,000 people would be on hand for a ceremonial launch if the canoe belonged to one of the chiefs, in part because the chiefs held significant banquets to show off their wealth and as a means to repay the canoe builder. Once the canoe was rigged with a mast and sail, it would make a trial run. While not a race per se, it was a display of the new canoe's operating effectively in conjunction with a fleet of other canoes. If it was a chief's canoe, it probably was the fastest and best, but even if it was not, the other canoes would hold back to allow the new canoe (and its owner) the privilege of finishing first. In this way the whole community could take pride in the craftsmanship of the builder of the new canoe.

Such an occasion in traditional times also would have been one of the few instances of generally peaceful gatherings between competing factions of a society, allowing for a rare opportunity to exchange news with far-off groups. Since travel to the festival setting would have been accessible only by canoe for villages of any distance, it also would have served to reconfirm the notion that extensive sea travel was not only possible but an actuality.

The largest vessels—and those most able to make long journeys—were usually double-hulled canoes equipped with an outrigger and sails. Some of these were huge. In Tahiti, Captain Cook reported a fleet of double-hulled war canoes, ranging from 50 to 90 feet long, with the largest carrying 120 people. The largest double-hulled canoe reported by early European observers was a Fijian model that was capable of carrying over 500 people.

Exactly how the Polynesian islands were settled is still a question of some debate, but in its simplest explanation the answer is by sailors who "hopped" from one island to the next in what at first glance would appear to be very primitive sailing canoes but were in fact remarkably seaworthy vessels. The fact that some of these voyages would have been upward of 2,000 nautical miles has been enough of an impetus for modern people to repeatedly try to re-create and explain these voyages by use of traditional canoes, usually of the double-hull variety. Simulations have had varying degrees of success, leading to a lingering mystery of exactly how remote locations like Easter Island (famous for its huge, stone-carved heads) were settled. Easter Island is isolated by 1,200 miles of ocean to the west and 2,200 miles to its east.

Suggestions for Modern Play

An old-fashioned model canoe race could make for an exciting and detailed class project. The first task would be to decide which type of canoe to build. Unless a mechanical rowing device were built, it would need to be rigged with a mast and sail. Choose one or two hulls and do some early experiments to decide how the outrigger should be lashed on or whether it needs to be on at all. During construction of the model, hold ceremonies to give the canoe spirit power when the wood is selected and again when it is first launched. Oliver is a strong source for many of the details of different styles of canoe construction.

Sources

Bollig, P. Laurentius. 1942 (1927). *The Inhabitants of the Truk Islands: Religion, Life and a Short Grammar of a Micronesian People*. New Haven, Conn.: Yale Cross-Cultural Survey.

"Easter Island." 1994–2001. Encyclopedia Britannica Online.

Firth, Raymond. 1970. *Rank and Religion in Tikopia: A Study in Paganism and Conversion to Christianity*. Boston: Beacon Press.

Howell, Reet. 1996. "Traditional Sports, Oceania." In *Encyclopedia of World Sport*, edited by David Levinson and Karen Christensen. Santa Barbara, Calif.: pp. 1083–1093. ABC-CLIO.

Malinowski, Bronislaw. 1922. *Argonauts of the Western Pacific: An Account of Native Enterprise and Adventure in the Archipelagoes of Melanesian New Guinea*. London: George Routledge and Sons.

———. 1929. *The Sexual Life of Savages in Northwestern Melanesia*. Vol. 1 and 2. New York: Horace Liveright.

Oliver, Douglas L. 1989. *Oceania: The Native Cultures of Australia and the Pacific Islands*. Vol. 1. 1989, Honolulu: University of Hawaii Press.

"Rotuma." 1994–2001. Encyclopedia Britannica Online.

Thompson, Laura. 1940. *Southern Lau, Fiji: An Ethnography*. Honolulu, Hawaii: Bernice P. Bishop Museum.

⊞   Dart Throwing

Polynesian dart throwing is a traditional outdoor activity that has fallen into disfavor among some native groups following the arrival of

European diversions. The Maori, the original inhabitants of New Zealand, are one such group that has discontinued the playing of dart throwing, even though it is tightly interwoven into local myth and legend.

Dart throwing, as played by the Maori, was a distance contest. It was a cross between the javelin throw of the ancient Greeks and the stick-throwing game of snow snake practiced by the indigenous people of what is now the northern United States and Canada. The dart was a long reed, and it was thrown underhand-style toward a mound of earth that had usually been smoothed out. The throwing motion was akin to that of a fast pitch in softball. The trick was to get the dart to glance off the mound, catch some air, and fly farther, as opposed to striking the mound in a way that would inhibit or abruptly stop the dart's flight. Imagine a skier going over a bump. If the skier times it well, a boost of acceleration can be achieved. The Maori would call upon divinity to help their darts by spitting on it and reciting a charm. One such charm was recorded by Elsdon Best, who wrote about the Maori in both 1924 and 1952: "Fly forward, my dart, like a meteor in the heavens. A dart of Tuhuruhuru cannot be passed. Fly directly forward, arise and descend beyond yon mountain range. May this dart be lucky" (Blanchard and Cheska 1985).

The dart is also the focal point of Maori stories about missing people in faraway places. The dart is thrown, the hero follows it and finds it and keeps repeating the process, and eventually the dart shows him the way. Sometimes the magic dart takes the hero to a destination that the hero didn't even know existed but is beneficial nonetheless.

The Samoans live on a large expanse of islands located in the Pacific, about 1,000 miles northeast of New Zealand; to keep going in that direction would send a Kiwi to Hawaii. Samoans enjoyed the traditional sport of dart throwing as well, though with some variations that seem to fit their general demeanor as large-living, fun-loving people as opposed to the Maori, who have been described as having a "cult of fitness."

The Samoan dart match, or *tika*, was essentially the same contest as the Maori's. The difference was that it would involve village against village and would include feasting, drinking, speeches, and ceremonies that could last for several days. The Samoan would shape and smooth his wooden dart until it was about four feet long but weighed nary more than two ounces. Samoans actually would take a few running strides before hurling the dart from the hip. Ideally it would glance off the ground (not a mound necessarily) like a stone skipping on water at about 30 feet, then float upward of 200 feet more. Since any number of people could play—particularly when a village's honor was at stake—they usually did. One village's team would line up, and all of them would throw their dart. The longest throw was left on the field; the others, picked up.

Then the next town would go. All darts that went beyond the first mark were scored as a point, and the longest throw was left out there for the goal. The team that went first then got a second turn, and so on. The game was to 10. If the teams were evenly matched, the game might last days.

Some 600 miles west of Samoa, in the Hebrides chain, are the Tikopians. They play the most formal of the Oceanic dart games. The field is more neatly arranged, and the darts are equipped with a five-inch head made of highly polished and close-grained hardwood, making them more like a javelin both in weight and in flight (150 yards, twice as far as top Samoan throws). What really matters, though, is the formation of the teams. These fall along rigid family and rank lines. Because the opposing groups are separate families, a traditional rivalry exists and is acknowledged by the dart throwers as well as the spectators. Team captains will be of similar rank, probably chiefs. There is a strong will to win. The game isn't just about fun (as the Maori's seems to be); it's about winning for the group (à la the Samoans) and for something extra, namely, to save face. The tika match becomes ritual and public function and is given the status of being significantly important. Not only are the competitors competing in something of vital personal importance, but they are also the sole focus of an entire community—something atypical in a society that usually emphasizes the whole community as opposed to the individual. It is also interesting to note that while the society in general enjoys engaging in good-natured taunts and ridicule in most activities, a poor dart throw is never jeered. Instead, it is simply greeted with silence since there is a social understanding that a poor throw in such a serious endeavor is difficult enough for the dart player to deal with.

Suggestions for Modern Play

Polynesian dart throwing could make an excellent school activity. Take the Samoan model, with the teams consisting of one teacher's class against another. Each person should be responsible for designing his or her own dart within specified parameters. Determine which style of throw works best. Also observe how competitive the event gets and whether the level of competitiveness increases as the game goes on and also from match to match.

Sources

Blanchard, Kendall, and Alyce Taylor Cheska. 1985. *The Anthropology of Sport*. South Hadley, Mass.: Bergin and Garvey.
Firth, Raymond. 1930. "A Dart Match in Tikopia." *Oceania*, Vol. 1, No. 1.

⊞ Prun

The *prun* is what the Aboriginal Australians call an intercommunity gathering that is the stage for regularly scheduled, rule-oriented, and community-based mock warfare games. It has also been referred to as the tournament.

The indigenous people of the island continent of Australia do not have a written language, and they are, in essence, a Stone Age people who subsist on hunting and gathering but do not grow their own crops. Their tools are quite rudimentary (throwing stick, spear, the unique boomerang, but not the use of the nearly universal bow and arrow). Because of cultural variations and different dialects, it is inaccurate to state that there is one, singular Aborigine. There are, however, more similarities in day-to-day subsistence than there are differences.

The lack of a written language, combined with the relative dearth of tools, makes it difficult to provide an accurate time frame to when a particular sporting activity started. It is known that humans first inhabited the continent between 25,000 and 20,000 years ago. This book makes the assumption that because of the Aborigines' lack of development in areas of technology, any of their traditional sports would fall into the realm of the ancient world.

Relatively widespread across the great expanses of desolate area in the continent of Australia, the prun is one of the few Aboriginal sporting endeavors that incorporate several different local groups. The prototype of a band, or horde, is that it is a small group of nuclear families, related to each other via the dominant male in each family. They migrate across a large area that is perceived to be the domain of that group alone. Most of the Australian Aborigines' sporting activities—various ball games, wrestling, avoiding the boomerang—are intraband affairs. The interesting game of keepaway called *mungan-mungan* might include several different bands, but the teams consist of young men versus old men. The prun is the one sport that actually pits one band against another. In fact, this intercommunity competition is the purpose of the prun.

The prun is used as a means to settle disputes, arguments, and building tensions between separate groups. It's also a great opportunity to test skills and attract attention. As Walter E. Roth wrote in 1902 of his firsthand accounts of the Aboriginal activities, the prun "gives the men a chance of showing off their prowess and courage to the women."

The prun is simply a mock war for people who seldom engage in the real thing. The host community sends out "invitations" to other competing groups to come to their encampment for a tournament. In the Tully River area, these tournaments are held every 7th or 13th day at an area specifically reserved for that purpose (Howell, Dodge, and Howell

1975). Men come to the prun in large numbers, selected by their local band, with their women helping to carry spears, shields, and boomerangs.

The elaborately painted and dressed men, accompanied by the women, enter the designated fighting area with great noise and boasts. Other groups enter in the same manner. The host tribe has the honor of starting the prun. They do this by either throwing a boomerang into the center of the band that they wish to engage or verbally taunting a group to provoke a fight. It has been reported that if there is no real quarrel between any of the groups, then one would be invented to get the proceedings started.

If a personal feud existed, it was usually taken care of first. This, however, was just a prelude to the chaotic scene that would follow in the center of the *puya*, or fighting area. Spears and boomerangs are thrown, shields are banged together, and then clubs are used at short range. Verbal parrying livened up the action and incited the crowd. There were two strict rules: no fighting outside the puya, and spears could be thrown only at the knees or feet. Remarkably, despite the absence of officials or referees, very few fatal or serious injuries were reported, though the minor mishap was common.

Usually, women came into the puya to aid their husbands and relatives. Naturally, this brought the women from the competing band into the puya, and then the women fight each other: "They are using their tongues all the time and with far greater effect than the men. The din is something terrible while the tournament lasts" (Roth 1902).

With such heated intensity, it would seem that anger would get out of control. That, however, is not the point of the prun. In fact, it is a way to relieve anger in a moderated way. That's why every 10 or 15 minutes the action comes to a halt, and while the participants are resting, their spears, boomerangs, and other implements are returned to them. Then the fighting begins anew. As the day wears on, other bands of men (and women) take up the challenge, sometimes coming to the aid of a weaker group. Often the tournament continues until dark and resumes the next morning. Winning is not the emphasis, and when it does happen, it is limited to individual confrontations.

The tournament serves the purposes of social intercourse, relieving the tensions of building rivalries, and amusement and entertainment. Because of its aggressive nature, simmering hostilities are released before they reach a breaking point when a real war might erupt. The formal and traditional structure, combined with the willingness of the groups to abide by the few, well-understood rules, makes sure that no one goes too far. "When the tournament is over, participants generally depart on good terms, old scores settled and a good time having been had by all" (Blanchard and Cheska 1985).

Suggestions for Modern Play

To try to duplicate the prun in a scholastic setting would be inappropriate. Still, in its base purpose, it is not that different from an idealized concept of interscholastic American football games. Like the prun, football is usually well attended by each local faction. It is very aggressive by its nature, and injuries do take place, but very few are life-threatening. The "fighting" is supposed to take place only on the field of play, and there are rules against actions that would increase the likelihood of injury. There are regular rest periods. It is an opportunity to get to know people from different towns. For the most part, participants and spectators leave the "fight" behind them.

Sources

Blanchard, Kendall, and Alyce Taylor Cheska. 1985. *The Anthropology of Sport.* South Hadley, Mass.: Bergin and Garvey.

Howell, Maxwell L., Charles Dodge, and Reet A. Howell. 1975. "Generalizations on Play in 'Primitive' Societies." *Journal of Sport History*, Vol. 2, pp. 145–155.

Howell, Reet. 1996. "Traditional Sports, Oceania." In *Encyclopedia of World Sport*, edited by David Levinson and Karen Christensen. Santa Barbara, Calif.: ABC-CLIO, pp. 1083–1093.

Roth, Walter E. 1976 (1902). "Games, Sports and Amusements." *North Queensland Ethnography*, No. 4, Brisbane, Australia: George Arthur Vaughan, Government Printer. Reprinted in Studies in Play and Games series. New York: Arno Press.

▦ Tug-of-War

The game that is commonly called tug-of-war is found across much of the world as a traditional sport, including Africa, Asia, Europe, and North America. Its genesis can be placed at a variety of locations, including the workers building the Sphinx in ancient Egypt, Chinese farmers, and sailors who have long practice at pulling heavy ropes to hoist their sails.

What is also known is that sports of tug-of-war are known to be traditional activities in several Oceanic cultures, including one that emphasized the sport to the point where damage of property and crops was considered a natural by-product of the competition, such was the passion of the participants.

Certainly, the Trobriands of Melanesia treated the tug-of-war, or *bi'u* (literally meaning "pulling"), as a great means of enjoying some physically demanding fun. The rope was a strong, creeping vine. The rules were relatively simple—an equal number of players on each side of the vine. Both men and women competed, sometimes against each other in a male versus female competition but usually as a mixed-gender team. The match typically began in the center of the village and was started by the reciting of a known song. First one side would chant the first half of the song, and when the other side had finished the chant, the pull would begin. What usually was not designated was a specific point where the tug-of-war would be finished, as is typically the case in a modern match. Instead, once a team proved itself superior and had a big pull going, it would end by dragging the other team around for a significant amount of time and space. In this way, houses, young trees, and household goods were often damaged or destroyed.

If the tug-of-war match was part of the Trobriands' *kayasa*, then the damage to goods and property was going to be even more severe. The kayasa was an obligatory and well-organized festival that centered around one specific activity (see Oceania: Canoe Racing), which was chosen by one of the headmen of the community. Sometimes the purpose of the kayasa might be work-related, as in the harvesting of food products. Usually, however, it had to do with some form of amusement. It was also expected that everyone who was physically able to would participate in the kayasa. It is not difficult to imagine that if a normal tug-of-war match could damage the houses in the village, then a kayasa bi'u could turn into a wild free-for-all that spread across the breadth of a village. "When it is played in the form of a *kayasa*, . . . houses, yam stores, and young trees are said to be destroyed and people sometimes injured" (Malinowski 1929).

As can be found in a review of tug-of-war practices, there were considerable differences in terms of how the contest was conducted across Oceania. In Melanesia, there was the standard rope-pulling competition, but also in a contest in Tonga hands were grasped without a rope. In the New Hebrides a contest from a sitting position (thus eliminating many of the leg muscles) was preferred.

In Polynesian communities the contests were usually a standard "pull" on a long rope or pole, but at times it started with team members gripping each other around the waist. It is known that prizes were awarded to winners in Hawaii.

Suggestions for Modern Play

Most people have participated at least once in a tug-of-war contest, usually two teams of even size pulling on a large rope trying to drag the opposing team to a centerline. Mix it up and use some of the different techniques like the ropeless competition where hands are joined around the person's waist in front of you, with the two leaders (as opposed to anchors) gripping the same, relatively short double-handled object. Or try the seated rope pull. Another tug-of-war option comes from South America, where one tribe has a seated push-of-war. The leaders of each group sit back-to-back, with their teammates then seated in front of them and between their legs. The objective is to get enough of a backward push with your leg muscles to get the other team sliding along on their buttocks or to "break" their chain.

Sources

Arlott, John, ed. 1975. *The Oxford Companion to World Sports and Games*. London: Oxford University Press.

Howell, Reet. 1996. "Traditional Sports, Oceania." In *Encyclopedia of World Sport*, edited by David Levinson and Karen Christensen. Santa Barbara, Calif.: ABC-CLIO. pp. 1083–1093.

Malinowski, Bronislaw. 1929. *The Sexual Life of Savages in Northwestern Melanesia*. Vol. 1 and 2. New York: Horace Liveright.

▦ Wrestling, with Notes on Boxing

The broad subgroup of Oceania that seemed to enjoy and support the physical sports of wrestling and boxing the most was the Polynesians, particularly the Samoans and Hawaiians, who considered them the favorite sports of both competitors and spectators. These were often well-organized bouts complete with referees and—at least in the case of boxing—even specific arenas for the competition. Wrestling and boxing were highly competitive in these two Polynesian outposts, but it should not be surprising that the large number of ethnic groups scattered across Oceania's thousands of inhabited islands would produce a variety of ways to wrestle with an almost equal number of reasons for wrestling.

The Samoans loved to wrestle and oiled their bodies for the sport. The object of adult males was to throw the opponent to the ground and then stand clear, with any means of making the throw allowed. Traditionally, the Samoan wrestling could be dangerous due to the suddenness and force of the throws.

The Hawaiian Games, which were in existence when Cook's expedition arrived in 1778 and were later suppressed by Calvinist missionaries who began arriving in 1821, featured several different types of wrestling, including the relatively common catch-as-catch-can, which resembles modern freestyle, index finger wrestling, and even wrestling on stilts.

This diversity of wrestling styles is one of the noteworthy traits of the Polynesian wrestlers. Throughout the greater Polynesian region there are also examples of seated wrestling matches, standing hand wrestling, hooked-finger pulling matches, and both foot- and chest-pushing matches.

In the Lau Islands, there was a combination of influences, from both the Fijians and the Tongans. When the Tongans were the ruling people, rough games of wrestling and boxing were quite common. The young

Boxing matches were a popular attraction for some of the Polynesian people, including the Samoans and the Hawaiians. Matches were usually well officiated and determined by a knockout. This print is from Captain Cook's third voyage of the Pacific and was based on an engraving done by Cook's primary artist. (Library of Congress, Prints and Photographs Division [LC-USZ62–102239]).

men had an interesting and stylized nonverbal method of issuing a challenge. They would hold their left arm across their chest and then slap their bent elbow with their right hand, producing a loud hollow sound. In boxing, the matches were contested with both hands or only one hand, and at times the fists were wrapped in bark cloth. Wrapping the fists was also practiced in Hawaii, but bare fists were the most common.

The outcome of a boxing match in Polynesia was generally very clear to all in attendance since it was usually decided only by a knockout. One victory did not make a champion, however. Instead, it usually produced only another challenger. The champion would be determined when there were no more challengers willing to step forward.

In Australia, a specific form of wrestling witnessed by Walter Roth in 1898 near Princess Charlotte Bay in the northeast corner of the continent sparked his interest because to that point he had seen little of the sport exhibited. Roth wrote that the match took place in a cleared, circular space that was about eight yards in diameter. The match began when "one person who fancies himself as good offers a challenge." The spectators offered words of encouragement to their respective group's favorite. The match apparently had some well-understood rules because it began when the challenger grabbed the originator around the loins and interlocked his fingers. The other person raised his arms and then remained passive, allowing himself to be lifted but trying to prevent himself from being thrown off-balance by means of steadying himself on the "lifter's" shoulders. The match was won if the challenger could throw the wrestler whom he lifted in such a way that any part of the body other than the feet touched the ground. "Strictly speaking, it is a throwing, rather than a wrestling match. Only males engage in this sport: as soon as one proves himself victorious, another challenges him, and so on" (Roth 1902).

Roth's description of the aboriginal wrestling in Australia has some commonality to the shared traits of wrestling and boxing matches in the Polynesian cultures. A specific and defined area of competition, the match began with a challenge, the rules were understood and specific, and as soon as one person was defeated, the winner would meet another challenger.

In later research into the play and games of the Aborigines, wrestling was found to be a common activity across tribes. These matches were both intratribal and intertribal, though the matches between different tribes were taken more seriously and contested more often. For this type of match, specific boundaries for it were designated, and prematch rituals included oiling of the body. The specific rules for the wrestling match differed by region, but almost always fairness was important, and winners were declared.

The Maori of New Zealand also wrestled frequently, using a modern freestyle approach. They would also occasionally have two women wrestle one man, not quite as unusual as it might first seem since the Maori women were known to carry weapons and fight alongside male warriors of their villages.

Wrestling is less frequently reported in the areas of Melanesia and Micronesia, but the Micronesian people known as the Chuuk had a unique version of what we would commonly call arm wrestling where the grip was held with only the thumbs. The two combatants, usually young men or boys, would lie down flat. Making sure they had a secure placement for their elbow, they would hook their thumbs and then try to bring down the arm of the other. For full-body wrestling, the Chuuk also had a challenge call similar to that of the Lau Fijians, although they would slap their hand onto their chest. The Chuuk's wrestling matches also shared the aspect of multiple challengers with the typical boxing matches of Polynesia. The Chuuk wrestler who won the first match would then face another challenger from the same group as the first challenger and so on. A person who had enough strength, stamina, and skill to win many matches in a row was treated with respect and given a special honorary title.

Suggestions for Modern Play

Types of limited body wrestling can be emulated, like the Chuuk's thumb-hold arm wrestling, the passive-aggressive match of the Charlotte Bay Aborigines, and the hooked-finger style of the Polynesians.

Sources

Arlott, John, ed. 1975. *Oxford Companion to World Sports and Games*. London: Oxford University Press.

Blanchard, Kendall, and Alyce Taylor Cheska. 1985. *The Anthropology of Sport*. South Hadley, Mass.: Bergin and Garvey.

Bollig, P. Laurentius. 1942 (1927). *The Inhabitants of the Truk Islands: Religion, Life and a Short Grammar of the Micronesian People*. New Haven, Conn.: Yale Cross-Cultural Survey.

Hocart, A. M. 1929. *Lau Islands, Fiji*. Honolulu, Hawaii: Bernice P. Bishop Museum.

Howell, Reet. 1996. "Traditional Sports, Oceania." In *Encyclopedia of World Sport*, edited by David Levinson and Karen Christensen. Santa Barbara, Calif.: ABC-CLIO, pp. 1083–1093.

Kramer, Augustin. 1932. *Truk*. Hamburg, Germany: Friederichsen, de Gruyter.

Roth, Walter E. 1976 (1902). "Games, Sports and Amusements," *North Queensland Ethnography* No. 4, Brisbane, Australia: George Arthur Vaugh, Government Printer; Reprinted New York: Arno Press.

PLAY

⊞ Archery

Archery among the island people of Oceania is best described as scattered and of marginal effectiveness. Compared to other regions of the world—especially the highly refined archers of Central and Eastern

Asia—the bows and arrows were rudimentary, and the archers themselves were not highly skilled.

Still, the bow and arrow were a common military weapon for offensive purposes in Oceania, particularly in the Melanesian societies. In Polynesia they were also well known but were used less frequently in warfare and more often for the purposes of hunting and sport.

Two factors define archery in Oceania, especially in comparison to other regions of the world: (1) archery was not developed by the indigenous people of Australia, making it the only continent not to develop the bow and arrow and (2) the bows and arrows in the other regions of Oceania were relatively weak and poorly made.

Probably the single most important reason that the archery of Oceania never advanced to a high level is the construction of the equipment, particularly the arrows. Throughout the region the arrows were not fletched, meaning that they did not have the feathers near the notched end that increase accuracy during flight. The fletching of arrows varies in its degree of effectiveness around the globe, but generally in the areas where archery progressed to a high level, the arrows were well fletched. One reason that the Native Americans' hunting practices often depended on stealth is that getting close to the target lessened the negative side effects of arrows that were often unbalanced and lacked great finishing detail.

The arrowheads of Oceania were also at times detrimental to an arrow's flight capabilities. As was also the case with spear points in Oceania, many different shapes were employed. While some of the barbed varieties of arrowheads look very imposing, they doubtless negated the arrow's ability to fly.

Two separate tribes from the New Guinea Highlands (part of the broader area known as Melanesia) provide significant information regarding the effectiveness of arrows in combat. The Dugum Dani of the Western New Guinea Highlands sustained the majority of their war wounds from arrows, but they were seldom fatal. This was because the bows did not provide enough power to cause the arrow to penetrate deeply. While the Dugum Dani could make their arrows fly up to 90 meters (by no means a long distance compared to other areas), they had to shoot them in a high arc to achieve that distance. Because the arrows were featherless, they wobbled perceptibly in flight, thus making them easier to spot and avoid. Further, it was reported that the archers seldom worked in conjunction with others; thus there were no reports of a horde of arrows flying into one spot in unison (which was a hallmark of the famous Persian archers, who held their own repeatedly against the powerful Roman forces; see Middle East: Archery).

The Mae Enga, also of the New Guinea Highland, did use volleys of multiple arrows shot simultaneously as a war tactic. Still, they were limited in their effectiveness by the lack of feathers, which made the arrows quickly lose their velocity and accuracy.

Another reason that the Oceanic archer may not have attained a higher level of skill is that in many of the ocean cultures the mark of a true warrior was one who had killed an enemy in close contact or hand-to-hand fighting. The war club was the primary weapon for several civilizations, particularly the often-merciless Fijians. Long-distance warfare, which naturally would include the use of bows and arrows, has at times been suggested to be a formalized type of game for the people of Oceania. Albeit a still-dangerous endeavor, this type of war would not have been taken as seriously as the hand-to-hand battles where lives would almost surely be lost and the potential gains of status in a society could be much higher.

Still, archery did have a place of honor within some Oceanic cultures and on occasion could be considered a sport. In Polynesia, chiefs and other notables recognized the imaginative power of an arrow shot into the sky and would hold long-distance shooting competitions, mostly for the sheer fun of the contest, but also to demonstrate their superior strength and help vouch for their fitness to rule. The use of archery as a symbolic act of prowess by the Polynesian chiefs emulates an often-repeated theme around the world. It shows up among the pharaohs of ancient Egypt, in Greek mythology, in the long-distance shooting competitions of Mongol invaders, and in chivalrous displays of marksmanship by a celebrated medieval thief from England's Sherwood Forest.

A looming and still relatively unexplained question is why the Australian Aborigines did not develop the bow when people everywhere else around the globe made the connection that a taut string could propel a small shaft with accuracy and distance. They did, after all, have perhaps the most advanced of all throwing sticks—the boomerang. Burke theorizes that throwing sticks should be considered the precursor to the bow and arrow in many civilizations. In addition, they developed and were quite effective in the use of a spear-thrower, a leverage device that was separate from the spear itself and was used to accelerate and extend a spear's flight distance in the same manner that the ancient Greeks used a leather thong for leverage and spin in the javelin throw.

"Why, then, don't the aborigines of Australia have the bow?" Burke himself asked. "Perhaps they had it once and did not develop it, because of a lack of interest or need" (1957, 12).

Sources

Burke, Edmund. 1957. *The History of Archery*. New York: William Morrow.
Oliver, Douglas L. 1989. *Oceania: The Native Cultures of Australia and the Pacific Islands*. Vol. 1. Honolulu: University of Hawaii Press.

Umminger, Walter. 1963. *Supermen, Heroes and Gods*. English ed. London: Thames and Hudson.

⊞ Ball Play

The Australian Aboriginal people played a variety of games with balls. One was simply trying to catch the ball while the person was in the air after jumping. Played individually and with teams, by both sexes, it can be an active game when played with teams. With everyone jumping in an attempt to intercept the pass, it has been referred to as kangaroo-play. The ball usually consisted of a piece of hide (opossum, wallaby, kangaroo) tied up with twine.

Even simpler was what Basedow referred to as "catch-ball," which was a game played "by the children of all Australian tribes." It was observed that seeds could serve as the ball. Perhaps reflective of the fact that most of their throwing implements (spear, throwing stick, boomerang) were not intended to be caught directly by another person, Basedow wrote that, "it is surprising, however, that despite the quickness of their eyes and the keenness of their sight, the natives, as a rule, are very backward at catching with their hands any object which is thrown at them" (Basedow 1925, 78).

Another popular ball game resembles the hoop-and-pole games played almost universally in traditional North American settlements. The Australian "bowl ball" game is a little different in that the ball (or sometimes a disc), which has been cut from the inside of a tree, is rolled down a smoothed descending slope and then jabbed with scaled-down versions of hunting spears. The more typical objective among Native Americans was to try to throw the spear at the spot where they felt that the hoop or stone would stop.

As has been pointed out in the introduction to this section, Oceania is far greater than just Australia, its largest island. With 10,000 islands (in its most limited definition) spreading from Australia to Hawaii, there is obviously a great opportunity for differences. Among several of the smaller groups, balls were made out of the large palm and banana fronds. Two strips of the fibrous material were shaped into a cube by means of plaiting, a process of criss-crossing, folding, or weaving.

In Micronesia, the Chuuk on Truk Island played a primitive handball game with their square ball made from pandanus leaves. These games consisted of two groups trying to knock the ball back and forth by using the palm of the hand. Similar balls and games were also found in the Gilbert Islands and among the Tikopia in the Solomon Islands.

In the Gilbert and Marshall Islands, particularly the latter, the game could also take a different shape, that of trying to keep the ball in play by means of kicking it. In basic form this is similar to the games known as *sepa, sepak,* and *takraw,* which are extremely popular in Thailand and other parts of Southeast Asia. The big difference in the Oceanic islands is that the game was not a competitive one that produced winners and losers but rather was played for the enjoyment of the cooperative effort with an emphasis on style and creativity of kicks. In this way it has a marked similarity to a modern derivative known commonly as hackey-sack, though a hackey sack is usually a small bag or pouch filled with seeds.

Suggestions for Modern Play

Learn how to "plait" and make your own cubed ball out of some type of thick plant growth, be it strips of palm leaves if you live in a warmer climate, thick marsh grass if you live near the ocean or possibly strips of pliable bark from a young evergreen in colder areas, or purchase a kickball at your local sporting goods shop. Then play the cooperative kick-ball game from the Marshall Islands with an emphasis on keeping the ball in the air and gradually adding more creative moves. The game can be played with one person or many people, but probably a number in the range from six to eight could form a circular enclosure to keep the game moving quickly. This is a fairly common training exercise for soccer players.

Sources

Basedow, Herbert. 1925. *The Australian Aboriginal.* Adelaide: F. W. Preece and Sons.

Bollig, P. Laurentius. 1942 (1927). *The Inhabitants of the Truk Islands: Religion, Life and a Short Grammar of the Micronesian People.* New Haven, Conn.: Yale Cross-Cultural Survey.

Levinson, David, and Karen Christensen, eds. 1996. *Encyclopedia of World Sport,* Vol. 3. Santa Barbara, Calif: ABC-CLIO.

Roth, Walter E. 1976 (1902). "Games, Sports and Amusements." *North Queensland Ethnography,* No. 4, Brisbane, Australia: George Arthur Vaughan, Government Printer. Reprinted New York: Arno Press.

⊞ Boomerang

Associated with Australia, the boomerang is known worldwide as the amazing flying stick that returns to its thrower. Consider the implications in this prehistoric version of the modern helicopter's rotary blade. If the hunter missed his target, he did not have to run after his spear or search for another suitable rock, thereby wasting valuable time. His tool would simply return to him or at least close to him, perhaps allowing a second shot at the same target.

Native to the Aboriginal population of the island country and continent known as Australia, the boomerang is also one of the more mis-understood tools. Even today, Australians like Duncan MacLennan, a noted retailer of the boomerang who offers free instruction, are of the opinion that kangaroos and ducks were brought down with the hard-ened carved and curved wood from the root of the mulga and acacia trees. Evidence that the boomerang was ever intended to bring down a kangaroo is questionable. It was probably a tool used for hunting small, ground-bound animals. Similar sticks have been found in other parts of the world, with the exception being that Australian boomerangs do re-turn to the thrower.

The precise reasons why a boomerang returns are complex and involve a number of scientific principles, including the gyroscopic effect of the earth's rotation, general aerodynamics, and the notion of airfoils. In gen-eral lay terms, the two "wings" of the boomerang create lift, or a hov-ering effect, while spinning horizontally. This is similar to a helicopter's wings. The spinning motion also results in a curved flight. Throwing the boomerang into the wind at an angle will produce a returning path as the boomerang hovers in an already curving path that is accentuated by the wind.

A hint at how the properties of the boomerang might have first been discovered comes from, ironically, a cave in Poland. An ivory mammoth tusk carved into a similar shape as the boomerang was discovered there in 1987. It measured over two feet long and just under two pounds. Because it was carbon-dated to be more than 20,000 years old (the oldest boomerangs are about 10,000 years), it was not thrown. A plastic replica made to test its aerodynamics showed that, while it was a good stick for throwing (90 feet with a tailwind, over 120 feet into a wind), it did not return. It did, however, hover a bit when thrown into the wind. Throw sticks are also found in ancient Egypt, South India, North Africa, and various Amerindian peoples. Perhaps Aboriginal Australians witnessed a similar effect, refined their carving, and developed the boomerang. Both the throw stick and the returning boomerang are used today.

The boomerang also was used as a digging implement, a club to kill a stunned or maimed animal, a type of flint to produce sparks for a fire, and a musical instrument in tandem with another or by being whirled above the head.

The irony of the boomerang is that it was developed by an ancient group that until the last century was considered still a Stone Age people by anthropologists. The Aborigines did not have metal tools, domesti-cated animals (except for the dog), agriculture, or a written language. They did not even possess the nearly universal weapon—the bow and arrow.

As can be evidenced by the community-oriented sporting events of *mungan-mungan* and the *prun*, the Aborigines did have ample time for

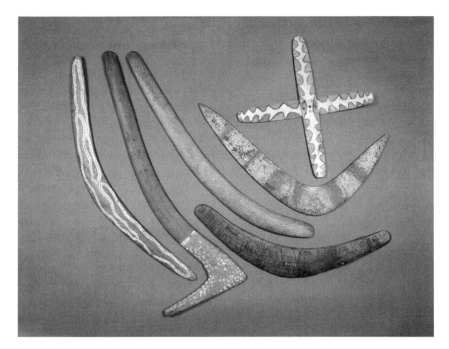

The Australian Aborigines had many different types of boomerangs, in part because the boomerang had many different uses, ranging from a hunting tool to a digging implement. (© South Australia Museum)

leisure activity. While the life of a hunter-gatherer was not an easy one, the natural order of the seasons did provide plenty of idle time, especially when food was plentiful. Without storage facilities or means of preserving meats and vegetables, Aborigines could not stockpile food and so had time for play.

The boomerang, by its returning nature, was both a hunting tool and an idle-time game. It could be used to flush animals, large and small, from an area, which then could be chased down (a common hunting tactic). Competitions for distance and accuracy have been recorded. It could also be used as a weapon against another human. Boomerangs were usually thrown during a prun. Therefore, it was also important to be able to avoid a boomerang, as indicated by a common play activity where six or more men would line up in a queue with their arms outstretched and on the shoulders of the man in front of them. One person would stand facing the line, then throw a boomerang over their heads, and each man was responsible for ducking the returning projectile. It was also used in spiritual rituals, as when hot embers from a fire would be pressed into a hole in the boomerang, and then the projectile would be hurled, glowing, into a night sky.

The boomerang has at times become a symbol of the Australian government's shameful treatment of the Aborigines, particularly prior to the 2000 Olympics, held in Sydney. The boomerang was chosen as the motif for the games. While perfectly natural to many, it was a visual reminder that the Aborigines are still the victims of racism. Aborigines make up 3 percent of the nation's population but are considerably more likely to be arrested and put in prison. An Aboriginal death in prison is reported every two weeks (Pilger 1998). Further, the overall life expectancy of Aboriginals is 25 years less than that of their white Australian counterparts (Pilger 1998).

While tens of thousands of boomerangs are sold in Australia annually (almost all to tourists), the sport of boomerang throwing is by no means a national obsession. As of 1998, there were about 2,500 members from 25 countries in the loosely organized World Boomerang Association. In terms of international competition, teams from the United States, Germany, France, and Japan have been dominant. Australia has not boasted a world champion since the 1980s.

Suggestions for Modern Play

For anyone interested in trying the boomerang; here are some basic pointers:

1. Face the wind. Then turn 45 degrees to the right (e.g., if the wind is from the north, you would face northeast).
2. Grip either end of the boomerang, making sure that the flat side is against your palm. Hold it upright and nearly perpendicular to the ground. It should tilt away from you slightly, about 10 degrees to the right.
3. As you step forward with your left foot, swing the boomerang back behind your head while maintaining the proper throwing angle.
4. As you step forward with your right foot, fling your boomerang arm forward, releasing the boomerang when it is even with your face. Snap your wrist at release to give the boomerang a rapid spin. If the boomerang circles to your right, next time turn more toward the wind before your next throw. If it lands too far to your left, turn away from the wind a bit more.
5. As the boomerang returns, it loses speed and spin. Catch it when it's chest-high by sandwiching it between your palms.

Sources

Blanchard, Kendall, and Alyce Taylor Cheska. 1985. *Anthropology of Sport*. South Hadley, Mass.: Bergin and Garvey.

Clayton, Mark. 1996. "Many Happy Returns." *Christian Science Monitor*, May 2, Vol. 88, Issue 110, p. 10.

———. 1998. "Boomerangers Prepare to Crown World Champions." *Christian Science Monitor*, July 28, Vol. 90, Issue 170, p. 16.

"The Killing Stick." 1995. *Discover*, June, Vol. 16, Issue 6, p. 28.

Pilger, John. 1998. "When Olympics Come to Sydney It Will provide a Facade for Shameful Australia." *New Statesman*, December 11, Vol. 127, No. 4415, p. 17.

Ruhe, Benjamin. 1982. *Boomerang*. Washington, D.C.: Minner Press.

Valenti, Michael. 1993. "Boomerang." *Mechanical Engineering*, December, Vol. 115, Issue 12, p. 68.

⊞ Mungan-Mungan

This is a contest that pits two distinct generations against each other in a team game of keepaway, popular among the Wargite tribe of Australian Aborigines in the Northern Territory of Australia. Like the more prevalent *prun* (tournament), *mungan-mungan* is relatively rare in that it is a sporting activity that can include participants from several different local groups. What makes it even more unusual is that membership on a team is not determined by group affiliation but rather by age. Mungan-mungan pits the old men against the young, giving sanction to the rather natural rivalry of a youth wanting to top his father while the father, just as heartily, wants to make sure that his superiority remains unquestioned.

Usually the old men take a tree limb about two feet in length and paint it white and then call it the *wormar*, which means "young girl." Then the word is sent out that a mungan-mungan contest will be staged.

Males from several local groups converge at the designated spot on the appropriate day. As they would do for the prun, their bodies are painted in preparation for the event. The old men possess the wormar (young girl), and their aim is to keep it ("her"). Whether this is out of a fatherly instinct of protecting a daughter's innocence or whether they are out to prove their own virility is not clear. Soon enough the challenge is issued for the young men to come and get the young girl, and they quickly rise to the challenge. What ensues is a wild, frenetic game of keepaway. The stick is often thrown through the air while men—young and old—are tripped and tackled, pushed and shoved. Spectators get in on the fun by expressing their rooting interests.

About the only rule of the contest is how the wormar is to be held. The old men hold the wormar behind their backs (maybe they are "protecting" her), while a young man who has her in his possession tucks her under his armpit. By this means, it is clear which team is in possession at any time.

The game goes on until one side is so exhausted that it surrenders. Whichever team has possession of the wormar at that time is the winner, at least of that round. The wormar is then hidden until the losers have enough time to recruit some additional players from their generation group to mount a rematch.

Suggestions for Modern Play

The game can be an easy one to duplicate. Instead of a stick, perhaps a Wiffle ball bat could be used (no sharp ends). It could easily be made into a coed sport, with women participating on both sides. A suggested format might be a preseason event where both the boys' and girls' soccer teams from a school join together to take on their coaches and as many parents as can be encouraged to compete. Instead of fighting over a "young girl," the object should be predetermined to represent something more acceptable but still desirable—like a week's worth of household chores.

Sources

Blanchard, Kendall, and Alyce Taylor Cheska. 1985. *The Anthropology of Sport.* South Hadley, Mass.: Bergin and Garvey.

Howell, Reet. 1996. "Traditional Sports, Oceania." In *Encyclopedia of World Sport*, edited by David Levinson and Karen Christensen. Santa Barbara, Calif.: ABC-CLIC, pp. 1083–1093.

▦ Surfing

Surfing today has become a symbol of freedom and adventure as men and women along ocean coasts around the world climb aboard a buoyant plank and ride the waves toward the beach. It could also be called the grandfather of the so-called extreme sports or action sports that have begun to carve out a very significant space in the modern sports world.

This "extreme" sport, however, is not the creation of modern people trying to break free from the stifling hustle and bustle of civilization. Like virtually all aquatic sports, the natural lure of surfing was felt long ago. Surfing was a central part of the Polynesian culture, especially in the areas of modern Hawaii and Tahiti. There were also reported instances of surfing in a few Melanesian territories and a traditional pastime in Australia that has strong similarities to surfing.

Surfing's date of origin, as with so many sports or games in this area of the world, is impossible to pinpoint. It is fair to say, however, that surfing was very much a part of the culture and endorsed by royalty when Polynesian waters were first explored by European navigators. Captain James Cook, writing with his lieutenant Captain King, detailed the surfing activities in Tahiti in 1777 and on the island of Oahu in modern Hawaii in 1778.

The early European visitors to Tahiti recorded seeing both men and women ride the waves on their wooden boards, and on occasion the Europeans were able to stand astride the board for a few scant moments. In Hawaii, the sport was refined to a higher degree, in part due to the important place that it had among the leisure activities of the ruling class.

Records discovered at the time of Cook's voyages showed that for fully three months of the year the Hawaiians' focus shifted from war and even work to a celebration of a god of sport and fertility commonly called Lono, with competitions in 100 or more games. Among them was surfing, with classes for both commoners and royalty. It has been suggested that the Hawaiian royalty used surfing, particularly with their huge boards known as *olo*, as a means of proving their physical superiority while improving their own strength and agility. Just carrying the boards, which were 14 to 18 feet long, required strength. Made from a light, buoyant wood from the wiliwili tree, they still could weigh 150 to 175 pounds. The shorter, 10- to 12-foot board used by commoners was called *alai* and was made from the denser koa wood. Not surprisingly, the elite, who kept the best boards to themselves, were reported to excel at surfing. On some occasions when the ocean was especially cooperative to the ancient "hotdoggers," the Hawaiian royalty even closed the surf to commoners so they could have all of the waves to themselves.

While Cook's records certainly indicate that surfing was a traditional activity participated in enthusiastically by the Hawaiians and Tahitians, there is limited physical and oral evidence to suggest surfing was a popular pastime many centuries before. Petroglyphs—or rock carvings—of the most basic stick-figure variety have been found in the Hawaiian lava rock landscape depicting a human on a straight line, with feet separated, knees bent and arms out to its side in a stance that seems to indicate a balancing act and bears a resemblance to a surfer riding a wave. Chants that tell of great surfing feats have been dated back to A.D. 1,500.

The process of making an early surfboard required significant preparation as well as paying the proper respect to a variety of deities. Before a tree was even cut down with the purpose of turning its trunk into a surfboard, a fish had to be placed in a hole near the tree's roots, and the craftsman prayed. After the ritual it was cut and hauled to a workplace, where it was chipped into its desired shape by the use of a bone or a stone adze (ax). As previously mentioned, the Oceanic people were still a Stone Age civilization in terms of their tools. The board would then be planed, or rough-sanded, with coral or a rough stone to remove the ax marks and treated with a black finish that was made from a variety of sources, including root, bark, fruit, or soot from burned nuts. A final touch was to treat the board with oil from the kukui tree. Before it reached water, more prayers were offered in a dedication ceremony. After each use the boards would be retreated with coconut oil and then stored wrapped in a cloth.

Surfing as an activity was squashed along with the other traditional sporting endeavors of the Hawaiian Games in the mid-1800s by the increase of Calvinist missionaries, most hailing from New England, who

At the time of the first European visitors to Hawaii, surfing was a well-established activity and especially popular with the local royalty. Surfing was strongly discouraged in the 19th century and had almost completely vanished as an indigenous activity until interest was rekindled by early "traditionalists" like these surf riders at Waikiki Beach, shown between 1906 and 1916. (Library of Congress, Prints and Photographs Division [LC-USZ62–120288])

became the overriding influence in the island culture. Surfing was virtually extinct in Hawaii by the late 1800s.

Surfing as a modern sport can be directly traced to the legendary Duke Kahanamoku, who organized the first surf club in 1920 in Waikiki. Because Kahanamoku was an expert swimmer who also was credited with developing the modern crawl stroke (freestyle), he had ample opportunity to spread his love of the traditional Polynesian sport around the world, first introducing it to the beaches of Sydney, Australia, in 1915.

That the Australians would take to such an activity is not particularly unusual, considering that the continent is an island, and that there seems to have been some surfing prehistory. A favorite pastime of Aboriginal children in Princess Charlotte Bay, Australia, at the end of the nineteenth century was to take a long piece of bark and scoot along the muddy riverbanks, balancing on one knee on the board while using the other leg to kick behind them; "with this movement rapidly repeated they can skim along the mudflats at a comparatively high rate of speed" (Roth, 1902) While not surfing, the activity does have a marked similarity to a couple of modern surfing "cousins"—the skateboard, the scooter, and the oceanside wakeboard.

Surfing and the use of the surfboard were also reported from other areas of Oceania. To the northeast of Australia, surfing has been reported among indigenous people in the Solomon and Caroline Islands as well as in the coastal islands of Papua New Guinea.

Suggestions for Modern Play

Surfing is now a worldwide sport that is riding a crest of popularity as the twenty-first century begins. While Pacific Ocean surfing is well known, particularly in Hawaii, California, and Australia, there is also a strong and growing surfing community along the Atlantic Coast, extending as far north as New Hampshire and Maine. This is one sport that requires a tutor or mentor, since learning about the potentially dangerous aspects of tides, undertows, and what lies beneath the surface of the ocean is essential. Most locations that have a significant surfing population have at least one surf shop that can provide lessons and rental equipment.

Sources

Arlott, John, ed. 1975. *The Oxford Companion to World Sports and Games*. London: Oxford University Press.

Drent, Les. N.d. "The History of Surfing." *Coffee Times* Web site, Captain Cook, Hawaii.

Firth, Raymond. 1970. *Rank and Religion in Tikopia: A Study in Paganism and Conversion to Christianity*. Boston: Beacon Press.

Oliver, Douglas L. 1989. *Oceania: The Native Cultures of Australia and the Pacific Islands*. Vol. 1. Honolulu: University of Hawaii Press.

Roth, Walter E. 1976 (1902). "Games, Sports and Amusements." *North Queensland Ethnography*, No. 4. Brisbane, Australia: George Arthur Vaughan, Government Printer. Reprinted New York: Arno Press.

■■■ Games of Tag

The notion of chasing other children in an effort to catch them—or tag them—is a simple, fun, and invigorating pastime that is to this day common playground activity throughout the world. The various Aboriginal children of Australia also enjoyed games of tag, usually going one evocative step further by ascribing an animal or spiritual characteristic to the person attempting to tag his or her playmates.

A series of "tag" games was described by Walter Edmund Roth in his short, but descriptive, pamphlet called "Games, Sports and Amusements," which concerned the native Australians and was published in 1902, based almost completely on firsthand knowledge. Because these cultures were still unaccustomed to "white" intruders, it is reasonable to consider these play patterns as being both characteristically innate and traditional to the areas where they were played.

Young children in the Cape Bedford region played a game of tag called "shark." The chaser twisted one arm over the other and held the arms in front and slightly below the waist. The posture of the arms was done to imitate the muscular undulation of a shark's swimming motion, not to physically mimic the shark's fin sticking out of the water. The boy or girl rushed about with hands in this position trying to catch whoever he or she could.

Very young children in a different region of the island continent called the Bloomfield played a game called "March fly." The chasers had to close their eyes and rush about. When they were successful in catching a player, then they had the thrill of making a very loud buzzing sound in that person's ear and giving them a pinch in imitation of a sting. Also in the Bloomfield were two games that involved more elaborate local knowledge and group cooperation but would ultimately lead to someone's being chased. Both involved the aspect of ghosts or evil spirits, from which the games take their name. *Wu-inggal* is a fire-starting spirit of either sex but known best as a beautiful woman. The children would pretend to have set up a camp and that it is nighttime, setting the stage for the wu-inggal to sneak into the camp brandishing a sharp digging stick, which is supposed to be red-hot. First the wu-inggal finds a victim and pantomimes running the stake through her victim. This accomplished, she would then begin to set the camp afire, at which point everyone "wakes up" and chases down the evil spirit and captures her. *Burakul* is a different spirit who was known for his loud, unpleasant noises. This spirit was the chaser; once he captured victims, he then had the privilege of tickling them extensively "until they are nearly dead from laughing" (Roth 1902) before letting them go.

Games similar to tag have been observed in other Oceanic regions. The Chuuk people (also called Truk), a very small ethnic group living on one of the Caroline Islands in Micronesia by the same name, played a tag game in which they were safe in the water but not on land. A favorite location for games of tag and other basic childhood games that involve random running about is the beach, particularly at nighttime. The Tikopia of the Solomon Islands in Polynesia reserve this time as appropriate for adult games, while daytime is the playtime for children. The Trobriands from Papau New Guinea often played communal games of hide-and-seek on the beach at night.

Suggestions for Modern Play

Certainly, American children know the concept of playing tag. It can be a physically demanding game if the person who is chasing is not as fast or old as her or his playmates. Conversely, if the strongest and swiftest person is the "tagger," it usually is relatively easy for her or him to be successful. Take a cue from the Australian Aborigines and add some handicaps to your next game of tag. Make the oldest or fastest runners be buzzing flies who must compete with their eyes closed to level the playing field, or give the younger or slower players the right to be burakuls, who will get to tickle their older competitors when they finally do make a tag.

Sources

Firth, Raymond. 1939. *Primitive Polynesian Economy*. London: George Routledge and Sons.

Fischer, Ann M. 1950. *The Role of the Turkese Mother and Its Effect on Child Training*. Washington, D.C.: Pacific Science Board.

Malinowski, Bronislaw. 1929. *The Sexual Life of Savages in Northwestern Melanesia*. Vols. 1 and 2. New York: Horace Liveright.

Roth, Walter E. 1976 (1902). "Games, Sports and Amusements." *North Queensland Ethnography*, No. 4. Brisbane, Australia: George Arthur Vaughan, Government Printer. Reprinted New York: Arno Press.

GAMES

⊞ Hand Games

Games that use hands as the central figure fall into two main categories among the Aboriginal Australians observed by Roth in the 1890s: those that used string and those played only with the hands.

Among the Australian Aborigines both sexes practiced string games, but the women and young children were extremely fond of the pastime. The women were quite expert in their craft and were adept at making elaborate string designs with their hands by using one or two "endless" strings. The concept of twisting, turning, and spinning string about the fingers and thumbs to create intricate designs is often called "cat's cradle" among English-speaking peoples. The construction of designs with strings, usually accompanied by some type of song or story, was also widespread throughout the other indigenous Oceanic people.

Roth detailed 67 distinct patterns of completed string art. Some were so elaborate and decorative that they could almost be considered folk art, but since the string was not a stable medium, meaning that the art disappeared basically when the hands were removed, they were considered a form of play by their practitioners. The string-game patterns were all intended to imitate something that was a natural part of the native life. They could be representative of human endeavors (two women fighting with sticks; four boys walking hand in hand), an animal (kangaroo, duck in flight), parts of an animal (a kangaroo's pouch), plants, insects, food, weapons, and parts of nature (the sun, the moon, and the stars).

Some of the designs required "not only the hands but even the mouth, knees, etc., to make certain loops, twists and turns" (Roth 1902). At times one or two assistants were needed to complete the tasks. The game was extremely widespread among the various ethnic groups of Australia, with most having given the amusement a specific name. In Cape

Bedford, for example, it was called *kapan*, which is also the name applied to other forms of making a mark or an engraving. When the Aborigines from this area first began to be taught to read and write by missionaries, and it was explained that letters formed designs that together made up words and thus stories, they ascribed the same word, kapan, to the literary process.

The Kapauku Papuans from the area of New Guinea that is now part of Indonesia called their game *gaa do gaa*. It was played by several girls at the same time with one string. The recitation of a song or story complemented the figure that was being made. The Trobriands of Papua New Guinea used the string games as a means to pass time indoors during the rainy season from November to January. Both children and adults played the games among the Trobriands, often for an audience. Each figure had a name, story, and interpretation, sometimes with a lyrical accompaniment.

String games were played throughout Fiji and western Polynesia, done chiefly by women and children as an artistic form passed down from the women to the young girls, who generally enjoy mimicking the older women as much as possible. The small tribe known as Chuuk (or Truk), a Micronesian group, were particularly adept and elaborate with their string games.

That these relatively primitive groups of people would develop elaborate designs with string can partly be explained by the example of the Chuuk. Most of the Chuuk's material goods were plaited. Plaiting is the process of weaving together pieces of fibrous plants to form a shape. The Chuuk used palm fronds to construct everything from a simple carrying basket to the sides of their homes. Naturally, they developed a great deal of dexterity and strength in their hands and would learn through experience how to make a simple, straight piece of fiber into a recognizable shape. Not all cultures used the method of plaiting as extensively. Still, the concept in this play, which a modern person often refers to as "working with one's hands," was universal in Oceania, and this handiwork was predominantly accomplished with relatively primitive tools, leaving the hand as the most sophisticated of all tools.

The Australians also had a variety of hand games that did not use string but usually employed many sets of hands in sequential and at times confusing configurations. Games played with multiple sets of hands include the "honey-game," "catching cockatoos," "bean-tree," and "cracking beans." In each a number of players' hands are placed in a certain pattern, often one on top of the other. Then a signal, usually in the form of ritualized dialogue, begins a movement of the hands.

In "catching cockatoos," the hands are stacked one on top of the other, with the index finger "of the hand below encircled by the thumb and three fingers above" (Roth 1902). The game begins when one index finger is left uncovered and one hand is free. That hand then "spears" the top cockatoo and raises it toward the spear-thrower's mouth so he or she can make a loud, lip-smacking display of eating the cockatoo. In this way the bird (hand) is passed around to each player, who also enjoys the dining pleasure. The game continues until all of the cockatoos have been speared and eaten.

Roth, despite his detailed descriptions, does not offer much in the way of social meaning to these hand games. A supposition about what the hand games, either with or without string, tell us about the indigenous people of Oceania can be made, in part, by recognizing that most of these people had relatively few material possessions. With few tools, simple things were often ascribed greater significance by means of imagination. As an example, a forked stick or pieces of bark wrapped into a cone shape would often constitute a doll. These simple sticks or cones would then be carried about and even nursed in an imitative fashion.

The hand games, particularly those with string, show that despite their limited means or "toys," Aboriginal children and adults could and did develop elaborate forms of play.

Suggestions for Modern Play

String games are a great opportunity for children and young adults to make a connection with older relatives or acquaintances, particularly women. Since they grew up in an era before video and computer games, they probably had firsthand experience playing cat's cradle games. This process of passing down the techniques and storytelling features of string games from one generation to the next is often repeated in Oceanic cultures. Once construction of a string design has been mastered, the next step is to create a story, chant, or song to accompany the process of making the design. The story can also lead from one design to another in a seamless production. Books with specific string games are available.

Sources

Firth, Raymond. 1951. "Privilege Ceremonials in Tikopia." *Oceania*, Vol. 21, pp. 161–177.

Kramer, Augustin. 1932. *Ethnographie: B. Mikronesian*. Hamburg, Germany: Friederichsen, de Gruyeter (translated from German).

Malinowski, Bronislaw. 1929. *The Sexual Life of Savages in Northwestern Melanesia*. Vols. 1 and 2. New York: Horace Liveright.

Pospisil, Leopold. 1958. *Kapauku Papuans and Their Law*. New Haven, Conn.: Department of Anthropology, Yale University.

Roth, Walter E. 1976 (1902). "Games, Sports and Amusements." *North Queensland Ethnography*, No. 4. Brisbane, Australia: George Arthur Vaughan, Government Printer. Reprinted New York: Arno Press.

Thompson, Laura. 1940. *Southern Lau, Fiji: An Ethnography*. Honolulu, Hawaii: Bernice P. Bishop Museum.

⊞ Mu Torere

Mu torere is a board game played by the Maori of New Zealand. It is an interesting board game that has an initial similarity in appearance to checkers but is more similar in philosophy to tic-tac-toe since if both players are proficient and do not make a mistake, the match should end in a draw.

The two-player game is played on a star-shaped board with eight points and a circle in the middle of the star. Each player has four stones or markers, and these are placed at the points in groups, so that four white stones are facing the four black stones, with the middle left open. The first move is by necessity to the middle. The object of the game is to block the opponent from having any open move. There is no jumping or "taking" of the pieces in this game.

The ways in which a stone can be moved are quite limited. The first option is to move to any adjacent point on the star. If the first option is not available and if the middle, known as the *putahi*, is open, then a stone can be moved to the middle. The final option is to move from the putahi to any point on the star.

The "board" was often just a drawing in the sand, which featured a center circle and eight equal-distance arms separated uniformly with a circle at the end of each arm. For greater permanence, it was occasionally marked on the inside of a strip of bark while the bark was green. When the bark dried, the lines of the "board" would remain etched. Bell notes that "it appears to have been played mainly on the East Coast of the North Island of New Zealand, by the Ngati Porou tribe" (Bell 1979).

Bell admits that there is some doubt as to whether this was an indigenous game, especially since the word "mu" is what the Maori assigned to European checkers, known as draughts, and means "move." Bell postulates that "mu" was added as a prefix and that this game was not derived from draughts because the Maori enthusiastically embraced draughts as a separate game.

If mu torere is truly an indigenous game, then it also has the distinction of being an oddity in Oceania, where the physical was stressed in play activities as opposed to sedentary games.

Source

Bell, R. C. 1979. *Board and Table Games from Many Civilizations*. 1979 Rev. double ed. New York: Dover.

▤ BIBLIOGRAPHY

Altherr, Thomas L. 1997. *Sports in North America: A Documentary History*. Vol. 1: *Sports in the Colonial Era 1618–1783*, Gulf Breeze, Fla.: Academic International Press.

Alvarsson, Jan-Ake. 1988. *The Mataco of the Gran Chaco: An Ethnographic Account of Change and Continuity in Mataco Socio-economic Organization*. Stockholm, Sweden: Almqvist and Wiskell International.

Anderson, Wanni Wibulswasdi. 1989. "Sport in Thailand." In *Sport in Asia and Africa: A Comparative Handbook*, edited by Eric A. Wagner. Westport, Conn.: Greenwood Press.

Arbena, Joseph L. 1986. "Sport and the Study of Latin American History: An Overview." *Journal of Sport History*, Vol. 13, no. 2.

Arlott, John, ed. 1975. *The Oxford Companion to World Sports and Games*. London: N.Y., Oxford University Press.

Arroyo, Raziel Garcia. 1969. *Five Mexican Sports*. Mexico: Publicaciones Internacionales.

Avedon, Elliott M., and Brian Sutton Smith, ed. 1971. *The Study of Games*. New York: John Wiley and Sons.

Azoy, G. Whitney. 1999. "Buzkashi." In *Encyclopedia of World Sport*, edited by David Levinson and Karen Christensen. New York: Oxford University Press.

Baker, Michael. 1999. "Korean Martial Art Kicks Its Way Back to Popularity." *Christian Science Monitor*, April 6, Vol. 91, Issue 90.

Baker, William J. 1987. "The Meaning of International Sport for Independent Africa." In *Sport in Africa: Essays in Social History*, edited by William J. Baker and James A. Mangan. New York: Africana.

———. 1999. "Traditional Sports, Africa." In *Encyclopedia of World Sport*, edited by David Levinson and Karen Christensen. Oxford and New York: Oxford University Press.

Baker, William J. and James A. Mangan. ed. 1987. *Sport in Africa: Essays in Social History*, New York: Africana.

————. 1988. *Sports in the Western World*. Rev. ed. Urbana, Ill.: Illini Books.

Barton, R. F. 1919. *Ifuago Law*. Berkeley: University of California Press.

Basedow, Herbert. 1925. *The Australian Aboriginal*. Adelaide: F. W. Preece and Sons.

Beaglehole, Ernest. 1937. *Notes on Hopi Economic Life*. Oxford: Oxford University Press.

Beauchamp, W. M. 1976. (1896). "Iroquois Games." In *Games of the Americas*, Part 2, edited by Brian Sutton-Smith. New York: Arno Press.

Beaumont, Lesley. 1994. "Child's Play in Classical Athens." *History Today*, August, Vol. 44, Issue 8.

Becher, Hans. 1960. *The Surara and Pakidi, Two Yanoama Tribes in Northwest Brazil*. Hamburg, Germany: Kommissionsverlag Cram, De Gruyter.

Bell, R. C. 1979. *Board and Table Games from Many Civilizations*. Rev. double ed. New York: Dover.

Bennett, Bradley C. 1992. "Plants and People of the Amazonian Rainforests." *Bioscience*, September, Vol. 42, Issue 8.

Bennett, Wendell C., and Robert M. Zingg. 1935. *The Tarahumara: An Indian Tribe of Northern Mexico*, Chicago: University of Chicago Press.

Bergman, Sten, 1938. *In Korean Wilds and Villages*. Translated by Frederick Whyte. London: John Gifford.

"Bid the Wind Blow." 1995. *Economist*, May 6, Vol. 335, Issue 7913.

Blacking, John. 1987. "Games and Sport in Pre-Colonial African Societies." In *Sport in Africa: Essays in Social History*, edited by William J. Baker and James A. Mangan. New York: Africana.

Blanchard, Kendall. 1996. "Traditional Sports, North and South America." In *Encyclopedia of World Sport*, edited by David Levinson and Karen Christensen. Santa Barbara, Calif.: ABC-CLIO.

Blanchard, Kendall, and Alyce Taylor Cheska. 1985. *The Anthropology of Sport*. South Hadley, Mass.: Bergin and Garvey.

Blank, Jonah. 1999. "Playing Hoops—for Keeps." *U.S. News & World Reports*, June 28, Vol. 126, Issue 25.

Bollig, P. Laurentius. 1942 (1927). *The Inhabitants of the Truk Islands: Religion, Life and a Short Grammar of the Micronesian People*. New Haven, Conn.: Yale Cross-Cultural Survey.

"Bororo File." 1996. *The eHRAF Collection of Ethnography*. New Haven, Conn.: Human Relations Area Files.

Bourland, Julia. 1998. "Breathing Lessons." *Women's Sports & Fitness*, November/December.

Boutros, Labib. 1977. "The Phoenician Stadium of Amrit." *Olympic Review*, No. 112.

Burke, Edmund. 1957. *The History of Archery*. New York: William Morrow.

Carroll, Scott T. 1988. "Wrestling in Ancient Nubia." *Journal of Sport History*, Vol. 15, No. 2.

Catlin, George, 1976 (1841). "A Choktaw Ball Game." In *The Games of the Americas*, Part II, edited by Brian Sutton-Smith. New York: Arno Press.

Chagnon, Napoleon A. 1968. *Yanomamo: The Fierce People*. New York: Holt, Rinehart, and Winston.

"The Challenge." 2001. Interactive Web site game from the British Museum (http://www.mesopotamia.co.uk/tombs/challenge/cha_set.html), played June.

Champion, Jean Rene. 1970 (1963). *A Study in Culture Persistence: The Tarahumaras of Northwestern Mexico*. Ann Arbor, Mich.: University Microfilms.

Chapin, Norman Macpherson, 1983. *Curing among the San Blas Kuna of Panama*. Ann Arbor, Mich.: University Microfilms International.

Chapman, Anne, 1982. *Drama and Power in a Hunting Society: The Selk'nam of Tierra del Fuego*. Cambridge: Cambridge University Press.

Chase, Guy. 1999. "Wrestling, Submission Wrestling" (Web site), www.guy chase.com, Multi-culture Martial Arts Academy.

Chehabi, H. E. 1995. "Sport and Politics in Iran: The Legend of Gholamreza Takhti." *The International Journal of the History of Sport*, December, Vol. 12, No. 3.

"Chess." 1994–2001. *Encyclopedia Britannica Online*.

Cifarelli, Megan. 1996. "Gesture and Alterity in the Art of Ashurnasirpal II of Assyria." *Art Bulletin*, June, Vol. 80, Issue 2.

Clark, Charles Allen. 1932. *Religions of Old Korea*. New York: Fleming H. Revell.

Clayton, Mark, 1996. "Many Happy Returns." *Christian Science Monitor*, May 2, Vol. 88, Issue 110.

———. 1998. "Boomerangers Prepare to Crown World Champions." *Christian Science Monitor*, July 28, Vol. 90, Issue 170.

Cobacchini, P., Antonio, and P. Cesar Albisetti. 1942. *The Eastern Bororo Orarimogodogue of the Eastern Plateau of Mato Grosso*. Rio de Janiero: Companhia Editora Nacional (translated from Portuguese).

"Colombia: Sports and Recreation." 1994–2001. *Encyclopedia Britannica Online*.

Conti, Mary. 1996. "Breeds." In *Encyclopedia of World Sport*, Vol. 1, edited by David Levinson and Karen Christensen. Santa Barbara, Calif.: ABC-CLIO.

Cook, William Azel. 1909. *Through the Wilderness of Brazil by Horse, Canoe and Float*, 1909, New York: American Tract Society.

Cooper, John M. 1917. "Analytical and Critical Bibliography of the Tribes of the Tierra del Fuego." *Bureau of American Ethnology 63*. Washington, D.C.: Government Printing Office.

———. 1946. "The Ona." In *The Marginal Tribes*, edited by Julian H. Steward. Washington, D.C.: Government Printing Office.

Corcoran, John, and Emil Farkas. 1983. *Martial Arts: Traditions, History, People*. New York: Gallery Books.

Corlett, J. T., and M. M. Mokgwathi. 1989. "Sport in Botswana." In *Sport in Asia and Africa: A Comparative Handbook*, edited by Eric A. Wagner. Westport, Conn.: Greenwood Press.

Courlander, Harold. 1982. *Hopi Voices: Recollections, Traditions and Narratives of the Hopi Indians*. Albuquerque: University of New Mexico Press.

Cox, A. E., R. G. Glassford, and Maxwell L. Howell. 1973. "Rubber Ball Games of Central America." In *A History of Sport and Physical Education to 1900*, edited by Earle F. Zeigler. Champaign, Ill.: Stipes.

Decker, Wolfgang. 1992. *Sport and Games in Ancient Egypt*. Translated by Allen Guttmann, New Haven, Conn.: Yale University Press.

———. 1996. "Chariot Racing." In *Encyclopedia of World Sport*, Vol. 1, edited by David Levinson and Karen Christensen. Santa Barbara, Calif.: ABC-CLIO.

Delp, Laurel, and Peter Charlesworth. 1998. "Land of the Rising Kite." *Travel Holiday*, April, Vol. 181, Issue 3.

De Voogt, Alex. 1998. "Going Full Circle." *Geographical Magazine*, December, Vol. 70, Issue 12.

———. 1998. "Seeded Players." *Natural History*, February, Vol. 107, Issue 1.

Drake-Brockman, Ralph E. 1912. *British Somaliland*. London: Hurst and Blackett.

Drent, Les. N.d. "The History of Surfing." *Coffee Times* Web site, Captain Cook, Hawaii.

Dumia, Mariano A. 1979. *The Ifuago World*. Edited by Jean Edades. Quezon City, Republic of the Philippines: New Day.

"Easter Island." 1994–2001 Encyclopedia Britannica Online.

Economist. 1993. July 10, Vol. 328, Issue 7819, p. 87.

Einarsson, Thorsteinn. 1988. *Glima—The Icelandic Wrestling*. Self-published.

Eisen, George, and David K. Wiggins, eds. 1994. *Ethnicity and Sport in North American History and Culture*. Westport, Conn.: Greenwood Press.

Erasmus, Charles John. 1971. "Patolli, Pachisi and the Limitation of Possibilities." In *The Study of Games*, edited by Elliott M. Avedon and Brian Sutton-Smith. New York: John Wiley and Sons.

Eubank, Lisbeth. 1976 (1945). "Legends of Three Navaho Games." *El Palacio*, July, Vol. 52, No. 7. Reprinted in *The Games of The Americas*, Parts 1 and 2, edited by Brian Sutton-Smith. New York: Arno Press.

Firth, Raymond. 1930. "A Dart Match in Tikopia." *Oceania*, Vol. 1, No. 1.

———. 1939. *Primitive Polynesian Economy*. London: George Routledge and Sons.

———. 1951. "Privilege Ceremonials in Tikopia." *Oceania*, Vol. 21.

———. 1970. *Rank and Religion in Tikopia: A Study in Paganism and Conversion to Christianity*. Boston: Beacon Press.

Fischer, Ann M. 1950. *The Role of the Turkese Mother and Its Effect on Child Training*. Washington, D.C.: Pacific Science Board.

Flannery, Regina, and John M. Cooper. 1976 (1946). "Social Mechanisms in Gros Ventre Gambling." *Southwestern Journal of Anthropology*, Vol. 2, No. 4. Reprinted in *The Games of the Americas*, Parts 1 and 2, edited by Brian Sutton-Smith. New York: Arno Press.

Flaskerd, George A. 1976 (1961). "The Chippewa or Ojibway Moccasin Game." *The Minnesota Archaeologist*. Reprinted in *Games of the Americas*, Part 2, edited by Brian Sutton-Smith. New York: Arno Press.

Fletcher, Alice C. 1994 (1915). *Indian Games and Dances with Native Songs*. 1915. Reprinted Lincoln: University of Nebraska Press.

Forbes, Clarence A. 1973. "The Spartan Agoge." In *A History of Sport and Physical Education to 1900*, edited by Earle F. Zeigler. Champaign, Ill.: Stipes.

Gaouette, Nicole. 1998. "Weighing in on a Sumo Match." *Christian Science Monitor*, February 27, Vol. 90, Issue 64.

Gillespie, Susan B. 1991. "Ballgames and Boundaries." In *The Mesoamerican Ball-*

game, edited by Vernon L. Scarborough and David R. Wilcox. Tucson: University of Arizona Press.

Gilmore, Melvin R. 1976 (1926). "The Game of Double-ball or Twin-ball." In *The Games of the Americas*, Part 2, edited by Brian Sutton-Smith. New York: Arno Press.

Glassford, Robert Gerald. 1976. *Application of a Theory of Games to the Traditional Eskimo Culture*. New York: Arno Press.

Godia, George. 1989. "Sport in Kenya." In *Sport in Asia and Africa: A Comparative Handbook*, edited by Eric A. Wagner. Westport, Conn: Greenwood Press.

Golden, Mark. 1998. *Sport and Society in Ancient Greece*. Cambridge: Cambridge University Press.

Goulstone, John. 1980. "The Northern Origins of the Olympic Games." *Olympic Review*, No. 152–53.

Gusinade, Martin. 1995. *The Fireland Indians*. Vol. 1: *The Selk'nam, on the Life and Thought of a Hunting People of the Great Island of Tierra del Fuego*. 1931. New Haven, Conn.: HRAF, (translated from German).

Guttmann, Allen. 1992. "Old Sports." *Natural History*, July, Vol. 101, Issue 7.

Han, Chungnim C. 1949. *Social Organization of Upper Han Hamlet in Korea*. 1970 copy. Ann Arbor, Mich.: University Microfilms.

Harris, H. A. 1972. *Sport in Greece and Rome*. London: Thames and Hudson.

Hocart, A. M. 1929. *Lau Islands, Fiji*. Honolulu, Hawaii: Bernice P. Bishop Museum.

Holcombe, Charles. 1990. "Theater of Combat: A Critical Look at the Chinese Martial Arts." In *Historian*, May, Vol. 52, Issue 3.

Howell, Maxwell L., Charles Dodge, and Reet A. Howell. 1975. "Generalizations on Play in 'Primitive' Societies." *Journal of Sport History*, Vol. 2.

Howell, Reet. 1996. "Traditional Sports, Oceania." In *Encyclopedia of World Sport*, edited by David Levinson and Karen Christensen. Santa Barbara, Calif.: ABC-CLIO.

Hulbert, Homer B. 1906. *The Passing of Korea*. New York: Doubleday, Page.

Hunter, Monica. 1987. *Reaction to Conquest: Effects of Contact with Europeans on the Pondo of South Africa*. Quoted in John Blacking, 1936, "Games and Sport in Pre-Colonial African Societies," in *Sport in Africa: Essays on Social History*, edited by William J. Baker and James A. Mangan. New York: Africana.

Itkonen, Toivo Immanuel. 1948. *The Lapps in Finland up to 1945*. Vol. 2. Helsinki: Porvoo (translated from Finnish).

Jernigan, Sara Staff, and C. Lynn Vendien. 1972. *Playtime: A World Recreation Handbook*. New York: McGraw-Hill.

Johnson, R. W. 1992. "The Irony of the Capac Nan." *Social Studies*, January/February, Vol. 83, Issue 1.

Josephsson, Johannes. 1908. *Icelandic Wrestling*.

"Kabaddi Canada Cup Tournament." 1992. *Macleans*, July 22, Vol. 105, Issue 25.

Kagwa, Apolo. 1934. *The Customs of the Baganda*. Translated by Ernest B. Kalibala. New York: Columbia University Press.

Kaneda, Eiko. 1999. "Trends in Traditional Women's Sumo in Japan." *The International Journal of the History of Sport*, September, Vol. 16, No. 3.

Karsten, Rafael. 1932. *Indian Tribes of the Argentine and Bolivian Chaco: Ethnological Studies.* Helsingfors: Akademische Buchhandlung.

Kennedy, John W. 2000. "Out of the Ashes." *Christianity Today,* January 10, Vol. 44, Issue 1.

"Killer Kites." 1996. *Civilization,* March/April, Vol. 3, Issue 2.

"The Killing stick." 1995. *Discover,* June, Vol. 16, Issue 6.

Knauth, W. 1976. "Sport Qualifications of the Ancient Persian Princes." *Stadion: Journal of the History of Sport and Physical Education,* Vol. 2, Issue 1. pp. 1–89.

Knez, Eugene Irving. 1960. *Sam Jong Dong: A South Korean Village.* Ann Arbor, Mich.: University Microfilms.

Knuttgen, Howard G., Ma Qiuei, and Wu Zhongyuan. 1990. *Sport in China.* Champaign, Ill.: Human Kinetics Books.

Kosambi, D. D. 1965. *Ancient India.* New York: Pantheon Books.

Kowalski, W. J. 1997. "Roman Board Games." World wide Web site, personal.psu.edu/users/w/x/wxk116/roma/rbgames.html

Kramer, Augustin. 1932. *Ethnographie: B. Mikronesian.* Hamburg, Germany: Friederichsen, de Gruyeter (translated from German).

———. 1932. *Truk.* Hamburg, Germany: Friederichsen, de Gruyter.

Kramer-Mandeau, Wolf. 1992. "Games and Festivals in Latin America, 1500–1900." *The International Journal of the History of Sport,* April, Vol. 9, No. 1.

Kyle, Donald G. 1990. "Winning and Watching the Greek Pentathlon." *Journal of Sports History,* Vol. 17, No. 3.

La Barre, Weston. 1948. *The Aymra Indians of the Lake Titicaca Plateau.* Menasha, Wisc.: American Anthropological Association.

Lamont, Deane Anderson. 1995. "Running Phenomena in Ancient Sumer." *Journal of Sport History,* Fall, Vol. 22, No. 3. p. 207–215.

Lankford, Mary D. 1996. *Jacks around the World.* New York: Morrow Junior Books.

"Latin America, Africa, Asia (Journal Survey)." 1995. *Journal of Sport History,* Vol. 22, No. 2.

Layden, Tim. 2001. "Long-distance Land." *Sports Illustrated,* April 23, Vol. 94, Issue 17.

Lema, Bangela. 1989. "Sport in Zaire." In *Sport in Asia and Africa: A Comparative Handbook,* edited by Eric A. Wagner. Westport, Conn.: Greenwood Press.

Levine, Donald N. 1965. *Wax & Gold: Tradition and Innovation in Ethiopian Culture.* Chicago: University of Chicago Press.

Levinson, David, and Karen Christensen, eds. 1996. *Encyclopedia of World Sport.* Vols. 1–3. Santa Barbara, Calif.: ABC-CLIO.

———. 1999. *Encyclopedia of World Sport* (paperback). Oxford: Oxford University Press.

Lewis, Peter. 1985. *Martial Arts of the Orient.* New York: Gallery Books.

Lhagvasuren, Gongor. 1997. "The Stele of Ghengis Khan." *Olympic Review,* Vol. 26, No. 13.

Lumholtz, Carl. 1902. *Unknown Mexico: A Record of Five Years Exploration of the Western Sierra Madre; in the Tierra Caliente of Tepic and Jalisco; and among the Tarascos of Mcihoacan.* Vol. 1. New York: Charles Scribner's Sons.

Malinowski, Bronislaw. 1922. *Argonauts of the Western Pacific: An Account of Native*

Enterprise and Adventure in the Archipelagoes of Melanesian New Guinea. London: George Routledge and Sons.

———. 1929. *The Sexual Life of Savages in Northwestern Melanesia*. Vols. 1 and 2. New York: Horace Liveright.

Man, Edward Horace. 1932 (1885). *On the Aboriginal Inhabitants of the Andaman Islands*. London: Royal Anthropological Institute of Great Britain and Ireland.

Mandell, Richard D. 1984. *Sport: A Cultural History*. New York: Columbia University Press.

Manners, John. 1975. "In Search of an Explanation." In *The African Running Revolution*, edited by Dave Prokop. Mountain View, Calif.: World Publications.

Marin, G. 1931. "Somali Games." *Journal of the Royal Anthropological Institute of Great Britain and Ireland*.

Marshall, Donald Stanley. 1950. "Cuna Folk." Thesis, Harvard University.

Masters, James. 1997–2001. "Pachisi." *The Online Guide to Traditional Games*. Web site address: eb.ukonline.co.uk/james.masters/TraditionalGames

———. 1997–2001. "Quoits—History and Useful Information." *The Online Guide to Traditional Games*. Web site address: eb.ukonline.co.uk/james.masters/TraditionalGames

McAdams, Mindy. 1995. "What Is Go?" Personal Web page, World Wide Web, well.com/user/mmcadams/gointro.html/

McGirk, Tim. 1996. "The National Game." *World Press Review*, August, Vol. 43, Issue 8.

McIntyre, Loren. 1975. *The Incredible Incas and Their Timeless Land*. Washington, D.C.: National Geographic Society/Special Publications Division.

Merker, Meritz. 1910. *The Masai: Ethnographic Monograph of an East African Semite People*. Berlin: Deitrich Reimer.

Messing, Simon D. 1985. *Highland Plateau Amhara of Ethiopia*. Edited by M. Lionel Bender. New Haven, Conn.: Human Relations Area Files.

Metraux, Alfred. 1943. "Suicide among the Matako of the Gran Chaco." *American Indigena*, Vol. 3.

Miller, S. G. 1991. *Arete: Greek Sports from Ancient Sources*. Berkeley: University of California Press.

Milne, A. A. 1928. *The House at Pooh Corner*. New York: E. P. Dutton.

Mitchell, Tracey. 1999. "Respiratory Therapists Give the Breath of Life." *Career World*, January, Vol. 27, Issue 4.

Morrow, Don. 1988. "The Knights of the Snowshoe." *Journal of Sport History*, Vol. 15, No. 1.

Mouratidis, John. 1985. "The Origin of Nudity in Greek Athletics." *Journal of Sport History*, Vol. 12, No. 3.

Mulling, Craig. 1989. "Sport in South Korea: Ssirium, the YMCA and the Olympic Games." In *Sport in Asia and Africa: A Comparative Handbook*, edited by Eric A. Wagner. Westport, Conn.: Greenwood Press.

Murie, James R. 1989. *Ceremonies of the Pawnee*. Edited by Douglas R. Parks. Lincoln: University of Nebraska Press for the American Indian Studies Research Institute.

Nabokov, Peter. 1981. *Indian Running: Native American History and Traditions*.

From Peabody Museum, Harvard College Web site: "Against the Winds: American Indian Running Traditions," posted 1999.

"Nadam Festival Opens in Inner Mongolia." 2000. *Xinhua News Agency*, June 7.

O'Brien, Richard, and Jack McCallum. 1994. "Weighty Concerns." *Sports Illustrated*, January 10, Vol. 80, Issue 1.

"Oceania." 1994–2001. *Encyclopedia Britannica Online*.

Oliver, Douglas L. 1989. *Oceania: The Native Cultures of Australia and the Pacific Islands*. Vol. 1. Honolulu: University of Hawaii Press.

"Olmec." 1994–2001. *Encyclopedia Britannica Online*.

"On Wings of Gold." 1992. *Economist*, July 25, Vol. 324, Issue 7769.

Oxendine, Joseph B. 1988. *American Indian Sports Heritage*. Champaign, Ill.: Human Kinetics Books.

Palmer, D., and M. Howell. 1973. "Sports and Games in Early Civilizations." In *A History of Sport and Physical Education to 1900*, edited by Earle F. Ziegler. Champaign, Ill.: Stipes.

Park, Willard Z. 1946–1949. "Tribes of the Sierra Nevada de Santa Marta, Colombia." In *Handbook of South American Indians*, Vol. 2. Washington, D.C.: Government Printing Office.

Parney, Lisa Leigh. 2000. "Sports 101." *Christian Science Monitor*, August 11, Vol. 92, Issue 183.

Paul, Sigrid. 1987. "The Wrestling Tradition and Its Social Functions." In *Sport in Africa: Essays in Social History*, edited by William J. Baker and James A. Mangan. New York: Africana.

Pilger, John. 1998. "When Olympics Come to Sydney It Will Provide a Facade for Shameful Australia." *New Statesman*, December 11, Vol. 127, No. 4415.

Poliakoff, Michael. 1984. Introduction to "The Significance of Sport: Ancient Athletics and Ancient Society," *Journal of Sport History*, Vol. 11, No. 2.

———. 1984. "Jacob, Job and Other Wrestlers: Reception of Greek Athletics by Jews and Greeks in Antiquity." *Journal of Sport History*, Summer, Vol. 11, No. 2.

Pospisil, Leopold. 1958. *Kapauku Papuans and Their Law*. New Haven, Conn.: Department of Anthropology, Yale University.

Rajtmajer, Dolfe. 1994. "The Slovenian Origins of European Skiing." *The International Journal of the History of Sport*, April, Vol. 11, No. 1.

Reefe, Thomas Q. 1987. "The Biggest Game of All: Gambling in Traditional Africa." In *Sport in Africa: Essays in Social History*, edited by William J. Baker and James A. Mangan. New York: Africana.

Reid, Craig D. 1994. "Cystic Fibrosis and Chi-Gong." *Nutrition Health Review: The Consumer's Medical Journal*, Issue 70.

Riordan, James, and Robin Jones, ed. 1999. *Sport and Physical Education in China*. London: E and FN Spon.

Rizak, Gene. 1989. "Sport in the People's Republic of China." In *Sport in Asia and Africa: A Comparative Handbook*, edited by Eric A. Wagner. Westport, Conn.: Greenwood Press.

Rosandich, T. J. 1991. "Sports in Society: The Persian Gulf Countries." *Journal of the International Council for Health, Physical Education and Recreation*, Spring, Vol. 27, No. 3.

Roth, Walter E. 1976 (1902). "Games, Sports and Amusements." *North Queensland*

Ethnography, No. 4. Brisbane, Australia: George Arthur Vaughan, Government Printer. Reprinted New York: Arno Press.

"Rotuma." 1994–2001. Encyclopedia Britannica Online.

Ruhe, Benjamin. 1982. *Boomerang*. Washington, D.C.: Minner Press.

Salter, Michael A. 1989. "Leisure Time Pursuits of the Quiche Maya." *Aethlon*, Spring, Vol. 6, No. 2.

Sasajima, Kohsuke. 1973. "Early Chinese Physical Education and Sports." In *A History of Sport and Physical Education to 1900*, edited by Earle F. Ziegler. Champaign, Ill.: Stipes.

Scanlon, Thomas F. 1982. "The Origin of Women's Athletics in Greece." *North American Society for Sport History (Proceedings and Letters)*.

Scothack, Cinaet. 1999. *Wrestling in Gaelic Culture*. Chattanooga, Tenn.: Clannada na Gadelica.

Seligman, C. G. (N.d.), *Bow and Arrow Symbolism*. from Web site "Asian Traditional Archery Research Network."

Sfeir, Leila. 1985. "The Status of Muslim Women in Sport: Conflict between Cultural Tradition and Modernization." *International Review for the Sociology of Sport*, Vol. 20, No. 4.

———. 1989. "Sport in Egypt: Cultural Reflection and Contradiction of a Society." In *Sport in Asia and Africa: A Comparative Handbook*, edited by Eric A. Wagner. Westport, Conn.: Greenwood Press.

Singer, Rena, "A Casino Quandary in Africa." *Christian Science Monitor*, November 27, Vol. 93, Issue 2, p. 1.

Soreq, Yehiam. 1985. "Diasporal Jewish Participation in Gymnastic Life." In *Sport History, Olympic Scientific Congress 1984 Official Report*, edited by Norbert Muller and Joacim K. Ruhl. Schors-Verlag: Niedernhausen.

Sorlin, Sverker. 1995. "Nature, Skiing and Swedish Nationalism." *The International Journal of the History of Sport*, August, Vol. 12, No. 2.

Soubeyrand, Catherine. 2000. "The Game of Senat." *The Game Cabinet* (Internet magazine), September, www.gamecabinet.com/history/

———. 2000. "The Royal Game of Ur." *The Game Cabinet* (Web site), September, www.gamecabinet.com/history/

Spears, Betty. 1984. "A Perspective of the History of Women's Sports in Ancient Greece." *Journal of Sport History*, Vol. 11, No. 2.

Spears, Betty, and Richard A. Swanson. 1978. *History of Sport and Physical Activity in the United States*. Edited by Elaine T. Smith. Dubuque, Iowa: Wm. C. Brown.

Stewart, Doug. 2000. "Scythian Gold." *Smithsonian*, March, Vol. 30, Issue 12.

Stokstad, Eric. 1999. "How Aztecs Played Their Rubber Matches." *Science*, June 18, Vol. 284, Issue 5422.

Terwiel, B. J. 1975. *Monks and Magic: An Analysis of Religious Ceremonies in Central Thailand*. Lund, Sweden: Curzon Press.

Thompson, Laura. 1940. *Southern Lau, Fiji: An Ethnography*. Honolulu, Hawaii: Bernice P. Bishop Museum.

Trillin, Calvin. 1996. "Kabaddikabaddikabaddi." *Time*, July 22, Vol. 148, Issue 5.

Tschopik, Harry, Jr. 1946. "The Aymara." *Bureau of American Ethnology*, Vol. 2, No. 143. Washington, D.C.: Smithsonian Institute.

"A Tuscan Village in South Africa." 2001. *Economist*, April 7, Vol. 359, Issue 8216, p. 49.

Umminger, Walter. 1963. *Supermen, Heroes and Gods*. English ed. London: Thames and Hudson.

U.S. News & World Report. 1995. July 3, Vol. 119, Issue 1.

Valenti, Michael. 1993. "Boomerang." *Mechanical Engineering*, December, Vol. 115, Issue 12.

Wagner, Eric A., ed. 1989. *Sport in Asia and Africa: A Comparative Handbook*. Westport, Conn.: Greenwood Press.

Walker, J. R. 1976 (1905–1906). "Sioux Games, Parts I and II." In *The Games of the Americas*, edited by Brian Sutton-Smith. New York: Arno Press.

Wallechinsky, David. 1996. *Sports Illustrated Presents the Complete Book of the Summer Olympics*. Boston: Little, Brown.

Watts, Jonathan. 1999. "Chinese Government Clamps Down on Falun Gong Sect Members." *Lancet*, August 7, Vol. 354, Issue 9177.

Westerfield, Jennifer T. 2001. "The Royal Game of Ur." The Suq, *Oriental Institute, University of Chicago*, April (Web site)

"What Is the Game of Go?" 1996. *American Go Association*. World Wide Web, usgo.org

Winn, Jasper. 1998. "Running Wild." *Geographical Magazine*, July, Vol. 70, Issue 7.

Wolkomir, Richard. 2000. "Shod for Snow." *Smithsonian*, December, Vol. 31, Issue 7.

Worley, Barbara A. 1992. "Where All the Women Are Strong." *Natural History*, November, Vol. 101, Issue 11.

Ziegler, Earle F., ed. 1973. *A History of Sport and Physical Education to 1900*. Champaign, Ill.: Stipes.

⊞ INDEX

Page numbers followed by "ill."refer to photo captions

About the Author

STEVE CRAIG is an award-winning sportswriter who has previously authored "Sportswriting: A Beginner's Guide."